Praise for *Phish: The Biography*

"Through a series of interviews informed by a genuine love for Phish's music and community, Parke Puterbaugh paints the picture of the band and their achievements year-by-year and album-by-album. With perspectives from the band members, management, crew and extended family, *Phish: The Biography* is worth reading for fans and curious music aficionados alike. In the words of Icculus, 'Read the book.'"

—Kevin Shapiro, Phish's archivist

"What sets [the book] apart are rare, first-hand accounts and details provided by Phish's inner circle . . . *Phish: The Biography*'s entertaining stories and pictures of key events in the band's remarkable history make it a must-read for fans."

—*Relix*

"The definitive Phish bio."

—*High Times* (4 out of 5 pot leaves)

"The real story."   —*Rolling Stone*

"[The] authoritative Phish-ography. . . . From the guys' early days at a Princeton prep school and the University of Vermont to success, fame, drug busts, breakup and reunion, it's all covered."   —*New York Post*

"Knowing Phish's story will enrich anyone's understanding of the American scene over the past quarter century."

—*New York Times Book Review*

"Puterbaugh delivers a consistently lucid and revelatory look at the twenty-six-year-long career of the legendary 'jam band' . . . his insider access allows him to get never-before-published comments and insights from the band, its management, archivist, crew, and close friends. . . . His solid reporting produces the best account so far."

"An even-keeled evaluation of an important American band—a must for Phishheads."

"Puterbaugh serves up everything one could want to know about jam-band supreme Phish. . . . Valuable enough as a comprehensive Phish file, this book is greatly enhanced by Puterbaugh's depth of knowledge."

"[This] book is stuffed with insider details."

PHiSH

Also written or cowritten by Parke Puterbaugh

Moon California Beaches

Moon Florida Beaches

Rhino's Psychedelic Trip

I Want to Take You Higher: The Psychedelic Era, 1965–1969

The 100 Greatest Albums of the Eighties

Bruce Springsteen: The Rolling Stone *Files*

Southeastern Wetlands

the biography

PHiSH

Parke Puterbaugh

DA CAPO PRESS
A Member of the Perseus Books Group

Lyrics from "Backwards Down the Number Line," "Fee," and "No Dogs Allowed" reprinted by permission. Copyright © Who Is She? Music, Inc. (BMI).

Text design by Trish Wilkinson

Library of Congress Cataloging-in-Publication Data

Puterbaugh, Parke.
    Phish : the biography / Parke Puterbaugh. — 1st Da Capo Press ed.
        p.   cm.
    Includes bibliographical references and index.
    HC ISBN 978-0-306-81484-6 (alk. paper)
    PB ISBN 978-0-306-81920-9
    1. Phish (Musical group) 2. Rock musicians—United States—Biography.
I. Title.
    ML421.P565P87 2009
    782.42166092'2—dc22
    [B]   2009030117

First Da Capo Press edition 2009
First Da Capo Press paperback edition 2010

Published by Da Capo Press
A Member of the Perseus Books Group
www.dacapopress.com

Da Capo Press books are available at special discounts for bulk purchases in the U.S. by corporations, institutions, and other organizations. For more information, please contact the Special Markets Department at the Perseus Books Group, 2300 Chestnut Avenue, Suite 200, Philadelphia PA 19103, or call (800) 810-4145, ext. 5000, or e-mail special.markets@perseusbooks.com.

10 9 8 7 6 5 4

To the troubadours from Gamehendge

CONTENTS

ACKNOWLEDGMENTS

It took just over a year to do the actual writing, but in many ways this book has been almost fifteen years in the making. That is to say, I first met and interviewed Phish in 1995 and continued to do so with relative frequency to the present day. It all began with a story assignment for *Rolling Stone* and evolved into much more than I ever could have imagined. Phish's management thereafter recruited me to write for them on an as-needed basis—album bios (group and solo projects), liner notes, "Halloween playbills," Web site interviews, and more. I spoke at length with them numerous times over the years. Thus I accumulated an oral history of their career in real time from 1995 forward, filled with reflections and reminiscences about the preceding years as well.

Even with a case full of taped interviews, it didn't occur to me that I might wind up writing a book on Phish. That's where Ben Schafer, executive editor of Da Capo Press, and Sarah Lazin, literary agent extraordinaire, entered the picture. A year after Phish's 2004 breakup—or second hiatus, as it turned out—Ben began casting about for someone to write a biography of the band and contacted Sarah for suggestions. She knew of my work with Phish and suggested me. All the pieces seemed to fit: I had plenty of firsthand material and, if a book was going to be written, I wanted to be the one to do it. I firmly believe they are one of the great American bands—and not just *jam* bands. A number of things over the years have struck me as miraculous: word processing, the Internet, compact discs, Google, hybrid cars, the Hubble space telescope, the Mars Rover, the Big Sur coastline, a breaching blue whale, and Phish. So let me tip my hand: I believe that Phish is better on their worst night than most bands are on their best night. Despite some bumps and bruises, I see Phish's career as a four-way street of envelope-pushing, risk-taking creativity undertaken at the highest level of effort and commitment. And this story definitely has a happy ending, with their triumphant reunion in 2009.

The Phish organization—band, management, and past and present employees—have been helpful and supportive of this project. Beyond extending their approval and cooperation, the group members allowed those who'd worked for them to speak to me. No conditions were imposed or strings attached. My candid conversations with longtime employees and associates only reinforced my deep respect for the band and the culture of their organization.

I'm especially indebted to Jason Colton, John Paluska, Tom Marshall, Beth Montuori Rowles, Amy Skelton, Kevin Shapiro, Chris Kuroda, Paul Languedoc, and Brad Sands. Jason has been my point man with Phish since 1995, and I got used to the calls from out of the blue: "Do you have time to talk to the band about the new album (or whatever)?" (Hell, yes, I have time!) As regards this book, Jason was extraordinarily helpful in all possible ways by opening doors, making contacts, offering insights, and much more. John generously made time for a lengthy interview, troubling himself to rise in the early-morning hours so that it could happen. Tom gave an illuminating interview atop the fabled Rhombus—brilliant suggestion, that—and subsequently answered piles of e-mailed questions in his witty, incisive way. Beth and Amy tendered lengthy interviews, sharing perspectives and recollections that brought the world of Phish on the road and in the office to life.

Anyone familiar with Phish understands how important Chris and Paul are to the band—the fifth and sixth Phish(es), without question, for many years. I got to watch them work their visual and sonic magic from the board on a few occasions and also got to talk with them along the way, including a memorable interview with both men at Paul's rural Vermont homestead in 2008.

Kevin Shapiro was an extremely important source. He can answer virtually any question about the band and its history off the top of his head. He gave up considerable time to be interviewed, to help track down photographs, to point me to the worthiest shows, and to share his opinions, information, and insights (and not just about Phish) with me. Our first talk lasted six hours. That was the beginning of not only a series of interviews but also a genuine friendship.

Others in the Phish camp also gave generously of themselves and their time to talk to me. I had illuminating interviews with Megan Criss, Ian McLean, Tony Markellis, and Eric and Jill Larson. Ditto Jim Pollock, Dominic Placco, Todd Phillips, and Sue Drew. Also within the band's sphere are Dave Werlin (of Great Northeast Productions) and Ellis Godard and Steve Paolini (of *The Phish Companion: A Guide to the Band and Their Music*), who shared their informed perspectives on Phish and their particular corner of that universe. Though I regrettably didn't get to speak with her specifically for this book, I have had pleasant encounters with Julia Mordaunt in years past.

In addition, I struck up a lively e-mail correspondence with Jesse Jarnow, jam-band expert and fellow scribe, about Phish and related bands. A word of thanks is due to Beth Jacobson, Phish's former publicist at Elektra Records, for all her help in the mid-1990s, and to Kaytea McIntosh for polling a pile of her Phishhead friends for thoughts on the band. Rebecca Adams and Matt Russ shared their erudition on the connections (and differences) between Phish and the Grateful Dead.

About the time I started writing about Phish, I also got to know Trey's sister, Kristine Anastasio Manning, because we were both, coincidentally, working on graduate degrees in environmental science at adjacent institutions: she at Duke University, me at the University of North Carolina. In a sense, she was Phish's first manager, arranging their earliests shows in New York City and starting up their newsletter.

In addition to having interesting talks about environmentalism, I learned much about Phish's early days from her. Sadly, she passed away from cancer in April 2009.

Having mentioned *The Phish Companion*, I should offer a word on sources. Any outside sources I've used are credited in the text. All uncredited quotes are drawn from interviews I've conducted. Because I've spoken extensively to the band members and those around them—I transcribed nearly a half million words of taped interviews—I didn't need to go far afield from firsthand sources in researching this book. The notable exceptions are *The Phish Companion*, which is the Encyclopedia Britannica of all things Phish, and Richard Gehr's *The Phish Book*, a band-authorized oral history published in 1997. In my opinion, every Phish fan must have a copy of the *Companion* close at hand. I've thumbed through mine so much that it's literally taped together. *The Phish Book* is an endlessly illuminating overview of the first half of their career. Moreover, Richard generously shared with me his raw transcripts from that project, which included much unpublished material.

I mentioned that this whole enterprise began with a *Rolling Stone* feature, and I'd like to thank Karen Johnston for making the assignment and Mark Kemp for editing the article. More broadly, I'd like to express my gratitude to Jann Wenner, Jim Henke, and the late Paul Nelson for making my career in music journalism possible.

With regard to this book, I am extremely fortunate to have Sarah Lazin as my agent and Ben Schafer as my editor; it is reassuring to know that your work is being handled by the best in the business. The combination of Ben's editing and Antoinette Smith's copyediting resulted in a better book, and I am grateful to both of them. Beyond his editing ability, I appreciate Ben's patience. I admittedly put him through the wringer of several blown deadlines, but I think it was ultimately worth waiting for. Collin Tracy expertly handled the book's production in its later stages, and Trish Wilkinson oversaw the design and layout.

Alan Bisbort, my collaborator on book projects and reckless antisocial mayhem dating back to our college years at UNC, provided useful advice and support. Old friends Mark Peel and Anne Zeman offered hospitality on one of my interview trips, while Bruce Eaton, another longtime pal (and fellow author), helped arrange a crucial interview. Ken Richardson, my editor at *Sound + Vision*, organized an expedition to Burlington, Vermont, in 2002 that yielded another opportunity to hang out with Phish and write one more article on the band. Mark Yates filled in some critical gaps in my live Phish collection.

My wife, Carol, and daughter, Hayley, abided my lengthy absences while I labored on this manuscript. Preoccupied in the extreme, I don't think I was particularly good company for a year or so. Thanks for encouraging (and putting up with) me. I love you both. A similar shout-out is due to Helen Puterbaugh, Mark Puterbaugh, and Anne and Tobe Sherrill, and to all my helpful homies in the Bull City and the Gate City, especially Mike Smith and Robbie Schultz.

Would it be too bizarre to thank a mountain? For a half-year, I hibernated atop beautiful Beech Mountain in western North Carolina to work on this book. It's a ski resort in winter and deserted hideaway at most other times. I am drawn to the quiet power of the place, and have now written two books there. I leased a ski condo that, purely by coincidence, was filled with pictures and knickknacks related to fish and fishing. It really helped when, casting about for inspiration while writing about Phish, I'd look around and see fish on every wall.

On a more serious note, Trey Anastasio—Phish's guitarist and mainstay—would often make references to intentions in our conversations. For many years Phish ritually engaged in critical self-assessment of every aspect of their work. It all boiled down to gauging and ensuring their purity of intent. In my estimation, their intentions have been unimpeachable and the creative effort expended by them extraordinary. My intention with this project was simple: I wanted to write a book about Phish that was honest and insightful.

I thank Trey, Page, Mike, and Fish for letting me write *for* them over the years and for trusting me to write *about* them in the pages that follow.

—*Parke Puterbaugh, August 2009*

PREFACE

My Phish Story

When I first met Phish in 1995, I knew too little about them even to have preconceptions, positive or negative. For me, writing about Phish looked to be another fun assignment for *Rolling Stone*, which I was doing a lot of at the time, and as a freelance music writer, I was simply grateful for work. While I might have preferred hanging out with R.E.M. or Robyn Hitchcock, you could send me on the road with anyone. (Well, maybe not Molly Hatchet or W.A.S.P.) Then and now, I love nothing more than traveling around and talking to musicians, who tend to be interesting and colorful even when their music isn't to my liking. And so I was excited at the prospect of flying to Vermont both to spend time with Phish and to hike to the top of Mount Mansfield.

To prepare, I acquired their catalog and began listening. I started with the most recent releases, *Hoist* (1994) and *Rift* (1993). It didn't take long to realize how exceptional these albums were. I couldn't have predicted anything like this. *Hoist* was all energy, speed and color. *Rift* was a deep, dreamy concept album about an unraveling relationship. The music was original and bracing, uncategorizable and without obvious influences. I marveled at the complexity and depth of songs like "Maze," "Mound," "Julius," and "It's Ice," as well as the lyrical cunning.

Chagrin at my ignorance quickly turned to delight at the realization there was a whole mother lode of Phish music to dig up and discover.

The studio albums were just the tip of the iceberg, as all manner of concert tapes and CDs circulated within Phish world.

My mounting interest in Phish's music was further fired once I saw my first concerts: Red Rocks, Morrison, Colorado, June 1995, both nights. As it turned out, I had plenty more opportunities to see and speak to Phish as the assignment became a lengthy, quixotic undertaking. It languished in editorial inventory, as a new regime in *Rolling Stone*'s music department sat on the story, uncertain about what to do with it or whether to publish it at all. But Phish kept ballooning in popularity, so eventually they realized the group had to be covered. Periodically, I'd get a call: "Can you freshen up that story on Phish? I think we're going to run it after all." I did four iterations of the piece over a two-year period before it finally ran.

Phish remained remarkably sanguine about the delays. The wholly unexpected outcome was that after I got to know Phish and vice versa, they tapped me to do writing for *them*. To top it off, when the *Rolling Stone* article finally ran in 1997, it was nearly 5,000 words in length— a virtual journalistic mini-epic.

And to think that everything, including this book, sprang from a story that very nearly didn't run.

ONE

Overview: A Tale of Two Cities (and Two Farms)

I

May 1989: Tapping Kegs on Ian's Farm

Ian McLean was an enthusiastic early fan of Phish. After high school, he was introduced to the band by some friends who'd moved to Burlington to attend the University of Vermont. McLean lived in Hebron, New York, having moved there with his family from Arizona. He'd been a Deadhead—turned on to them by a much older brother who'd been a camp follower dating back to the Fillmore days—but like a lot of Deadheads of younger vintage, McLean ultimately found Phish's music and scene more viable after a certain point in time.

"They were the first band that was taking all the shit we really liked from the Grateful Dead shows and doing more of it: free-form jamming and real spacy, out-there music," said McLean. "That's what attracted me to it, and that was at a time when the Dead seemed much less genuine. The transition for me was like, why would I go on tour to watch that fricking sad junkie [meaning Jerry Garcia] croak onstage when there's these sick dudes that are playing right down at Nectar's? That's what got me going."

McLean regularly made the hour-and-a-half drive to hook up with his buddies at Phish shows—particularly at Nectar's, a funky restaurant, bar, and live-music venue in downtown Burlington. Nectar's served as Phish's creative incubator through 1988. On its cramped stage, they took their music as far out as they dared, and a small but growing fan base hung with them through every bizarre gag, unpredictable meter change, and lengthy jam. By the time Phish began venturing away from their home base in Burlington, they had amassed a group of supporters who followed them, helping to light a fire in other communities.

Anchoring the circle in which McLean ran was Eric Larson, a former dormmate of guitarist Trey Anastasio's and ardent early fan who hired the group to play at his house parties in Burlington. (In the 1990s, Larson got hired as Phish's chiropractor, masseur, and videographer.) Larson and McLean had been to "a million Dead shows together," in McLean's words, but had now cast their lot with the hometown band. Their crew was a fixture at Nectar's, and they also traveled to see Phish gigs at campuses and pubs in Vermont villages like Waitsfield and Rutland. The raucous, outgoing McLean was a particularly vocal fan and booster. If you listen closely to the live cuts from Nectar's that were appended to Elektra Records' expanded reissue of *Junta*, you can hear him whooping and shouting between songs.

McLean lived on a farm in Hebron with his friend Brad Condon. Every Memorial Day, they'd throw a big bash with food and music. It was McLean's job to book the bands and Condon's to roast the pig. These were no small affairs; at one of them, McLean booked six bands. The farm occupies several hundred acres, so there was no worry about annoying the neighbors. McLean twice recruited Phish to play on the farm: a late-summer party in 1987, attended by roughly thirty people, and a Memorial Day blowout in 1989 that attracted upward of four hundred party maniacs.

The first of these, held August 21, 1987, was notable for the sheer number of animal companions in attendance. Phish never missed a trick, and they performed a number of dog-themed songs for the occasion. Barking was as audible as applause. Anastasio's faithful retriever, Marley, was designated "head of security." The first set opened, logically enough, with "Dog Log" and also included "Shaggy Dog" and "Funky Bitch." The middle set included "Harpua," a protracted narrative about a monstrous canine that devours a beloved feline named Poster Nutbag.

The audience was tenfold larger when Phish again played the farm not quite two years later, by which point they'd become a good deal more popular in New England and were beginning to conquer other parts of the country. They were still a homegrown phenomenon but were on the cusp of something much bigger and evolving by leaps and bounds. This day-long bacchanal, referred to among fans and tape collectors as "Ian's Farm," occurred on May 26, 1989. It was a cool, clear late-spring day—perfect party weather. You can just imagine how idyllic and intoxicating the gathering must have been. As McLean observed, "What can you say about a party that's got eighteen kegs and a band like Phish playing?"

There was one hitch. For a few nervous hours, McLean worried that the group wasn't going to show. There'd been a van breakdown somewhere on the rural highway between Burlington and Hebron, and in that time before widespread cell phone usage, Phish couldn't call the farm to explain the delay.

"I was a little freaked out, like, 'Oh my God, my boys aren't gonna be here,'" McLean said. But they made it in time to fire up their first set with the sun still in the sky, initiate the second as it was setting, and perform a raucous final set after nightfall. At the end of the first set, Phish relayed the hosts' pleas for a sober driver to make a beer run. This dialogue between band members and partygoers is a non-musical highlight of tapes from Ian's Farm. Phish's loose, danceable final set included ZZ Top covers ("La Grange" and "Jesus Just Left

Chicago"), the funky New Orleans groove of Robert Palmer's "Sneaking Sally Through the Alley," and the jaunty Caribbean calypso of the Mustangs' "Ya Mar."

Even after three sets and four hours of music, the revelers at Ian's Farm weren't ready to let go of Phish.

"The music was pretty killer, it really was," McLean recalled. "I remember at the end we were like, 'C'mon, a hundred bucks a song, keep on going!' And they were like, 'No, we're fucking done. We're going home.' The show's gotta end sometime, but they definitely played a long time at that one."

The cost of hiring Phish to play all day at a private party in 1989? According to McLean, the band got paid $600—a hundred bucks for each member and their crew guys, Chris Kuroda and Paul Languedoc. Those were the days, in more ways than one.

"America was a different place back then," McLean mused. "I think if you throw a party like that anymore, you're gonna have problems. Now there's all sorts of liability issues and the rest of it."

Another thing he recalled of Phish in that time frame was their intense dedication to the music they were creating, almost to the exclusion of everything else.

"They were all pretty straight," McLean said of Phish. "We were always trying to corrupt those guys, and they would never play along with our little tricks and games.

"We tried to be a bad influence as hard as we could," he added, laughing, "but they were really focused at that point. They were really committed to what they were doing."

II
August 1991: A Perfect Day on Amy's Farm

Amy Skelton was Phish's first fan. She attended their first show (and was among the few paying attention) and, in fact, befriended drummer Jon Fishman before there even was a band. She can recall sitting in on an early rehearsal: "I remember Jon saying he had just met Trey and those guys and was starting to jam with them, and I remember going to one of those practices at somebody's house. So I was at all of those first gigs because my buddy Fish was playing."

Amy and Jon shared an interest in dropping acid that pretty much deep-sixed the academic side of their second semester at the University of Vermont. Skelton went on to excel at UVM as an animal science major, while Fishman ultimately found his niche at Goddard College, where he and Anastasio joined keyboardist Page McConnell. (Of the four of them, only bassist Mike Gordon started and finished his studies at UVM.) All the while, Skelton's fandom and friendship with Phish remained at a high level. In 1992, she began working tours for the band on the merchandise side, and signed on in 1997 as a full-time salaried employee.

The reason Skelton didn't hire on earlier, despite the fact they implored her to do so, was that she took a job running a horse farm in Maine shortly after graduating from UVM in 1989. On August 3, 1991, Phish played a legendary show on the farm that served as a precursor or blueprint for the outdoor festivals that would become a significant part of their legacy. In Phish-fan lore, the event was forever branded as "Amy's Farm."

The official name of this equine enterprise was Larrabee Farm, and it was located in Auburn, Maine, where Skelton grew up. Skelton boarded thirty-five horses, including thirteen of her own, and gave riding lessons. To save money in the cash-poor early days, the band would bunk down at the farm whenever they played in the area—in Portland or at Bates College in Lewiston, for instance. In 1991, Phish were beginning to break out into bigger venues on a more national level. They hatched the idea of playing a free gig to thank their New England fans, who'd sustained them with enthusiastic support from the beginning.

"They were doing well in Boston, and it just grew from there," Skelton recalled. "There was this groundswell of kids who were telling other kids, and it was spreading by word of mouth. That was a really cool thing, and by '91, they really wanted to say thank you. It was as much a thank-you as the big gigs were in the later years. Give it back to the fans."

Amy offered the farm, and on one of Phish's visits she saddled them up and rode them out to look at the field she had in mind. "They were like, 'Wow, this is amazing! We could have a great gig out here! It'd be so cool!'"

On the way back, the horses carrying Mike Gordon and Jon Fishman bolted for the barn. "I was terrified that I'd be the cause of one of their deaths," Skelton said, laughing. "But they survived it."

Skelton subsequently sorted out the "mass gathering" regulations with the Auburn city council, widened a tractor road and bridge to make the fire department happy, and hired a water truck to placate the health department. They built a stage, rented a generator, and mailed a postcard to fans containing a map, date and time, and instructions on what to bring (e.g., "It's a hay field, so it will be stubbly, and your feet will hurt if you come barefoot, so bring shoes").

Skelton and Phish had no idea how many people would show up. Previously, the biggest crowd they'd played for hadn't been much more than a thousand or so. Amy's Farm drew three thousand Phish fans. It was a strong three-set cavalcade with a "Harry Hood" encore and guest spots from the Dude of Life and Sofi Dillof (Page's then-girlfriend and future wife). Every bit as impressive as the music was the sense of community. Amy's Farm marked the moment when Phish fans began to come together and revel in their swelling numbers.

A swimming hole on the property gave the horde a place to take a dip when the band wasn't playing. There was a keg behind the stage, where Phish hung out with their girlfriends and pals from Burlington. Skelton informally patrolled the fields on her horse. They'd erected chicken-wire bins where people could deposit garbage and recyclables. When the show ran long and night fell, Chris Kuroda fired up the one light he'd brought along and manually changed colors with gels he carried in his pocket. "It was a great day," Skelton recalled. "The show went off without a hitch."

Afterward, the band and entourage repaired to the farmhouse and partied till three in the morning. A few hours later, after they'd crashed, it started to rain. It dawned on someone that Phish's gear was still sitting onstage, exposed to the elements. "We all went, 'Oh, shit!'" Skelton recalled with a laugh, and they scrambled outside to rescue it.

In the big picture, Amy's Farm opened the door for further adventures on a grander scale. "I think it gave them the can-do attitude," she continued. "You know, that they could do things their own way and do things themselves."

III
August 1996: Peaking in Plattsburgh

This was surreal.

I was gazing across an endless runway at the heart of a decommissioned U.S. Air Force base three miles south of Plattsburgh, New York. The runway could accommodate the Space Shuttle, and indeed Plattsburgh AFB still rated fifth on NASA's list of contingency shuttle landing sites, despite the fact the base had been decommissioned the previous year. With its closing went 10,000 jobs and the small city's largest employer. As a result, there had been nothing but ghostly quietude on the vast concrete expanse.

However, in late summer, Plattsburgh AFB sprang to life again as a tie-died multitude of 70,000 flew high to the music of Phish at their rock-festival-in-the-middle-of-nowhere, the Clifford Ball.

I piloted a rented car down the runway. After about a mile or so, clumps of wandering bodies and parked cars came into view like a mirage. Instead of warplanes streaking in from practice runs, the flight line was overrun with a civilian army of beatific Phishheads who had amassed for Phish's summer tour finale and first multiday concert and campout. Cars and vans parked in endless orderly rows on the runway, while acres of green-domed tents were pitched tightly together on the broad, grassy strip between the runway and the forest's edge.

The community that materialized almost overnight became the ninth largest city in New York. It wasn't Woodstock, the original rock festival, which at half a million strong could boast of being the third largest city in the state. But the Clifford Ball was pretty damn big—and they all came to see just one band. There was, in fact, an uncanny Woodstock connection. The timing of the Clifford Ball coincided with the dates of the original Woodstock Festival in 1969. All in the Phish camp professed surprise when they later learned of this. It was just one of these serendipitous, synergistic things that routinely happened to this band.

As a live-music event, the Clifford Ball was a late-summer bonanza that blew the other warm-weather tours—H.O.R.D.E., Lollapalooza, and Perry Ferrell's doomed Enit Festival—out of the water in the summer of '96. Unlike those other festivals, however, only Phish played at the Clifford Ball. They performed three sets per day, each lasting around ninety minutes. Held on August 16 and 17, the Clifford Ball offered the novelty of Phish performing in broad daylight for a midafternoon opening set on the second day.

The impetus for playing at different hours of the day came from Jimi Hendrix. "A lot of his monumental concerts—Monterey, Woodstock, Rainbow Bridge, Isle of Wight—were at different times of day," explained Trey Anastasio, Phish's guitarist and nominal leader. "I wanted us to be able to play at all different times of the day at one concert to capture all those different moods."

He likened Phish's Saturday afternoon opening set to his daily wake-up ritual of putting on a pot of coffee and a bluegrass record. And so, on Saturday, the members of Phish got up, drank their coffee, and began picking a bluegrass tune, "The Old Home Place." A happy, howling crowd fanned outward from the stage to the distant campground as far as the eye could see.

Over the course of the weekend, Phish performed for roughly nine hours without repeating a song. As if that weren't enough, Phish literally went the extra mile and played an unannounced jam at 4 A.M. on Saturday. For this, they were drawn through the campground on a flatbed truck. Astonished Phishheads bolted out of their tents and wordlessly joined the swelling, Pied Piper-like procession. This side trip was the musical highlight of the Clifford Ball for Gordon, who felt he'd approach his goal of "bridging the gap between playing music and dreaming."

The festival was named after Clifford Ball, the man who pioneered the idea of air-mail delivery. While passing through the Pittsburgh airport some years earlier, Phish had noticed a commemorative plaque describing Ball as "A Beacon of Light in the World of Flight." They first used the phrase on *A Live One*, their 1994 double-disc concert compendium, which bore the notation "Recorded live at the Clifford Ball." Phish even suggested Clifford Ball as a festival name to Blues Traveler's John Popper, who instead went with H.O.R.D.E. ("Horizons of Rock Developing Everywhere") for the jam-band tour he organized. So the Clifford Ball went from *A Live One*'s make-believe ballroom to Phish's (sur)real-life festival, the first of eight weekend campouts they have hosted in isolated places.

As befits an event named for an aviation pioneer and held on an Air Force base, planes and aeronautics were a recurring motif. During the festival Phish arranged for flybys from F-14s, biplanes, and stunt planes. Prop planes trailed banners like those you'd see at the beach or ballpark, but the messages ran to Dadaist philosophy ("Hopeless Has Exceptions") and bizarro-world humor ("Running Low on Fuel— No Joke," with a stunt pilot sputtering his plane in the sky).

There was even more to see in the sky at the Clifford Ball. An acrobat did gymnastic flips and twirled on circus ropes while Phish played "Run Like an Antelope." On Friday, they launched into "The Divided Sky" as the setting late-summer sun colored half the sky a rosy orange and the other a darkening indigo. They dusted off a faithful version of David Bowie's "Life on Mars"—a timely nod to headline-making revelations from NASA's Mariner spacecraft that there might indeed be life on the red planet. A fireworks display painted the heavens as Phish played "Harpua" at the close of Friday night's set.

Leaving no stone unturned, Phish even invited a relative of Clifford Ball—a grandson of the old gent—to attend as their guest. I spoke to him for a while, and he professed awe both at the event and his invitation to participate. Ben and Jerry—who are to ice cream as Phish is to music, with both entities calling Burlington, Vermont, home—made a cameo appearance onstage. "Phish Food" would soon be introduced as Ben and Jerry's newest flavor, joining Cherry Garcia in the realm of frozen musical tributes.

The only other musical act that appeared onstage at the Clifford Ball was the Plattsburgh Community Orchestra. They played soothing, impressionistic works by Debussy and Ravel late Saturday afternoon. While the orchestra cooled the crowd with Debussy's "Nocturnes," a glider accompanied the orchestra with an aerial ballet.

Phish even operated a completely licensed, fully functioning, FCC-licensed radio station ("Clifford Ball Radio," 88.9 FM) twenty-four hours a day during the festival. Deejays played everything from hip-hop to Iggy Pop and conducted off-the-wall interviews with characters like Fred Tuttler, a retired dairy farmer from Vermont. (Q: "Which is better, Jersey milk or Holstein milk?") Anastasio dropped by to cue up favorite discs by Pavement and bands that had influenced them. Kevin Shapiro delved into Phish's live vault for his "From the Archives" radio show.

The massive audience for Phish's sets fanned outward toward the runway. They throbbed to the music like a single organism. Onstage, Phish was arrayed in a straight line—from left to right, McConnell, Anastasio, Gordon, and Fishman—the customary formation for much of their existence. From a platform on the scaffolding to the side of the stage, I could clearly see the expressions on the musicians' faces, somewhere between concentration and rapture. Anastasio flashed smiles at the others as he counted off each number with rhythmic downstrokes on his guitar.

The Clifford Ball represented a mid-career peak for Phish. At the end of what had been an atypically abbreviated summer tour of the States—owing to the fact they had been touring in Europe—attendance at their first festival was twice the size of the largest audience for whom they'd previously played. That prior milestone had occurred barely a week earlier, when 35,000 turned out to see Phish at Wisconsin's Alpine Valley outdoor venue on August 10, 1996. According to *Pollstar*, the Clifford Ball was the largest concert in North America in 1996.

More than a triumph of numbers, the Clifford Ball stood as a feat of imagination and logistics, driven by a desire to entertain and inspire fans that almost seemed antiquarian in its total indifference to the bottom line. In fact, the idea was to provide an experience that money couldn't buy. The band members themselves emerged from the event as agog as the audience. That was because the denizens of Phish Nation, much like the throng at the original Woodstock Festival, behaved as a relaxed, peaceable, and self-regulating body. There was one wedding, one death (by drug overdose), and just a handful of arrests among the blissed-out crowd. The only complaints weren't about brown acid but green grasshoppers, which infested the campground.

"It felt like so much more than just a big concert with 70,000 people," Anastasio reflected a few weeks later. "It felt like some kind of exciting new thing. We did as much of it as we could, but most of the feeling came from the way people were. That's the part I couldn't have anticipated and that just kept blowing me away."

It was all about peaceful coexistence and phenomenal music, and it was Phish that imagined it into being. Those three days at the Clifford Ball were unlike anything I'd ever seen. It was as close to an Edenic scene of peace, love, and musical bliss as I've ever experienced, and many who were on hand echo that sentiment. The memory of that weekend remains as hopeful evidence that even in this politically muddied, corporately hog-tied, culturally degraded, and violence-wracked world, something approaching utopia still is possible.

No one who was there will ever forget it.

IV
August 2004: Bottoming Out in Coventry

This was surreal, too, albeit for very different reasons than the Clifford Ball.

For one thing, this was the end. Phish's last hurrah. They'd announced that they were breaking up, and the village of Coventry, Vermont, was the site of their final concerts.

It had been raining for days. Rain fell in relentless sheets that turned the land in and around the sylvan village of Coventry into the world's biggest mud puddle. And it wasn't even what they call the "mud season" in Vermont, following the spring thaw. The timing couldn't have been worse, as an army of Phishheads—estimated with remarkable imprecision between 25,000 and 70,000—were descending upon a small state airport bordered by farmers' fields outside of Coventry. This was supposed to be a grand finale. Instead, it turned out to be a waterlogged disaster, dampening already disillusioned spirits within Phish Nation. There was no joy in Mudville.

The only thing worse than being there was not being there. Traffic had backed up for thirty-five miles along Interstate 91. And yet the festival site could not accommodate another car, because the fields were too saturated for parking. Many among the army of pilgrims who'd come from every corner of the country—and from other countries, too—couldn't get to the festival because of the interstate gridlock and untenable parking situation at the festival site. The police, promoters, and Phish saw a calamity in the making and called on fans to go home, promising reparations at a later date. Gordon broke the bad news on the radio.

And then something remarkable happened: In a mass act of civil disobedience, they didn't go home. They parked their vehicles on the interstate's breakdown lane and walked, like a ragtag army of refugees, toward the festival site. Some walked twenty miles or more. They were not going to be denied a final chance to see their band, rain and mud and discomfort and inconvenience be damned. If ever there were a demonstration of loyalty to a rock band that went above and beyond the call of duty, the determined mass march to the Newport State Airport at Coventry to see Phish was it.

Musically, Phish made a disappointing exit. Their relatively dispirited and untogether playing—so atypical of a band that had always operated on principles of musical tightness, infectious joie de vivre, mind-boggling concentration, and continuous improvement—appeared to jibe with rumors of drugs and disarray within the Phish camp.

The stage was rumored to be sinking in the mud. Truckloads of wood chips, gravel, hay, and plywood rolled in to stabilize the grounds. This was the inspiration for some lines from "Invisible," a song from Anastasio's first post-breakup solo album, *Shine*: "Fall down good, sink in the water / But you're walking on wood." It was a reference both to the state of the band during Coventry and the state of the land as the musicians trod the boards to navigate the sodden site.

Fortunately, the rain stopped falling on Saturday, when the music was set to begin. But the damage was done. The sea of mud had taken days to form, had been worked over and stirred up by all the vehicles and human feet, and would not vanish as quickly as had the clouds.

"I want to welcome all of you to this incredibly special night and weekend," Anastasio told the crowd as Phish took the stage on Saturday night.

"In twenty-one years, I've never ever been nervous going onstage before a Phish concert—ever, ever, ever," he said a few songs later. "Tonight, I'm a little nervous."

It sometimes showed in his playing. Coventry was not his, or Phish's, finest hour. Clearly, he was a man in pain. Combining the long-simmering issues that led him to break up the band, guilt and uncertainty over that decision, and the use of drugs to numb those emotions with the meteorological mayhem that wreaked havoc and dampened spirits, Coventry in a sense became Phish's Perfect Storm.

Even loyal friends had a hard time coming to the group's defense at Coventry, though they stopped short of outright criticism. What, for instance, did Ian McLean—a veteran fan of "Ian's Farm" fame who saw at least one show on virtually every tour—have to say about Phish's performance that weekend?

"No comment."

Phish subsequently refunded unused tickets to those 10,000 ticket-holders who hadn't gotten in to Coventry. In addition, each was sent a limited-edition photo book hand-signed by every member of Phish.

"I hope people appreciate the gesture, because it was heartfelt," manager John Paluska told *Billboard* magazine. "The band put a lot into it, and I think it was therapeutic."

That was an example of Phish at their finest, going the extra mile for their fans even after they'd broken up.

Between the ecstasy of the Clifford Ball and the agony of Coventry, something slowly started going wrong. There is some irony in this. First of all, Phish were in many ways at the top of their game, playing some of their best tours and individual shows in those later years, especially, 1997, 1998, and 2003. Second, although Anastasio's bust in 2006 seemed to affirm long-held perceptions by outsiders about Phish and their following as degenerate druggies, the group—aside from occasional recreational use of soft drugs like pot and mushrooms—had been longtime innocents in the world of hard drugs. Cocaine didn't even enter their scene until sessions for *Billy Breathes* in 1996, and the drug didn't take hold as a backstage staple for another year or two after that. Even then, it wasn't a problem for the entire band and crew, some of whom were merely dabblers or even nonusers. Through it all, Phish still played solidly, with only a handful of obvious exceptions.

Summarizing the overall impact of drugs, there were a handful of years in which they insinuated themselves into Phish's scene, without apparent ill effect on the music, and a handful of years beyond that in which the drugging became internally problematic, to the music's occasional detriment. If the jams were sometimes less consistently in-spired in later years—well, even the greatest careers and most creative endeavors experience their share of bumps and complications over time. And as Anastasio pointed out after it was all over, "We had a great run. It was amazing, everybody is okay, and nobody died."

With regard to Coventry and everything leading up to it, if Phish's career were a baseball game, then you might say they played eight great innings and a bad final one, which didn't change the game's out-come. They won decisively, building a legacy that made them heirs to the jamming legacy of groups like the Grateful Dead, Santana, and the Allman Brothers and purveyors of a whole new paradigm all their own. Moreover, the game has now gone into extra innings, with Phish's well-received reunion in 2009. As if to affirm that metaphor, they kicked off their Summer 2009 tour at Boston's Fenway Park, home of Major League Baseball's Red Sox.

Throughout their career, regardless of phase, stage, or size of crowd, the key question that Phish asked and answered is this one, articulated by Anastasio onstage at Coventry. He was recalling his goal in writing "David Bowie," one of his earliest and most challenging compositions for Phish: "How far can you push it in the harmonic and rhythmic language and still have people dancing?"

That question carried with it an assumption that became a truism among those who follow Phish—namely, that Phish is a live band. Creating collectively in the moment is Phish's forte, and it is why they matter. It explains why fans follow them around the country, even to out-of-the-way locales like far northern Maine and a Seminole Indian reservation in South Florida. It's also why tens of thousands trekked to an unforgiving mudhole outside the village of Coventry to witness what they believed at the time was Phish's final show.

Phish's strength has always been the stage, the live situation, where they could improvise with fire, purpose, and a risk-taking group mind-set. Every show is a musical adventure, supported and urged on by Phish's devoted following. Unlike the typical rock concert, you don't go to a Phish show expecting a fixed set list of greatest hits and radio favorites. For one thing, there were no greatest hits or radio favorites, since Phish's singles never dented the Top Forty (or even the lousy Hot Hundred), and they didn't exactly conquer mainstream FM rock radio, either. For another, the notion of a recurring clump of favorites performed night after night was anathema to both the band and its fans. You'd go to see Phish expecting them to introduce new material, rearrange old songs in fresh ways, or break out something that hadn't been played in a multitude of shows.

"Nobody ever comes just to hear a single," Trey Anastasio told *Spin* in 1995. "Everybody is there for the same reason, including us: to get to that point where you'd kind of step through the membrane or something, and all of a sudden you're in this *wwwusshhht*—and it's so much fun to be there."

If certain songs did show up on set lists with some regularity—say, "You Enjoy Myself" and "Tweezer"—they were never performed the same way twice. In fact, such compositions served as launching pads for adventurous jams that would go on for ten or fifteen minutes or even half an hour. "Runaway Jim" and "Tweezer" have each lasted nearly an hour. Phish themselves didn't know what would happen when they set off on these expeditions, trusting the mood and the muse to guide them. Songs might also be strung together or snippets of tunes woven in and out of a central piece, making for a continuous, free-flowing set. It was all about spontaneous creation and deep exploration. The Phish experience, in its purest terms, stems from the symbiotic energy between band and audience. Performing without a net in real time, Phish in concert yields visceral peaks that can't be matched by sound waves emanating from a CD player. In other words, you have to be there to really "get it."

"The times I most treasure are jamming onstage," said bassist Mike Gordon.

"To me, Phish is a live band," agrees Kevin Shapiro, the band's archivist since 1996. He's seen upward of three hundred Phish concerts, by his reckoning.

"A peak show for me is New Year's Eve 1991," he continues, referencing a three-set extravaganza in Worcester, Massachusetts. "That was the first show where I hopped into a car and drove that far. The 'Tweezer' they played at that show changed me pretty much for good. At that point I realized seventeen hours was not too far to drive, and I would do that each way, anytime."

Many others felt similarly, running down their gas gauges while chasing Phish from gig to gig.

Between December 2, 1983 (Phish's debut), and August 15, 2004 (the final night at Coventry), the group performed 1,435 concerts. That is the most accurate figure to date, though it is always subject to revision as new information emerges about forgotten gigs played in the less well-documented early years. Given that the average Phish show runs for about three hours—two seventy-five-minute sets plus an encore—that's a lot of hours spent onstage. Added up, it is the equivalent of 175 full days, or six entire months. In other words, Phish has spent at least half a year of their lives onstage—and that's before they reunited in 2009.

They've spent more time than that rehearsing, too. This was the real secret to Phish's success as a jam band: For years, they assiduously practiced four-way improvisation using self-devised exercises. They learned how to listen to one another and how to play as a unit. Phish is ideally a musical conversation, not a monologue. That conversation began way back in 1983 in the college town of Burlington, Vermont.

TWO

Getting Their Feet Wet, 1983–1987

October 1983. Room 210, Patterson Dorm, on the campus of the University of Vermont. You might call this dorm room ground zero for Phish, the point at which all of the fun and games began.

The occupant of the second-floor room was Jon "Fish" Fishman, a drum-playing freshman with a minimal commitment to classwork. His roommate, by contrast, was a studious engineering major named John Thomas. They used to joke that if you added Thomas's 3.6 grade-point average to Fishman's 0.36, you'd almost have a perfect 4.0.

Fishman was studious in his own way, although as more of an autodidact than a traditional student. His preferred area of study was drumming, and he practiced in the dorm room for much of the day. You might think that a drumming dormmate would be a nightmare, but because most everyone else attended classes while he practiced, the disturbance was minimal. Often he'd take acid and drum all day long.

One day Fishman was having a particularly good time banging away when a stranger barged into the room. It was Trey Anastasio, a long-haired, red-headed sophomore philosophy major from Princeton, New

Jersey. Anastasio lived on the fourth floor of Wing Dorm, also on the UVM campus, and his musical obsession also took precedence over academic pursuits.

Eric Larson, a fellow dormmate (and future Phish employee), recalled his first impressions of Anastasio as a newly arrived freshman. "Literally, within the first two weeks of school he was up in his dorm room with a guitar and amplifier, and he's got either Zeppelin or Hendrix cranked up and is playing along with it," said Larson. "And so I go and knock on the door—*who are you?*

"He was definitely a wild young college student, long hair, that kind of thing. We liked the same music, so I was attracted to that. Our whole dorm floor had a great vibe to it. So I stayed friendly with him the whole year, and it wasn't long after that he rounded up the rest of the band members."

He started with Fishman. Always on the lookout for kindred musical spirits, Anastasio had followed the sound of drumming to its source in Room 210. His expression turned incredulous when he saw the determined-looking troll behind the drum kit.

"Oh my God, it's *you*?!" Anastasio exclaimed. "*You're* the one playing the drums up here? I'll be right back!"

Fishman's face was not unfamiliar to Anastasio. He'd seen him before on campus. One day Anastasio and his friend Steve Pollak had stationed themselves outside the UVM library, where they amused themselves by observing passing students and deciding who did and didn't look like they belonged on campus. When Fishman approached, both of them fell down laughing.

"They pegged me from a hundred yards away in a crowd of people, going, 'He doesn't look like he belongs here,'" Fishman recalled with a giggle.

Neither Fishman nor Anastasio really belonged at UVM, as it turned out. It is an outstanding state university with a storied history, but a regimented approach to learning cramped their idiosyncratic styles. Anastasio was more interested in learning music composition than becoming a music teacher, which was the department's strength. While he learned from individual teachers, including guitar instructor Paul Asbell and classical music instructor Jane Ambrose, he generally recoiled from the detached, clinical approach of academia, which was antithetical to the barnstorming enthusiasm with which he pursued every musical endeavor. As for Fishman, well, the only thing he really wanted to study was drumming, in his own way and on his own time.

Fishman started playing drums at the age of five, and his lifelong aspiration was to be in a rock band. He grew up in Syracuse, where his father, Len Fishman, worked as an orthodontist. His mother, Mimi, was one of Phish's biggest boosters, playing mother hen to hordes of parking-lot kids. She was the Phish parent most likely to be spotted on tour. Toward the end of her life, she organized fund-raising concerts in Syracuse involving other noted jam bands. Her charitable organization, the Mimi Fishman Foundation, remains active.

At his parents' insistence, Fishman briefly took piano lessons, but drumming was his destiny. At age seven he acquired his first drum kit—oddly, a gift from the family's plumber—and retired to the basement, where he worked at becoming Syracuse's answer to John Bonham. During his senior year in high school, Fishman was in a band called Frodo "for like five minutes," he recalled. "It was all cover tunes and stuff. Most bands I saw around campus at UVM were all covers, too. Here was this guy, Trey, who right off the bat was writing originals, and the covers we did do were things we had in common, so that was fine, too."

By the time he arrived at UVM, Fishman was a self-taught drumming addict who'd assimilated elements of style from rock (power), Motown (groove), and jazz (polyrhythmic complexity). Like every member of Phish, he listened deeply, remaining open to outside influences while cultivating a singular, recognizable style. In addition to Bonham, Fishman has sung the praises of Bill Bruford (drummer for Yes and King Crimson) and virtually everyone who drummed with Frank Zappa. Fishman's enthusiasm for Zappa led to his recruitment by the Rykodisc label to compile a Zappa anthology in 2002. Primus's Larry LaLonde did one as well; each was titled *Zappa Picks*.

In 1986, both Anastasio and Fishman transferred to Goddard College, a small, experimental school located an hour east of Burlington near Plainfield, Vermont. There they would finish their educations in a self-directed environment more suited to their nontraditional temperaments. But UVM was where Phish came together, and the small city of Burlington served as the band's home base for many years. Even Phish's management company, Dionysian Productions, would relocate there from suburban Boston in 1995. And though Dionysian itself dissolved shortly after Phish's breakup in 2004, the band's archive remains in Vermont, as does a core team of employees who oversee archival releases and work closely with Phish's new management on current projects and other business.

For reasons that would become clear as Phish progressed, Burlington made for a perfect crucible. It had much do with the fact that Burlington was a college town and therefore provided the right combination of affordable housing, places to play, and a potential fan base among the student population. Beyond that, Burlington's relative isolation gave Phish the ability to develop at their own pace. They could experiment on the stages of Burlington's clubs without having to worry about competition from more commercial-minded acts. Moreover, they weren't prematurely "discovered" and hustled down a crash-and-burn trajectory by prying music-industry types, as might have happened in a locale that registered on their radar. For many years, Phish remained Vermont's best-kept secret. The cat really didn't get out of the bag until the early nineties—a decade after their formation.

"The luckiest thing that ever happened to them was that they played a lot of shows and practiced a lot of hours before anybody really paid any attention to them," said manager John Paluska. "That might not have happened somewhere else, New York or wherever, where people would've caught on to them sooner. They put in an extraordinary amount of time compared to the average band, especially by the time they got noticed. I think you'd be hard-pressed to find a lot of bands who'd worked as hard and played as much together as those guys have."

In a broader sense, everything about Vermont nurtured their creativity. The stoic New England temperament values intellectual rigor and self-discipline, while its countervailing hippie subculture exhibits vestiges of sixties open-mindedness and musical obsession. Anastasio, McConnell, and Mike Gordon found tutors and teachers who kept them challenged and focused.

Then there's the physical environment to consider, with Burlington nestled in an inspirational setting of rolling green mountains (*vert monts* in French, ergo "Vermont") and limpid glacial lakes. Vermont's frigid, snowy winters, lasting half the year, tend to keep folks indoors with their nose to whatever grindstone they've gravitated toward. As Gordon has suggested, Vermont is the proverbial "freezer" to which one of Phish's signature songs, "Tweezer," makes reference.

Anastasio returned to Fishman's dorm room with another UVM student, electrical engineering major Jeff Holdsworth, who also played guitar. The three of them jammed for a while. Between that experience and the four-track tapes of his music that Anastasio later played for him, Fishman was completely sold on their collaboration.

"As soon as I heard him play guitar, and then soon after I'd heard some of the songs he'd written, I was like, 'Ah, this is it. I'll play drums to this guy's music.' Because I could see immediately that he really thought in an original way and that he was really into writing his own stuff and jamming. He had all the right elements, and I was just psyched to play with him."

The next step was finding a bass player. Anastasio hung handmade signs around the dormitory. Nothing cute, just straight to the point: "Looking for a bass player with a P.A." Bassist Mike Gordon was simultaneously posting handbills of his own about getting a band together. He was an engineering major at UVM, though he would ultimately switch to film and communication.

Anastasio recalled the first time he jammed with Gordon as the moment he realized something unique was coalescing. As he told interviewer Charlie Rose in 2004, "The first time Mike and I played together was pretty groundbreaking. I remember it, every note of it. We were in a little room and we were playing, and we just connected."

So now there were four. In no-nonsense fashion, they hashed out a repertoire of cover tunes and booked their first gig. It was a Christmas dance in the cafeteria of Gordon's dorm, which housed a lot of students in the ROTC program. Their first band practice was held in the fourth-floor lounge of Wing Dorm. In a 2002 *Billboard* interview, Gordon recalled the band working up a few oddball originals (such as "Skippy the Wondermouse" and "Fluorescent Gerbils"), as well as covers of Talking Heads ("Pulled Up"), the Allman Brothers Band ("Whipping Post"), and Wilson Pickett ("In the Midnight Hour"). The last of these had been a mandatory item in the repertoire of every rock and soul band that hoped to get people dancing in the sixties. Even the Grateful Dead played it in their early years. John Belushi and Dan Aykroyd had lately made it popular all over again with their comedy flick–cum–soul revival, *The Blues Brothers*.

According to Gordon, the nascent combo's practice session attracted a crowd of students who danced along to the music—a harbinger of things to come. The foursome of Anastasio, Gordon, Holdsworth, and Fishman billed themselves as Blackwood Convention. Someone's parents must've played bridge, because the name is a term for a popular bidding convention in contract bridge that was devised by one Easley Blackwood Sr. The date of Phish's live debut was December 2, 1983. For years, the band mistakenly recalled the show as having been a Halloween dance on October 30, until eagle-eyed archivist Kevin Shapiro made some inquiries and set the record straight. (When you realize that they were off by more than a month, you start to understand how easily historical inaccuracies can creep into the record—*any* record.)

The quartet's performance had all the hallmarks of a scene from *This Is Spinal Tap*—particularly the one where the heavy-metal foursome was booked to play a weekend mixer on a military base. Their cover-heavy set included the Hollies' "Long Cool Woman in a Black Dress," Creedence Clearwater Revival's "Proud Mary," the Doors'

"Roadhouse Blues," "In the Midnight Hour," and the Grateful Dead's jammy tandem of "Scarlet Begonias" and "Fire on the Mountain." Anastasio also recalled them playing "Can't You Hear Me Knocking" by the Rolling Stones—a song with a riff that Phish would tease from time to time—and the Motown classic "I Heard It Through the Grapevine." Holdsworth, who had more band experience than the others, picked and sang most of the tunes.

Blackwood Convention went over like a lead zeppelin. During their second set, they were rudely drowned out by Michael Jackson's *Thriller*, which had been placed on the turntable and turned up to goose the party along with something more contemporary. But every band's got to start somewhere, and as Anastasio has pointed out, they still got paid for the gig. Moreover, the experience provided them with comic fodder once they became famous. In 1995, at the second Halloween show where they covered another act's album in its entirety, they teased songs from *Thriller*—the riff from "Beat It," the intro to "Wanna Be Startin' Somethin'"—to fool the audience into thinking that was what was coming. *Thriller* was the trick, and the Who's *Quadrophenia* was the treat.

They played another dorm gig, in Marshall/Austin/Tupper Hall, within a few days of the abortive cafeteria show. They set the bar high, filling the dorm's basement with banks of equipment, including a rudimentary, handmade light show; a gigantic backdrop; and multiple speakers and turntables for generating ancillary noise and special effects while they played. It was a bit like Pink Floyd's multimedia assaults, albeit with a minuscule budget (and audience). Yet even at this nascent stage, one could detect seeds of what the future Phish would become: a band that aimed high and did their best to turn big ideas into reality.

It would be their last public performance for nearly a year. The short answer why the foursome got put on the back burner so soon after forming is that Anastasio got in trouble. The long answer requires some consideration of Anastasio's complicated, risk-taking, envelope-pushing personality. Without question it helped drive Phish to extreme and sustained heights of creativity. But it has also gotten him into trouble at various points in his life. This was one of those occasions.

Anastasio and a friend in Colorado had been competing to see who could send the other the more outrageous package through the mail. Anastasio upped the ante by liberating a hand and heart from the school's anatomy laboratory. (Tom Marshall swore the heart was human, while others claimed it came from a goat.) He boxed the body parts, enfolding the heart in the hand and enclosing a note with the bloody mess: "I've got to hand it to you, you've got heart." For this macabre prank he received a semester's suspension from UVM. He actually got off lightly, as he risked running afoul of U.S. Postal Service regulations regarding the sending of potentially infections biological materials through the mail. You might call it the group's first hiatus, but they hadn't even named themselves Phish yet.

Back home in Princeton, Anastasio moved in with his unamused dad, Ernest G. ("Ernie") Anastasio. Ernie was an executive vice president with the Educational Testing Service (ETS), the company responsible for the Scholastic Aptitude Test (SAT) and the Graduate Record Exam (GRE). His parents had divorced, and his mother, Dina Anastasio, now lived in New York City, where she edited *Sesame Street Magazine* and wrote children's books. Given that Anastasio was returning to live with a no-nonsense Italian father who placed a premium on educational attainment, he wasn't allowed to slack off during his collegiate suspension. And so his fitful education resumed, for the time being, at Mercer County Community College.

Another piece of the Phish puzzle fell into place with uncanny timing. Anastasio and Tom Marshall bumped into each other for the first time in years. Anastasio and Marshall had become friends while attending junior high at the private Princeton Day School. They were part of a crowd of precocious music addicts who'd written songs together as far back as eighth grade. "Golgi Apparatus," which would become part of Phish's repertoire, was one of them.

Their friendship had largely been put on hold when Anastasio headed off to prep school in Connecticut. Now fortune found both of them back in Princeton. Ironically, each had involuntarily left college—Anastasio ejected from UVM for his anatomical pilfering, and Tom yanked from Carnegie Mellon in Pittsburgh for poor grades and hanging out with the "wrong element"—when they crossed paths on the community college campus. Anastasio spent just one semester at Mercer before returning to UVM, while Marshall would stay for two years before transferring to Rutgers, the state university of New Jersey. His father had been an engineering professor at Rutgers, and Marshall wound up earning his degree there in computer science.

Marshall recalled the moment in early 1984 when he and Anastasio bumped into each other on the Mercer County campus: "I was walking out to my car and he was walking in. This was the first time we'd seen each other, really, since tenth grade. He looked at me and said, 'Tom?' And I looked at him—unmistakable person, huge hair down to his ass, red hair—and I said 'Trey?' It took him about five seconds to decide not to go to school that day. He said, 'Do you want to come to my dad's house and make a recording studio?' And I said, 'Of course.'"

They spent the afternoon tacking carpet scraps onto the walls of a basement alcove to dampen the sound. Down there, Anastasio made four-track basement tapes of what would turn out to be some of Phish's earliest original material: "A Letter to Jimmy Page," "You Enjoy Myself," "Run Like an Antelope," and "The Divided Sky." Many Phish fans, myself among them, regard the last of these as the quintessential Phish composition.

"'Divided Sky' was funny," recalled Marshall. "Back then it was called 'Log,' because Trey recorded it with a log outside. He just started hitting the log and it made such a cool sound that hitting the log was entirely one track, and then he had some metal thing he was hitting. That's how that one started."

During this period, Marshall got a glimpse at how seriously Anastasio valued music as both his salvation and vocation. One afternoon

Marshall entered the kitchen of the Anastasio house to find his friend with his hand in the garbage disposer, trying to dislodge a dropped utensil. When he saw Marshall, he began screaming: "Get the hell out of here . . . Get the fuck out of here!" ,

"It really caught me off-guard, and I was like, 'What's wrong with you?'" said Marshall. "I guess he thought I was going to bump a switch and turn it on. And he said to me, 'Tom, *my hands are my life!*'"

On another occasion, Marshall got a preview of what would become a popular stage routine of Phish's. This time he entered the house through the basement door, unbeknownst to Anastasio, who was wailing loudly on guitar in front of the bedroom mirror. He bounced up and down as he played, watching his hair go weightless and then falling down.

"I was like, 'What the fuck are you doing?' and he was cracking up," said Marshall. "Years later, when I saw him and Mike hopping up and down on the trampolines at a Phish show, I'm like, 'Shit, I remember when he came up with that.'"

The rekindling of their friendship began in 1984 and evolved, by decade's end, into a prolific songwriting partnership. The Anastasio–Marshall byline has yielded four hundred songs to date. About three hundred have been played by Phish or Anastasio's solo band at some point, while another one hundred are lost soldiers that never made it beyond the duo's demo sessions. As with lyricist Robert Hunter and Jerry Garcia in the Grateful Dead, Anastasio and Marshall have been the primary source of material for Phish, and their partnership carried over to Anastasio's solo career, too.

"When I used to write more lyrics, it took me so long, and I always wished I was focusing my energy more on music," Anastasio said in 1995. "Lyrics on a certain level are my thing, but I was really happy to start a partnership with Tom. I can produce so much more and have more fun, because music is more the language that I speak."

Back in 1998 I asked Marshall what was the first song he and Anastasio wrote together. His e-mailed answer:

I think Trey and I might differ on this. Probably the first song with my lyrics was "Wilson" . . . although I wrote that with Aaron Woolf. "McGrupp and the Watchful Hosemasters" has some of my earliest lyrics, but it hasn't been recorded by Phish—in the studio anyway. Ditto for "Makisupa Policeman." The first recorded song with my lyrics might be "Squirming Coil," although that was written by Trey alone looking at the lyrics I sent him in a letter. We also wrote "Lawn Boy" over the phone, I believe. We recorded "I Am Hydrogen" together a long time ago . . . but I wrote that with Marc Daubert [another Princeton Day School alumnus], and it doesn't have lyrics. The first Phish song with my words on it, some people say, is "Run Like an Antelope"—I wrote the famous "Rye Rye Rocco . . . " part—but realistically I had no part in writing that song. So which is the first song that Trey and I wrote together, face-to-face? I don't know—there are some old ones, "Mathilda" and "Little Squirrel," but they're not Phish songs. "NICU," maybe? I guess I really don't know.

That may be another way of acknowledging that the their friendship and collaboration is so prolific and long-lived it's difficult to completely untangle the threads.

The Anastasio–Marshall friendship started back in eighth grade, when Marshall switched from public to private school. His parents had sent him to Princeton Day School, figuring there would be fewer troublemakers to fall in with. They were wrong.

"It turns out Trey was sort of a misbehaving-type character, and I was happy to find people like him existed," Marshall said with a laugh.

There were other misfits and social outcasts at Princeton Day as well, and they all gravitated to music. In addition to Anastasio and Marshall, the core of the "Princeton mafia" comprised Aaron Woolf (immortalized as "Errand Woolf" in the *Gamehendge* saga), Dave Abrahams (an inspiration for several Phish numbers, notably "Dave's Energy Guide" and "Guelah Papyrus," which also name-checks his par-

ents), and Marc "Daubs" Daubert. Their personalities and contributions left their mark on Anastasio, especially in the band's early years.

"It was a really amazing thing how musical our grade was and how
many bands we had," said Marshall. "People like Aaron, Marc, Dave,
Roger Halloway, Pete Cottone, Trey and me, plus at least ten and
maybe even fifteen other guys out of a total class of a hundred, had
bands, played an instrument, or were very interested in music. *Extremely* interested in music."

Anastasio was born in Fort Worth, Texas, on September 30, 1964. His
family moved to Princeton when he was two. Exhibiting musical pre-
cocity from a young age, he took up drums at age eight. The guitar
wouldn't enter the picture until ninth grade, and even in high school
he still regarded drums as his primary instrument. His drumming
background would strongly influence his approach to the guitar,
with his rapid-fire soloing, snare roll–style chording, and impeccable
timing.

As a schoolkid, he would also learn lessons he would later draw
upon with Phish in an unlikely place: the hockey rink. Anastasio was
a solid hockey player who played right wing, and his dad coached
the team. Many years later, Anastasio adapted the knuckle-down work
ethic Ernie Anastasio imposed in hockey practice to Phish's rehearsals.
These practice sessions were legendary for their duration, focus, and
intensity. So Phish fans can thank Ernie Anastasio for cracking the
whip on the ice.

Anastasio, Marshall, and his Princeton pals came into musical
awareness at a time when classic rock was the rage. Anastasio sifted
through it all, choosing his influences well. Jimmy Page and Jimi
Hendrix topped the list, with a shot of Frank Zappa and a host of
progressive-rock outfits from the familiar (Robert Fripp's King Crimson and Peter Gabriel–era Genesis) to the obscure (France's Gong
and Italy's PFM). At home, his parents provided a sound musical
foundation of music from the sixties.

"I grew up with my dad and mom playing Hendrix's *Band of Gypsies*, the Rolling Stones' *Sticky Fingers*, and the Beatles' *White Album* in the next room," he recalled. Zappa also was a key discovery, attitudinally no less than musically. It was Zappa who posed the rhetorical question: "Does humor belong in music?" In Zappa's case, humor—specifically, corrosive social satire—was a huge part of his music. Humor figured in Phish's music, too, though in a more whimsical, surrealistic way than Zappa's increasingly puerile jibes at obvious targets. Surely the notion that music could both amaze and amuse registered with Anastasio, though he wisely didn't buy in to Zappa's lowbrow socio-sexual japes. Phish never wrote anything as juvenile as "Titties & Beer" or "The Illinois Enema Bandit." As Anastasio noted, "A better question for Zappa might've been, 'Is humor the *only* thing that belongs in music?' You have to be careful about that, too."

For Zappa, the ultimate joke might have been his conjoining of intricate, sophisticated music with juvenile lyrics depicting elements of American society at their most vulgar and degraded. However, Anastasio was Zappa's opposite when it came to how he viewed people. Anastasio was optimistic and gregarious, whereas Zappa became the ultimate curmudgeon and misanthrope. Still, Zappa set a powerful example as a fluid guitarist who could compose for and conduct an orchestra, exhibiting a far-ranging overview that encompassed everything from Igor Stravinsky and Edgar Varèse to doo-wop harmonies and avant-garde jazz.

"I have the highest respect for Zappa, for who he was, what he represented, and the fact that he didn't give a shit what anybody else thought about him or his music," he told biographer Richard Gehr. This attitude of self-sufficiency would serve Phish well during those periods when they were overlooked or misunderstood by the rock press.

At the same time he was digesting all these superlative sixties influences, Anastasio experienced and understood the sociology of the suburbs in the seventies—that peculiar time and place where he came of age. In 1997, he expounded on how its banality acted as an impetus—for him and his Princeton pals, as well as the other members of Phish—to reach for something greater.

"The life that is put before you is so meaningless and boring: Just go to the mall for the weekend, get good grades in school, get a job at a corporation, and that's your life," Anastasio said. "And you're thinking to yourself, 'This can't be it!' It's like, *c'mon.*"

That skepticism carried over to the music they were hearing.

"I can remember way back in the sixth, seventh, and eighth grades always feeling like there was something better out there," Anastasio recalled. "Yet still you go to parties, you listen to the radio, you hear it. You can't help but hear it. I grew up going to hundreds of parties where people put on *Fly Like an Eagle*, Pink Floyd, Meat Loaf, and stuff like that.

"That was the soundtrack to my youth, regardless of how much I wanted to be like my idols, like Jimi Hendrix or something. But the experiences are different, and you just aren't Jimi Hendrix. So all those different experiences add up to who you are. And all the while you're striving for some kind of meaning, and we found that meaning in music."

Life in Princeton wasn't all soul-sapping suburban sterility. This leafy, attractive college town with its venerable tradition of education and culture actually had much to offer. The Princeton University campus was an oasis of ivy-covered Gothic buildings and bikeable brick walkways. Anastasio and his pals made Princeton part of their playground.

"We were always on the Princeton campus, and we knew it like the back of our hand," said Marshall. "We biked on it, we walked on it, we were there all the time. That was our thing. We'd also always break into the Princeton parties at an extremely young age. Back then, it felt like one big community, and a lot of us even thought we were going to go to Princeton eventually, just stay here and go."

Amid all the partying, they took their music quite seriously. Anastasio was the drummer in an eighth-grade band called Falling Rock. They had one of those diamond-shaped yellow road signs with the words "Falling Rock" printed in block letters. The band played hard rock by the likes of Deep Purple ("Space Truckin'") and others in that vein. Toward the end of ninth grade, Anastasio picked up the guitar. He had a natural aptitude for the instrument and before long he quietly shut down a lot of the six-string hotshots in the vicinity.

"I went to a party," recalled Marshall, "and a bunch of the regular guitarists were sitting around in a circle trying to decipher 'Skronk' by Genesis. Over in a corner I heard this little amp plugged in, and I went over to see who was playing, and it was Trey. He was playing guitar by himself, and it sounded like Duane Allman. And I didn't even know he could play!

"I said, 'Trey, what's going on? You play guitar?' And he said, 'Yeah, I'm picking it up.' 'Picking it up? You're playing better than anyone over there.' He was by far better than anyone in our grade. They were struggling note by note with an easy song, and he was improvising on 'Rambling Man' or something and just nailing it. And I asked, 'How long have you known how to play guitar?' And he said, 'Tom, I've just always sort of known.'"

The social life of Anastasio, Marshall, and their pals at that time sounds like a collage of scenes from *Dazed and Confused*, *That 70's Show*, and various smoke-filled Cheech and Chong farces.

"I remember a party at Trey's house," said Tom. "Of course, there's some drug stuff, and it's my first exposure. But I was just drinking beer, which was bad enough for me. It was like the standard ending to all movie high-school parties. The headlights swept across the yard, someone yelled, 'Your dad's home,' and people just began piling out the back door, sprinting across the yard, hiding in closets, and crazy shit."

Having become a handful for his parents, Anastasio was sent to the Taft School, a prep school in Watertown, Connecticut. Founded in 1890, Taft has a motto of "Not to be served but to serve," though it's hard to imagine many of the troubled kids from good homes there taking it seriously. At Taft, Anastasio befriended Steve Pollak. He was christened "the Dude of Life" by his pals after uttering a series of mock profundities while they were all under the influence of mushrooms. They formed a short-lived band named Space Antelope, for which Anastasio was the drummer. Pollak, like Anastasio, wound up attending UVM and finishing elsewhere. He was on the scene during Phish's germinal years, and several songs he wrote with Anastasio— "Slave to the Traffic Light," "Fluffhead," and "Run Like an Antelope" (an amended Space Antelope leftover)—became standards in the group's repertoire.

Anastasio was also at Taft when Talking Heads' *Remain in Light* was released in 1980. It was the New Wave quartet's fourth album— and the third in a row produced by Brian Eno, who had become a de facto member.

"It was a really influential record for me," Anastasio said a few weeks before Phish played *Remain in Light* in its entirety at their 1996 Halloween show in Atlanta. "When I think about it, I may have listened to this album more than any other album, ever. I practically learned how to play guitar listening to this record. It was literally my guitar-practicing album. Anytime I wanted to learn something new and practice it, I would put on *Remain in Light* and kind of jam to it. I used to use it instead of a metronome."

Knowing this deflates the exaggerated notion that the Grateful Dead figured prominently in his musical upbringing. In 1980 he knew how to play a Talking Heads album, but it would be two more years before he even attended his first Dead show. He didn't get into them the first time around, either. But, as was the case with a generation of concertgoers, everything became perfectly clear when he saw them again after dropping acid.

"It was just incredible," he recalled. "Blew my mind. It was just surreal, you know: improv. Hooked up. I had never really seen anything like it before. That's what I mean when I say different musicians have validated different aspects of music for me."

Beyond the obvious, noted procession of influences—Jimmy Page, Jimi Hendrix, Carlos Santana, Frank Zappa, Robert Fripp, David Byrne, and Jerry Garcia—Anastasio absorbed and refracted elements of style from others who crossed his radar. These included another classic-rock guitar hero, Queen's Brian May, with his fat, multitracked midrange sound; musical brigands like Miles Davis and Bob Dylan, who stuck to their guns when the audience revolted; jazz guitarists Joe Pass, Django Reinhardt, and Pat Metheny; and Igor Stravinsky ("who simply had it all").

Anastasio also understood that the ultimate goal of any artist is to discover his own voice. From amid the welter of guiding lights that set him on his musical path, he would do so fairly rapidly in Phish.

Meanwhile, back in Princeton, Marshall, Dave Abrahams, and Marc Daubert had their own high-school band, And Back. An enlarged version of that group included the aforementioned Pete Cottone and Roger Halloway. Marshall and Aaron Woolf also had a group, A Dot Tom, which is where "Wilson"—the inspiration for Anastasio's *Gamehendge* saga—originated. "Wilson" makes passing mention of "Rog and Pete" in yet another name-check of Princeton friends.

Though Anastasio and his pals back home were playing in different bands, there was still much informal collaboration. "They were my jamming buddies in high school," he recalled in 1996. "All we ever did on Friday and Saturday nights was get together and jam and make four-tracks. That was it.

"Tom and I made a couple of four-track albums starting in high school and have been writing ever since, and he always sang and played as much as I did. That's why I'm such a big fan of Ween, because it reminds me so much of all these hundreds of four-track tapes we've made."

Ween, incidentally, comes from Hopewell, New Jersey, the next town over from Princeton. Matthew Sweet and Mary Chapin Carpenter hail from the area as well. More relevantly, Blues Traveler and the Spin Doctors—jam-band mainstays, friends of Phish, and core acts on the H.O.R.D.E. tours—have solid roots in Princeton, too. All four members of Blues Traveler and Chris Barron of the Spin Doctors attended Princeton High, a public school. There must be something in the water or, more likely, in the schools' music departments. In any case, the solid push those budding musicians got in high school did not go unnoticed. When Phish's *A Live One* received gold certification (500,000 copies sold) from the RIAA (Recording Industry Association of America), Anastasio sent a gold album to Princeton Day School's music department.

I asked Anastasio whether any of those high school–era four-tracks survived.

"Yeah, I'm looking at 'em right now. I'm in my studio and there are stacks of them," he said. "It's hilarious stuff, from five o'clock in the morning when we were up all night."

"It started out to be about making people laugh," affirmed Marshall. "That was almost the whole point of getting together, because we would just laugh our asses off when we were writing this shit. If the tape recorder was rolling, then we'd stop it, play it again, and play it fifty more times, laughing harder each time."

Anastasio also had another collaborator: his mother, Dina. They wrote songs together, selling them for $250 a pop, and several of them wound up on kids' albums. In 1995, he could still sing them from memory:

> *Well, there was a little frog and his name was Joe*
> *The frog jumped up and then he crashed down low*
> *He jumped a little higher and a little higher, oh*
> *And he stopped and he said, "Hi, my name is Joe!"*

The mother and son would be given a theme, such as "self-esteem," and write accordingly: "I like me, I like me, I like me." Their most adventurous effort was a musical called *Gus, the Christmas Dog*. They envisioned it becoming a made-for-TV Christmas special, but there were no takers. That's not to say the songs went to waste. The main theme from *Gus, the Christmas Dog* became the final section in "The Divided Sky." Other parts of *Gus* were appropriated for Phish songs as well. One of its numbers, "No Dogs Allowed," became part of Phish's early repertoire and their first stab at barbershop quartet. A cadre of early fans used to follow Phish around and scream for them to do "No Dogs Allowed," and occasionally they'd oblige. The song tells the tale of a lost puppy who enters a New York subway station and is turned back:

> No dogs allowed, no dogs allowed, no dogs allowed
>   on the subway
> So climb up the stairs and be on your way
> 'Cause there's no dogs allowed on the subway.

Thump-thump-thump-thump.

With his fists, Tom Marshall pounds out a deep, reverberant rhythm atop a giant hunk of metal in the shape of a rhomboid solid. In 1966 an artist named Tony Smith designed this metal sculpture, giving it the generic name "New Piece." Marshall, Anastasio, and their friends simply called it "the Rhombus." It figures heavily in Phish lore.

The Rhombus sits in a grassy field behind the Institute for Advanced Studies, where some of the great minds of our age have come to puzzle out the world's mysteries. Albert Einstein, who clearly understood the wages of fame in ways that Phish would eventually appreciate—"It certainly gets in the way of your work," declared the genius—was among them. To one side of the Rhombus is a pond, and pathways meander through the peaceful, shady surroundings, designed to provide a serene, inspirational setting for all the brains at the institute.

A pack of Princeton schoolkids—mainly Marshall, Anastasio, Dave Abrahams, and Marc Daubert—had different designs on the Rhombus. They went there to drink beer, smoke dope, make music, and commune with the cosmos. Hanging out at the Rhombus became a kind of pagan ritual that allowed them to tap into a primordial energy source and get a good buzz in the process. For one thing, it was far enough from the main road to escape the prying eyes of the authorities. Out by the road, the local cops would periodically sweep the former battlefield with their lights, rounding up all the potheads who were in the grass, so to speak. If they did smoke dope there, their little group learned to hide behind the columns of the memorial so the cops' sweeping lights wouldn't expose them.

Back then, mounting the Rhombus was part of the ritual. On a warm afternoon in May 2008, at Marshall's suggestion, we scaled the metal sculpture and talked atop its summit for hours, as he and Anastasio had so many times in years past. Of course, ascending the eight-foot-tall Rhombus in middle age was not as easy as it had been in junior high and high school. Marshall tried to ascend its slanting side with a running start, letting his momentum skip him to the top, as they'd done effortlessly way back when. He succeeded on the third attempt, a testament to his athleticism and height. (He's a rangy six foot four.) Before doing so, he gave me a leg up so I could grab a corner and hoist myself to the top.

"So this is the magical Rhombus," said Marshall. "A lot of the energy of the Rhombus came out when you hit it, and we'd ruin our hands by slamming into the late hours. But when you're laying back on it, it feels like it's echoing up into the solar system. It's an incredible feeling. It's definitely a power source. There's enough room to get four or five people up here, and you all chant and sing, and there has to be a guitar and a six-pack to do it right."

In my notes from that day, I wrote, "Birds twittering, Rhombus rumbling, geese honking, wind howling."

There *was* something alive about the Rhombus. The steel skeleton seemed to vibrate with an elemental energy. The Rhombus is where the chant for "The Divided Sky" originated, inspired by a phenomenon Marshall and Anastasio witnessed one night.

"We'd always lay on our backs and start with a drum pulse," Marshall recounted. "This one night, we noticed that half the sky was dark and half was light. It was an effect that came from the clouds being really low and the institute tower being lit in such a way that one-half of the lighting appeared to be off. It cast this incredible beam of light right over our heads. Half of the sky was fully lit and the other half was completely black. And we began chanting, 'Divided sky, the wind blows high.'"

Marshall got married in 1992, and he held his bachelor party at the Rhombus. Phish were almost nine years into their career at that point, and it was a pivotal time. That year saw the release of their first album on a major label (*A Picture of Nectar*, Elektra Records); the re-release of their prior indie-label albums (*Junta* and *Lawn Boy*), and the recording of the concept album *Rift*—which, in part, addressed Marshall's marital jitters. (Just listen to "Fast Enough for You.") Phish also gigged 112 times in 1992. Amid this bustle, Anastasio returned to Princeton for Marshall's marriage. At the wedding ceremony, Anastasio and Dave Abrahams performed a Bach processional on acoustic guitars. The bachelor party was somewhat less sacrosanct, ending with a fiery, heavy-metal exclamation by the Rhombus.

"There were six or seven of us," Marshall recalled. "Trey had his guitar, and we played and drummed and smoked and drank. At the end of the night, we had quite a lot of garbage—six-packs and bags and shit. My resourceful friend John Sprow opened the hatch of the Rhombus. It has since been welded shut, but back then it was just held down by gravity and we knew how to open it. He threw all the bags and stuff into it, which was blasphemy for us since we'd always treated the Rhombus nicely. Here's a guy who didn't know our ceremony and just figured, 'Oh, wow, what a nice garbage can.' Then he threw a lighted match on top of it, and before long our butts were getting hot.

"This is a quarter-inch or more of solid steel, and the heat was becoming an issue, so we threw the door back down on top of it. All of a sudden we heard a howling, and it really was *howling*. Each screw hole began making this jet-like sound and shooting flame about a foot high. The Rhombus became a blast furnace. It really was the night the Rhombus came to life. It was either saying 'thank you' or 'get the hell out.' We'd like to think it was saying thank you for all the years of fun."

Every so often during Phish concerts, Anastasio would provide what the fans called "Rhombus narration" from the stage. Seeking out the Rhombus became a kind of holy grail for serious Phishheads. It's hard to understand why the Phish following had such difficulty finding the Rhombus, since this unmistakable metal icon sits in plain view in a park behind a well-known building in Anastasio's hometown of Princeton.

No doubt part of the reason is that Anastasio offered clues from the stage that actually threw them off the track. For instance, during "Colonel Forbin's Ascent" at a 1995 show in Hershey Park, Pennsylvania, he purported to reveal that the Rhombus was located in King of Prussia. And so the Rhombus largely remained a mystery well into the nineties.

Anastasio returned to the University of Vermont for the fall 1984 semester. During his absence, Mike Gordon and Jon Fishman played in a group called the Dangerous Grapes—another two-guitar outfit that mined an unoriginal but satisfying blues-rock groove, drawing from the usual suspects: the Allman Brothers Band, the Grateful Dead, Stevie Ray Vaughan. If nothing else, their afternoon jam sessions entertained the members of the UVM fraternity at whose house they rehearsed. The return of Anastasio, however, promised fresh challenges and original material, and Fishman unhesitatingly threw in his lot with the prodigal guitarist.

Gordon also came around, but with a proviso: He wanted the band to continue to include covers in their sets. In this he had an ally in Jeff Holdsworth, who was also still in the fold, though his role would diminish as original material and musical charts increasingly entered

the repertoire. That said, Holdsworth provided Phish with two original songs—"Camel Walk" and "Possum"—which they continued
to perform long after he left. In fact, "Possum"—a catchy, finger-
popping country-blues shuffle—became a live favorite. Anastasio
even made it part of his original *Gamehendge* song cycle.

As for the covers, Gordon had an interesting point to make, as he
usually does: "We always talk about getting away from our egos," he
told Richard Gehr in *The Phish Book*, "but there's a certain egotism
about who wrote whatever song you happen to be playing, so that's
another part of the ego to do away with. The source of what you're
playing shouldn't make any difference if you're attempting to be true
to the moment."

The foursome finally settled on Phish as a name. Amy Skelton, who
was around for Phish's birthing, doesn't remember exactly when or
how it emerged. They first mused about calling themselves Phshhhh
(without a vowel), based on the sound that brushes make on a snare
drum. Someone even came up with a poster that had *Phshhhh* on it,
but the lack of a vowel ultimately presented problems. (Imagine a promoter's confusion: "You call yourself *what?* How do you spell that?")
And so Phshhhh became Phish, the decision made the afternoon before they played a Halloween party in 1984. This was also their first
gig since resuming the band after Anastasio's one-semester suspension
from UVM.

The name Phish was intriguing but ambiguous, and it didn't tie
them to any particular sound or movement. Phish played on Fishman's name and on fish in general, much like the minor alteration of
animal names that turned beetles into "Beatles" and birds into
"Byrds." To clear up one oft-repeated misconception, Phish was only
coincidentally a contraction of Phil Lesh, the name of the Grateful
Dead's brilliant bassist, despite speculation by fans that this might be
some sort of nod to the Dead.

"Definitely not," stated Skelton. "Definitely not remotely on any
of their radar screens."

"The band is called Phish, because Fish is the drummer," Anastasio said matter-of-factly in *Specimens of Beauty*, a band documentary made during the recording of *Undermind* in 2004. "If I went and saw Phish, I'd be watching Fish." It was Anastasio who designed the clever band logo, which depicts a rather circular fish with the five letters in Phish artfully outlining the piscine creature. Air bubbles that look like eyes stream from its open mouth as it swims from right to left. The elongated letters are reminiscent of sixties psychedelic art.

Mike Gordon is the *x* factor in Phish. He is a maze of seeming contradictions. For everything you can think of to say about Gordon, virtually the opposite is true, too. He is introverted and outgoing. He is warm and congenial, wary and reserved. He is spontaneous and process-oriented. He is low-key and high-strung. He is an utterly unique individual who willingly submerges himself within a group dynamic. He's also hilarious in a subtle way, possessing a dry wit and deadpan delivery.

The youngest member of Phish, Gordon was born on June 3, 1965, in Waltham, Massachusetts. He spent most of his childhood in Sudbury, another town within commuting distance of Boston, where the family moved when he was three and a half. His father, Bob Gordon, founded a chain of convenience stores (Store 24) in New England. His mother, Marjorie Minkin, is a renowned artist, painting large abstract shapes on various media, including Lexan—a thick, clear plastic—in bright, iridescent colors.

For many years, from 1987 and well into the 1990s, Minkin painted Phish's stage backdrops. She troubled herself to measure the wall space behind the band at Nectar's (seven feet by twenty feet) to get it exactly right. Later on, when the venues got larger, she painted a series of four-feet-by-eight-feet sheets that hung side-by-side. Her work explores the interplay of light and color, and Chris Kuroda's lights brought out different properties in the paint that made them come alive. His illumination of her paintings was another aspect of the band's shows that was uniquely Phish.

Born into a family of observant Jews, Gordon had what he calls a "very religious upbringing." He spent much of his youth roaming the outdoors. Near Gordon's home in Sudbury were acres of fields and streams that he explored with his friend Steve Andelman. Down the hill is a network of five square miles of fields and paths. "My whole childhood was spent walking through these fields," he reminisced. "There are stone walls hundreds of years old. It was just magical going there with my various friends, exploring streams and climbing trees." For more on this, listen to "Andelmans' Yard," a dreamlike, autobiographical reverie from Gordon's 2008 solo album, *The Green Sparrow*.

He credits music with helping him break out of his shell socially. He played bass in a few high-school groups, including the Tombstone Blues Band. There's a charming picture of Gordon with his fellow adolescent bluesmen, instruments clutched earnestly while wearing matching half-sleeve baseball jerseys with "Tombstone Blues Band" printed across the chest. Gordon moved on to more contemporary sounds with The Edge, which included numbers by Talking Heads and the Police in its repertoire.

As Phish's most devout Deadhead, Gordon has freely acknowledged the role of bassist Phil Lesh in shaping his approach to the instrument. But Gordon remains open to any and all sources of expertise and artistry across the musical spectrum. He immerses himself completely, almost obsessively, in his effort at continuous improvement. In one recent year, for instance, he spent a few hours a day learning Benny Goodman's clarinet solos on the bass guitar. He's also the band member who brought the bluegrass element to Phish. Perhaps the simplest way to explain his perspective is to observe that he's into honoring roots while breaking new ground, too.

Gordon also has an interest in cinema that has paralleled his career in music. He studied film at UVM, and one professor in particular, Ted Lyman, became something of a mentor. As a cineaste, he cites as his favorite directors such existential wits as Woody Allen and David Lynch, as well as the linchpins of the French New Wave, Jean-Luc Godard and François Truffaut. He has wielded the camera for Phish's lone video ("Down With Disease"); for *Tracking*, a half-hour documentary about the making of Phish's fifth album, *Hoist*; and for two full-length films, *Outside Out* (a cryptic, quasi-comedic tale featuring Col. Bruce Hampton as an anarchic mentor) and *Rising Low* (a fine documentary about bass players and bass playing). *Rising Low* paid tribute to Allen Woody, the bass player for the Allman Brothers Band and Gov't Mule, who died of a drug overdose in August 2000. In the same movie, Gordon blurred the lines between fact and fiction by contriving a bassist named Joey Arkenstat and having some of the instrument's real-life legends pay verbal tribute to this nonexistent "influence." Somewhere in all this can be discerned the broad outline of his serious yet playful personality.

An inescapable similarity between Anastasio's and Gordon's upbringing is that both musicians had a practical, business-oriented father and a creative, artistically inclined mother. In their career you can see this merging of art and practicality. Both sets of parents divorced, too. Moreover, Anastasio's and Gordon's siblings each went on to careers in the environmental field. David Gordon earned a degree in environmental law at Harvard and worked abroad in the area of environmental diplomacy. Kristine Manning (Trey's sister) earned her degree at Duke University and worked as an environmental journalist, editor, and advocate before her untimely death in 2009.

"Between my sister and Mike's brother, they're gonna save the world," Anastasio noted in 1995.

"We're going out there to destroy it," cracked Gordon, "and we're counting on them to rebuild it."

Gordon's first original contribution to Phish bore the prosaic title "Mike's Song," which he recorded as a four-track. Both Anastasio and Gordon were pretty proficient with their four-track machines by 1984, and a good portion of material that wound up on Phish's first release, *The White Tape*, stemmed from their individual efforts.

"Mike's Song" went on to become a Phish concert staple, formed into a triptych with "I Am Hydrogen" and "Weekapaug Groove" (or, after 1992, with an ever-unpredictable middle in place of "I Am Hydrogen"). In the beginning, however, "Mike's Song" was "just a little four-track experiment I did in my sophomore dorm room," according to Gordon. "We never played the groove that was on the four-track, which was kind of like Motown."

"Weekapaug Groove" came about in typical seize-the-moment fashion. A high-school friend of Anastasio's had a family house in Weekapaug, Rhode Island, a beach town, and Phish played at the yacht club. As they were returning from the gig, the Four Seasons' cheesy disco-era hit, "Oh, What a Night (1963)," came on the radio. Mishearing the lyrics of the bridge, Gordon began singing, "trying to make a woman that you move." To that bit of doggerel—"It never occurred to any of us that it has any meaning"—he added "Sharing in a Weekapaug groove," and the germ of a song was born. For some inexplicable reason, the town fathers of Weekapaug took offense to the song and had a threatening cease-and-desist lawyer letter sent to the band, which they sensibly ignored.

Page McConnell entered the picture in 1985, when he enlisted Phish to play Springfest at Goddard College. Ultimately, he joined the band and also convinced Anastasio and Fishman to transfer to Goddard, which had a self-directed, open-ended curriculum. Goddard students set their own goals and agendas for learning and then meet with an adviser for weekly evaluations in order to track progress. In their final year, a senior study project is undertaken and submitted.

McConnell studied jazz piano with a teacher named Lar Duggan, who lived in Burlington, and his musical mentor at Goddard was named Karl Doyle. Anastasio was tutored in composition by Vermont composer Ernie Stires and wrote *The Man Who Stepped into Yesterday* (aka *Gamehendge*)—for his senior thesis. Fishman played drums and penned a how-to manual on drumming. All three graduated from Goddard.

During the 1985 Goddard Springfest, the institution seemingly didn't have much to celebrate, with its student body having shrunk to a historical low of 33. (In 2002, Goddard completely terminated its traditional-age on-site bachelor's degree program. Now it exists solely to provide a low-residency education for working adults.) McConnell recalled that the '85 Springfest included a dozen bands besides Phish.

After recruiting Phish to play Springfest and then jamming with the group at a UVM gig in May 1985, McConnell set his sights on actually joining Phish. It was a good fit and, for sure, more challenging than the groups he'd fallen in with at Goddard. In his desire to join Phish, he had an ally in Gordon. While Phish went on another hiatus in the summer of 1985—during which Anastasio and Fishman spent the summer bumming across Europe—McConnell moved to Burlington and Gordon rehearsed Phish's repertoire with him. When Phish revved up again that September, Gordon made sure McConnell was on hand.

McConnell and Fishman recalled what ensued:

McCONNELL: "I joined the band under protest."

FISHMAN: "There was this brief period where we didn't really know who we were gonna get in the band. It was like 'This doesn't necessarily mean you're in the band.'"

McCONNELL: "That lasted like a week and a half."

FISHMAN: "It was kind of awkward. Then it was like, 'Who are we kidding?' But it's worked out pretty good. I'm glad we didn't fire him. I think down the road it wouldn't have worked nearly as well not having a keyboardist."

McCONNELL [*dryly*]: "Thanks, Jon!"

The sticking point had to do with the fact that Anastasio wasn't entirely sold on the concept of Phish with a keyboardist in their ranks. "Phish is a two-guitar band," he protested. But this was one time his opinion did not hold sway, fortunately, for all concerned.

Anastasio and Fishman's European vacation in the summer of 1985 is a story worth relating in its own right, not just because it was eventful but because a couple of Phish's most renowned songs ("You Enjoy

Myself," "Harry Hood") came out of it. As Fishman recounted, he and Anastasio painted houses for a month to make enough money for a summer abroad. The two of them, joined by Anastasio's Princeton school chum, Pete Cottone, set off for Europe with about $400 in each of their pockets. By the end of the summer, they were relying on Pete's dad's credit card. Their travels carried them to England, Belgium, Italy, France, Holland, and Germany, culminating in a three-week beach campout on the Greek island of Corfu. In a sense, this was Phish's first tour of Europe, although the full quartet wouldn't make the trek for purposes of performing for seven more years.

Their experience of living in a bamboo hut on Pelekas Beach sounds something like a more exotic preview of Phish's festival campouts, albeit a bit more edgy and real-world. Fishman recalled the scene:

> The mix of people was just outrageous. There were these Greek punks who had this little village, like four or five black tents and a huge bonfire pit in the middle. Everybody else's little bamboo huts were down at the other end of the beach. Every night they would burn a huge effigy of one of those Greek things with a big hard-on. They'd hang it from a noose and burn it. Their leader had a Mohawk and a ripped white sleeveless T-shirt. On the front it had a guy's head splattering against a wall, and the blood running down the wall spelled the word "gross." They were "the evil people," we called them, and somewhere along the way we ended up becoming pretty good friends with the evil people.
>
> Me and Pete and Trey would jam on the beach every night. There were these two big German guys, Rudi and Jürgen, who really wanted to hear us play. Rudy would be really high and drunk and say, "We play now music! Play us music!" So we'd play for him and Jürgen, and they'd get into it. We told them, "We're in this band Phish and someday we're gonna come to Germany."
>
> One night we were jamming and the evil people came over to check it out. They didn't speak any English, and this guy set a big boom box down in the sand, looked at us, and went, "Lynyrd Skynyrd?" And we're like, "Yeah, Lynyrd Skynyrd!" "Deep Purple?"

"Yeah, Deep Purple!" We listened to "Free Bird" and "Child in Time."
We hadn't heard music for a couple months. Things like that made
the whole European trip just amazing.

The two also had a portable Sony cassette recorder upon which
they recorded their travel experiences, dubbed the "Tape of Life." On
one side of the tape was the Beatles' *Magical Mystery Tour*, and on the
other was Pink Floyd's *Meddle*. The unit's erase head was broken, so
instead of recording over the music, it simply added sounds from
their travels to it, such as a voice repeating the line, "Hello, my name
is Yannis, I come from Cyprus."

"Everyone we met would talk into this thing—weird people we
met on the street and weird events," Anastasio recalled. "By the time
it was over we had this incredible collage tape. We camped under the
Matterhorn one night and were singing, drinking wine, and that was
on there. It was all on there."

One night in Paris, they were busking in the street—Anastasio on
a mini-guitar, Fishman on a Flexatone (an odd little percussion instrument dating from the early twenties), Pete on bongos—alongside
fire-eaters, glass-walkers, and other freaks. They drew a large crowd
that really got into the music, dancing and digging the scene as Phish
crowds would in years to come. Unwilling to break the spell, even
though they were getting separated from their belongings as the surg-
ing crowd pushed them back, they discovered afterward that someone
had stolen the Sony unit with the "Tape of Life" in it. The loss of their
tape recorder wasn't the worst thing that happened to them abroad.
While tripping on their German friends' acid one day on Pelekas
Beach, they decided to swim out to a raft offshore just as a violent
storm was blowing in, and Anastasio nearly drowned. After this har-
rowing experience, he sat on the beach and wrote the music for
"Harry Hood."

Once McConnell was in, there followed a half-year period during
which Phish carried on as a five-piece band, with him and Jeff on-

board. This was not the most convivial period in the band's history. While McConnell was on the same musical page as the other members of Phish, in terms of breaking ground and moving forward, Holdsworth began to detach from the group. His anchoring influence became less essential as Phish increasingly set sail for uncharted waters. With his interest waning and days numbered, Holdsworth began shedding gear and downsizing his role. Anastasio has cited as a "defining moment" the day he brought sheet music for "You Enjoy Myself" to band practice. Everyone but Holdsworth was gung-ho about the idea of tackling original, scored music.

In March 1986, Holdsworth bailed out. He graduated from UVM, left town, and underwent a religious conversion. Having heard tales about the abundance of pot, mushrooms, and acid within the student community at UVM and Goddard in general and within the local musical community in particular, it's reasonable to speculate that someone like Holdsworth, who didn't navigate easily through that world, might've wanted to extricate himself from it. Moreover, Holdsworth didn't have the compositional mind of the others, nor did he share with them the compulsion to bend old forms into new shapes and sounds.

Holdsworth eventually paid his erstwhile bandmates a return visit, sporting short hair and a tweed jacket to which a "Jesus Is Love" button was pinned. He was a lot thinner, they noticed.

"None of us really knew him that well, when I look back on it," noted Fishman. "None of us knew him well enough to pinpoint what caused that, except for the fact he was always kind of a loner."

"Really quiet and nice guy, too," added McConnell.

Having found the Lord, Holdsworth made a stab at converting them. But by then they were pursuing a higher calling of their own. As Fishman put it, "We all have a certain desire to honor the roots and traditions of music, but there's also this persistent desire to find out what else we can do rather than the common forms, the things you always hear."

McConnell can remember the first time the foursome (minus Holdsworth) realized they had something unique among them. "One afternoon in the practice room we were playing a song with a jam in it. All of a sudden this jam started to take off and I was having this experience like, 'Oh my God, this could really work as a foursome, this is really happening.' I have a real vivid memory of that."

It wasn't all smooth sledding for Phish as a reconfigured foursome. Even as late as 1995, McConnell quipped, "We're still getting used to it."

Yet McConnell was indisputably the piece that completed Phish. Like the others, he possessed self-discipline, tremendous ability on his instrument, a willingness to put in long hours of rehearsal, and the desire to aim high. Less eccentric than Gordon, less extroverted than Fishman, less extreme than Anastasio, he was kind of a grounding force—the one who instinctively knew when the gags were going too far or the jams were getting off-course.

Now no one recognizes his worth more than Anastasio. "Page's piano is what sets us apart from the million other two-guitar bands," Anastasio told Richard Gehr. "He truly makes the band something special."

Beneath his outward reserve lurks a subtle but incisive sense of humor. He'd wisecrack in a quiet deadpan. During a joint interview with McConnell in 1995, Fishman spoke of wanting to get new faces backstage to freshen up the scene.

"I think it'd be cool to throw a bunch of random passes into the audience," he proposed. "Throw them into a fan and blow 'em out there, just to meet some new people."

With the barest hint of a smile, McConnell cracked, "You tell me what night you're gonna do that, Jon."

"That might not be the smartest idea," Fishman conceded.

Another time McConnell was playing chess at a friend's house in Burlington when a few acquaintances dropped by. One was a die-hard fan who, spying McConnell, rather too enthusiastically exclaimed, "Dude, I caught you guys in Rochester, I caught you guys in Buffalo, I caught you guys in Colorado, I caught you guys in Miami. . . ." Page looked up and quipped, "And now you've caught me at Max's house, too."

McConnell is the product of genes touched by genius. His father, physician and scientist Jack McConnell, was co-inventor of Tylenol, helped develop magnetic resonance imaging (MRI), devised a TB test, and was an expert in gene technology. The impetus for creating Tylenol stemmed from the fact that his wife, Mary Ellen, was allergic to aspirin. Dr. McConnell, who worked for Johnson & Johnson, researched an aspirin substitute. He also started a free clinic in Hilton Head, South Carolina, that served as a national prototype. Most germane to Phish, Dr. McConnell was a big fan of Dixieland jazz, and both parents encouraged their son to stick with the piano. Many years later, when Phish would swing through the South, Dr. McConnell joined his son's band for a rousing version of "Won't You Come Home, Bill Bailey?"

Like Fishman's revelation about drumming at age five, McConnell realized he wanted to play piano at four years of age. He spent a couple years studying music at Southern Methodist University in Texas before transferring to Goddard. Prior to Phish, he played keyboards in a few college bands, including Tom's Sub Shop and Good Soup. The former group included future Phish poster and T-shirt artist Jim Pollock, who lived in McConnell's dorm. Pollock played guitar and sang. They played "R&B kind of stuff, just for the fun of it, on porches and places like that," according to Pollock. According to McConnell, they had four songs from Velvet Underground's *Loaded* album in their repertoire. "We were really bad," Pollock said with a laugh. "Page carried the band because of his musical expertise, and fortunately he found those guys in Burlington."

Good Soup covered groups like Talking Heads, the Police, and Bob Marley. McConnell cites *Talking Heads '77*, the David Byrne–Brian Eno collaboration *My Life in the Bush of Ghosts*, and Eno's more ambient works as albums that turned his head during the New Wave era. McConnell was also in an R&B band called Love Goat, which opened for Phish at an end-of-semester gig on the UVM campus, when McConnell sat in with Phish for the first time.

At Goddard, he delved into jazz piano. Bill Evans, Art Tatum, and Thelonious Monk rate high on his list of favorite pianists. McConnell brought a jazz influence to Phish, providing the impetus for the group's short-lived alter ego, the Johnny B. Fishman Jazz Ensemble, which performed jazz standards with local horn players. Alto saxophonist Russ Remington, trumpeter Carl Gerhard, and tenor sax player Dave Grippo were subsequently christened the Giant Country Horns—and, in an expanded lineup, the Cosmic Country Horns—touring with Phish for spells in 1991 and 1994. (Anastasio would recruit Grippo and Remington for his horn-oriented solo band in 2001.) Every tangent the band undertook over the years, be it jazz, bluegrass, barbershop quartet, or Anastasio's fugal compositions, served to broaden their already eclectic musical purview. For such reasons, McConnell credits Phish with providing the bulk of his music education.

"A lot of the formal training I've had has been in the band," he said in 1995. "Trey's material and some of the stuff Mike has written is really challenging on the piano. There were a lot of two-part invention sort of compositions that really challenge your left-right brain. I was cursing Trey at the time when he would write this stuff—not to his face, of course—but I developed a lot of dexterity and technical ability just through learning the Phish songs."

Goddard was working well for McConnell as a laboratory of self-directed piano studies, and UVM wasn't working out particularly well for Anastasio and Fishman, so it didn't take a hard sell on McConnell's part to convince both to transfer. For their enrollment, Page received a $100 headhunter's fee—$50 apiece—as part of Goddard's effort to shore up its sagging enrollment.

"It wasn't like I was really recruiting them," said McConnell. "It was more like, 'Hey, look what I'm doing over here.' It made sense, especially for Fish."

"I remember checking it out and going, 'You can do anything you want here and get credit?'" Fishman added.

Goddard called its program a twenty-four-hour curriculum, in the sense that you're always learning since you're theoretically following a study plan of your own devising. "And you don't stick to it," cracked Fishman. "Then you write an evaluation saying why you didn't stick to your study plan."

"It can be like that," McConnell acknowledged, "but if you want to get something out of it, you can. And we were all pretty focused."

"The good thing about Goddard was as soon as I wasted a semester partying my ass off and then wrote an evaluation and got away with it, I realized I was wasting my own time," conceded Fishman. At that point he buckled down with his drumming studies. "Basically I locked myself in a room for three years and played drums and went to band practice." During this period, Phish shared a house just over the Winooski River from Burlington. Fishman didn't even have a bedroom, just an alcove off the kitchen, where he slept on a futon. Overflowing kitchen garbage pails sat close by, and the place was so filthy that Anastasio claimed it was infested with maggots.

"From a distance, it looked like a pattern in the carpet," recalled Anastasio, "but up close you could see all these little creatures wriggling around."

Around this time Fishman went through a hard bout of the lovesick blues. A serious girlfriend split up with the drummer, plunging him into a chronic funk. The relationship ended over what she saw as his laziness. One day he had awoken with the revelation "work sucks" and decided not to show up for his job shoveling snow in downtown Burlington. She issued an ultimatum: "Either you go to work or I'm leaving."

He didn't go to work and she made good on her promise, so Fishman retired to his bedroom, rising only for band practice. Actually, he didn't even have a bed at that point, just a growing mound of dirty clothing that he sprawled upon. Each day he began sleeping later and later. The cycle was broken one day when Mike Gordon brought a plate of eggs and toast to his room.

"I thought you might enjoy breakfast in bed," he said with the barest flicker of sarcasm. It was five o'clock in the afternoon.

"That was the first thing that made me laugh in a long time," said Fishman, "and from there, things got better."

Over dinner, where this tale was told, the band members all cited it as a turning point. The next time Fishman saw his ex was backstage at Madison Square Garden, where Phish headlined in 1994. The reluctant snow shoveler had made good after all. In any case, there were no hard feelings.

"We each wound up doing what we dreamed about," he said. "She's an ornithologist, and I'm a rock and roll drummer."

While attending Goddard, McConnell studied improvisation and led a jazz band that included Fishman, Gordon, a saxophonist, and a female singer.

"It was great for me," McConnell concluded. "I can't imagine ever having had that experience anywhere else."

Anastasio, as noted, studied composition with Ernie Stires, whose mentoring proved significant in shaping his approach to much of the material he would write for Phish. He would spend hours at Stires's home in Cornwall, Vermont, where they would drink coffee, listen to music, and discuss theory and composition. For homework, he might have Anastasio write a fugue. The idea was to expand his musical palette, and Anastasio—always up for a challenge—made the most of this one-on-one education. It's worth noting that Stires provided extensive tutoring of Anastasio and others, including fellow Vermont musician Jamie Masefield of the Jazz Mandolin Project, for absolutely nothing. He shared his knowledge and overview purely for the love of music.

As a result, Anastasio was able to yoke his imagination to a base in music theory. The musical pieces written during his years of instruction in Stires's living room uniquely defined Phish's sound and approach. The typical piece of Phish music from this period had intricate sections that opened into an often lengthy group improvisation. Originating from densely composed music, Phish's subsequent jams exhibited tightness, discipline, and vigor. The group essentially composed in the moment, listening and reacting intently to one another, as opposed to noodling aimlessly.

It's curious to realize, however, that Stires never really grasped the extent of his achievement in helping to guide one of the great musical minds of modern times, largely because he had no use (or ear) for rock and roll. Stires was a product of the jazz age and also had a grounding in the classics. He saw rock and roll as endlessly repetitive and harmonically limited. As for the musical revolution he helped incite with his mentoring of Anastasio, he didn't quite get it—culturally or musically.

"Trey wouldn't be so enormously successful unless he was hitting some major vein in the psyche of his generation," Stires said, acknowledging his most famous charge. "What he's hitting is a mystery to me."

Like the other members of Phish, Mike Gordon got something out of Goddard, though he remained a UVM student. On November 23, 1985, Gordon had a life-changing experience while playing a gig there with Phish. He reminisced about it in a 2003 conversation:

"It was the night I decided I wanted to make music a full-time career. I wrote two full journals just about that one night of playing. I had this incredible self-actualization, and I dedicated all future journals to figuring out what happened that night and what makes a peak experience like that occur."

I asked whether that particular show was taped and whether the band might ever release it.

"I taped it, but I've never even listened to it," he said. "I vowed never to listen to it. There's no possible way that listening to it would ever be the same. It would be like being an entirely different person listening. So I just wanted to save the memory."

Burlington, with a population of 40,000, is by far Vermont's largest city. Yet it's still a small city in a small state isolated by geography. Its relaxed cultural climate in no small way influenced Phish's development.

"Burlington is an excellent womb for a band," said Fishman. "It's relatively easy to get a gig, you get paid decently, and it's not a cutthroat situation at all."

Phish's first club gigs were at a place called Doolin's. They played a midweek happy-hour gig from 5 to 7 P.M. Anastasio maintains that in the beginning there'd literally be only two people there: Amy Skelton and Brian Long, the "first fans." It was, after all, a frat bar, and they weren't catering to that type of audience. Still, they did slowly accumulate a crowd, as fresh converts brought their friends to the Doolin's gigs.

Nothing happened overnight, though. While small club gigs were easy to find, campus gigs were hard to come by at first, and even Slade Hall (the "hippie dorm") proved a tough nut to crack. This all worked to Phish's advantage, as they weren't swamped by success but experienced a slow, steady climb, during which they nurtured their craft in an environment where they gained a following one fan at a time. They gradually cultivated a varied audience of college students and hipsters from Burlington and environs.

"It wasn't like one big crew," explained Ian McLean, an early fan and friend of the band. "You'd go to parties and see people you recognized from Phish shows, but we didn't really hang out together at all."

On December 1, 1984, Phish ascended a rung on the local club scene by playing their first gig at Nectar's. This combination restaurant, bar, and music venue on Main Street in downtown Burlington, with its familiar revolving sign over the sidewalk, has long been a local institution. The operation was owned by Nectar Rorris, a Greek entrepreneur with a soft spot for music. Through the years, Nectar's has served as a place for bands like Phish to develop their repertoire and following. There was no cover, because Nectar never charged a cover. Hungry students could grab a cheap plate of food—gravy-covered fries were a specialty—and hear a little music. There was nothing not to like about Nectar's. Anastasio even met his future wife, Sue Statesir, at Nectar's when he dropped by for a drink.

At first, Phish performed not on Nectar's main stage but at the less prestigious upstairs room (which is currently Metronome Club). For a brief spell, including this gig, the group was augmented by Marc "Daubs" Daubert, one of Anastasio's Princeton pals, on baliphone and percussion. Although there's not much accurate documentation on how many times Phish played upstairs at Nectar's—*The Phish Companion* lists just December 1, 1984—Amy Skelton maintained, "They played upstairs a bunch in the early days before they moved downstairs."

Phish also played plenty of private parties, whose dates and numbers also remain largely undocumented. Eric Larson presided over a party house at 39 Dorset Street Extension in Burlington where Phish played a number of times. Larson has a video of one such affair from May 1987.

Hunt's, a cool club that presented music most nights of the week, also played a critical role as a live venue for Phish in their developmental years. It was a long, narrow room with tables and chairs near the entrance and a dance floor by the stage. As many as 300 or 400 could squeeze onto the floor on a busy night. Phish got their first break there when the local reggae band for whom they were supposed to open dropped out at the last moment, leaving Phish to play the entire evening. Their fans were decent in number and enthusiastic in response, and Phish went down well enough to earn regular bookings thereafter. By the fall of 1986 they were playing well-attended gigs at Hunt's and getting to play downstairs at Nectar's, too. It was on Nectar's main stage that Phish really gelled. From November 1986 through March 1989, they had an informal residency at Nectar's, performing every month or two on some combination of Sunday, Monday, and Tuesday nights. Their increasingly loyal fans would show up every time they were booked, even if it was a three-night stand. That's not to say Nectar's was always packed, although it got that way toward the end of their time there.

The way the Nectar's stage was configured influenced how Phish aligned themselves as a band, even after they graduated to large arenas and outdoor stages. The stage was long and narrow, forcing the musicians to array themselves in a line, without the drummer behind the other musicians, as is typical. What was a pragmatic necessity at Nectar's turned into one of Phish's most visible quirks thereafter: a straight-line arrangement across the stage, with McConnell and Fishman at opposite ends and Anastasio and Gordon in the middle.

The band all lived within walking distance of Nectar's, with Anastasio around the corner and the other members sharing a red house on King Street, across from the Harry Hood milk plant and overlooking Lake Champlain. "The house was "in the pit of Burlington, a funny little house down low, low as you can get without going into the lake," Anastasio recalled. The fourth roommate was Brian Long, a former dormmate.

Anastasio remembered the crowd dynamic at Nectar's: "Usually there wouldn't be that many people at the beginning of the night. People would come and go, and it would just kind of swell. Eventually, it started getting really packed, which is why we had to stop playing there. But for a long time, it wasn't."

Chris Kuroda recalled seeing Phish at Nectar's. Despite his best intentions of attending to schoolwork and forgoing late sets on school nights, he found himself reeled in by Phish time and time again.

"My experience of Phish at Nectar's was that I couldn't leave and I couldn't stay away," Kuroda said. "And that was a very common thing. Many times I said, 'One set and I'm going home,' and it never happened. It was addicting. *Unbelievably* addicting."

Imagine the scene: a wildly enthusiastic crowd, everybody dancing, hair flying, the band and audience trading wisecracks between numbers. It was a musical experiment unfolding in a sociable laboratory. The crowd would slam-dance, like mock punks, whenever the band played the Gordon-penned hardcore sendup "Big Black Furry Creature from Mars."

It was a varied crowd, too. One could see long-haired hippies, buzz-cut frat boys, and plenty of students and natives who fell into no obvious clique. In this sense, it was a preview of Phish's fan base once it blew up in size and scale in the nineties.

"It was kind of like a Phish show [in the later years] where you had serious hippies who were doing the whole tour and sleeping in their cars," said Amy Skelton, "and then you had kids coming out who were pretty clean cut and did well in school and obviously came from money. You had that same thing going on even at the Nectar's stage of the game."

"For five years we had Nectar's and other places around town to play from nine until two in the morning," recalled Fishman. "We'd get three-night stands, so we didn't even have to move our equipment. Basically, the crowd was our guinea pig. We'd have up to five hours to do whatever the hell we wanted."

"We really took things out at Nectar's," added Anastasio. "We did the play [*Gamehendge*] there, and we did a lot of songs where people would come onstage and do weird things."

For instance, Steve Pollak provided surreal comic relief on occasion as the Dude of Life, sporting bizarre outfits and props that included a shower curtain, pool goggles, and rubber chickens. In some way, large or small, Phish would try something new every time they played Nectar's.

The group taped some of the early gigs but, preoccupied with the shows and their execution, eventually relegated that task to various friends and fans. Many of the Nectar's sets, for instance, were taped by Del Martin, a friend of the band. Phish hasn't yet come to terms with him or others who want money and/or an assurance of their release, and therefore none of the Nectar's shows have turned up as official LivePhish releases or downloads.

"We would have picked more shows from the eighties, if more were available," said Gordon. "A couple of ones that were on my list of favorites, the early ones, just weren't taped at all."

Phish started taping every show, or nearly so, in an organized way starting in the fall of 1991. Prior to that, taping was much more sporadic and haphazard, which leaves about seven years of Phish history that is incompletely documented. Band archivist Kevin Shapiro has this to say about the years for which Phish possesses relatively few tapes:

"In some situations, people they trusted to make tapes at the time won't give us what they made and want big payoffs or promises to release certain things. So far Phish hasn't been willing to do that. To this day, we haven't bought out any collections. There are a few we *should* buy out, in my opinion. But so far, as a matter of principle and financial reality, they haven't done that."

Nectar's figured so prominently in Phish's development that the band put its owner on the cover of their third album and cited him in the title, *A Picture of Nectar*—a phrase from the song "Cavern" that can be taken two ways: "a pitcher of nectar" or a photograph of the mustachioed Greek club owner. The group also appended a note to the CD jacket paying tribute to the man who let them develop as a band on his stage. In part, they wrote: "Eight and a half years ago, we played our first bar gig at Nectar's in Burlington. Nectar . . . was happy to give us a gig despite our lack of experience, organization or a song list long enough to last two sets. . . . Those nights at Burlington taught us how to play."

Anastasio unequivocally stated, "There wouldn't be a Phish without Nectar's."

The group later granted Rorris permission to print up and sell T-shirts that read: "Nectar's—Home of Phish." He told the band, "You wouldn't believe, these things are selling like *pancakes!*"

What's curious about all this attention given to Nectar's is that Phish actually played more gigs—or at least more documented gigs— at another Burlington club called The Front, a larger venue where they moved after outgrowing Nectar's. Phish played The Front fifty-six times, compared to forty-three known gigs at Nectar's. McConnell ventured that "we must've played Nectar's a hundred times," and Chris Kuroda guessed there were upward of seventy-five shows. Either McConnell and Kuroda, who were in a position to know, are both way off in their count or there are many more than the known number of Nectar's gigs. Perhaps they were so eventful that it *seemed* like there were a hundred of them.

The emphasis on Nectar's has to do with the fact it was Phish's laboratory and playpen. There was no compulsion to be "professional," just entertaining, and that came naturally. They treated the Nectar's shows like open band rehearsals, with false starts, abandoned tangents, between-song chatter about what to do next, good-natured banter with the audience, gags and laughter, and ever more adventurous jams. This freedom gave Phish confidence to experiment and progress as they learned what did and didn't work before a crowd. What they found out was surprising: The more risks they took, the more people liked them. While honing their act at Nectar's and other local venues, they discovered a sizable audience in Burlington with an appetite for musical adventure. What they couldn't have imagined was how widespread that hunger would turn out to be.

During the mid-1980s, before Phish began recording as a band, Anastasio and Gordon had been recording on their four-tracks at school and at home, and the fruits of these labors saw casual release as *Phish* (aka *The White Tape*). It was something they could send out as a calling card to get gigs, and they also sold it at shows and gave it away to friends. Depending on your point of view, this is or isn't Phish's first release. Only three of its sixteen songs—"Alumni Blues," "AC/DC Bag," and "Dog Gone Dog"—have all four members playing on them. Four of them are Gordon's songs, and nine are by Anastasio, cut alone or with his Princeton comrades. This low-fi assemblage doesn't really cohere as an album and, despite its charm as an embryonic glimpse at the band and its repertoire at an early stage, is hard to regard as a finished release.

On the other hand, *The White Tape* was distributed as a Phish release, and those three group endeavors do mark the spot at which Phish debuted on record (or, rather, tape). Moreover, five of Anastasio's endeavors, cut alone or with his Princeton co-conspirators, went on to become key items in Phish's repertoire. These numbers—"You Enjoy Myself," "The Divided Sky," "Slave to the Traffic Light," "Fluff's

Travels," and "Run Like an Antelope"—appear here in rough form. "Slave to the Traffic Light" is the most developed, in terms of a band arrangement. "Run Like an Antelope" was a straggler from Anastasio's Taft School days with Steve Pollak in Space Antelope that had been re-recorded by Anastasio with Tom Marshall on a tape they called *Bivouac Jaun* before showing up on *The White Tape*. Drawn out to nearly seven minutes, it is an impressive one-man show and would become one of Phish's longest-lived and most beloved numbers. In fact, its key lines were practically a rallying cry for Phishheads: "Set the gearshift for the high gear of your soul/You've got to run like an antelope, out of control."

As for the rest, they're mere snippets, with "You Enjoy Myself," "The Divided Sky," and "Fluff's Travels" running only for a brief, skeletal minute or so. Gordon's four numbers aren't so much songs as experiments in sound, such as the audio-vérité dentist-chair tor-ture chamber of "NO2," or surreal spoken-word tracks with musical accompaniment, like "Minkin" (about his mother's art) and "He Ent to the Bog" (a disorienting narrative that includes recited jokes about hamburgers). In a more hardcore vein, Gordon is solely responsible for the rock-music-as-middle-finger message of "Fuck Your Face." His tongue was in his cheek, but there's evident venom in his rebel-lion, too.

The White Tape was released on compact disc in 1998, coinciding with a ramping up of the band's merchandise arm. It still sounds like the equivalent of a very weird bunch of baby pictures. And while it is hardly essential listening, one can hear the groundwork of a band that was unafraid to break with convention and follow their own path.

Meanwhile, Phish were improving with every gig and gaining new fans as a result. Their fans turned friends on to live tapes and dragged them to gigs, where Phish made good on all the word-of-mouth that preceded them. Converts became proselytizers themselves, and the au-dience grew in an organic way. The band worked on their weaknesses—which were mostly vocal in nature—and tightened up instrumentally through incessant practice and regular gigging.

"They sort of sucked when we first started seeing them," admitted Tom Baggott, a Phish fan and acquaintance. "They were getting it together. They were sort of sloppy, you know, but that was the fun of it. That was the magic of it. It was like there was a big joke going on and all the early Phish fans knew the punch line—which was that this was gonna be something big."

"I thought they needed to work on the vocals," noted Ian McLean, "but as far as the musicianship and the songs they wrote, I was like, 'If they're this small and people are that into it, then there's no limit to how big it could get.'"

"I was noting increasing dexterity, polish," Amy Skelton recalled of Phish circa 1986–1987. "They rounded out the rocky edges."

Skelton spent her final year of college attending the University of New Hampshire in Durham. Bitten by the Phish bug, she'd commute back to Burlington for their gigs, packing her pickup truck with fresh converts from UNH.

"I brought lots of live tapes with me to UNH, and Phish was good enough by that point that people who'd never heard them could be caught by the music. That's saying a lot. You're talking about crappy audience recordings of somebody's friend's band, so there's no real reason for people to listen. But they were listening. I was making tapes for lots of people in New Hampshire who were asking for them."

"They were my friends," Skelton conceded, "but they were getting darn good. It was really danceable, you could get a good groove going, and the musical changes—even by 1985—were pretty right on. The whole band moved together and moved well. And they practiced hard."

From the beginning, Eric Larson would tell anyone who'd listen, "These guys are going to be famous. These guys are going to make it."

You could argue that it was miraculous that four musicians from four states, each possessing unconventional passion, talent, and vision, found each other in Vermont. McConnell has noted that he was within a hair of leaving the state when he finally connected with the others, and Anastasio's misadventure with anatomical parts easily could have scuttled Phish, as well. This much is true, however: They made the most of the opportunities their unique chemistry offered them.

Having gained momentum on the local scene, Phish next turned their attention to the world beyond Burlington.

THREE

Phish's Lost Masterpiece: The Legend of *Gamehendge*

Trey Anastasio, Page McConnell, and Jon Fishman all graduated from Goddard College's performing-arts program after submitting their senior study projects to their faculty advisers. McConnell—the group's original Goddard enrollee—titled his paper *The Art of Improvisation*. Fishman wrote a manual called *The Self-Teaching of Drumming*.

Anastasio titled his project *The Man Who Stepped into Yesterday*. It was a musical fable set in a fictional land called Gamehendge. Many Phish fans simply refer to the suite of songs as *Gamehendge*. Though the piece was rarely performed in its entirety, various individual songs became highlights of Phish's live repertoire. A few other *Gamehendge*-related tunes were added along the way, and the story line got fleshed out onstage, as Anastasio would elaborate about Gamehendge's inhabitants and power struggles.

Gamehendge defies easy description or categorization. Being that Phish is a rock band and *Gamehendge* unfolds as a series of songs that tell a story involving various characters, the first inclination would be to label it a "rock opera." But Anastasio had been exposed to the

Broadway theater by his mother while growing up, so *Gamehendge* might just as easily be considered a musical. In framing its main conceit, Anastasio drew from C. S. Lewis's *The Chronicles of Narnia*, and the abundance of spoken narration takes it further into the realm of theater and literature. Because it was never officially released on CD—although it has been bootlegged—you can't exactly call it a "concept album." Maybe a "concept tape"? That's the form in which Anastasio submitted it. The prized cassette is stored in the Goddard College archives.

So just what is it? *Gamehendge* might best be described as a rock musical in which challenging, multipart compositions are interspersed with expository narration. The songs, eight of them on the original tape, were preceded by spoken sections that set the scene and moved the story forward.

The inspirations for *Gamehendge* ran the musical gamut. Phish made discernible nods in their early music to various prog-rock and New Wave precursors, so it's not surprising to hear echoes of these informing *Gamehendge* and other early work. For instance, "The Squirming Coil"—from Phish's second album, *Lawn Boy*—could have easily passed for a track from one of Genesis's weird and whimsical albums, such as *Nursery Cryme* or *Foxtrot*.

By Anastasio's own admission, *Gamehendge* took some cues from Genesis's magnum opus, *The Lamb Lies Down on Broadway*, released in 1975, particularly the scene-setting "Chamber of 32 Doors." Genesis's musically ambitious and lyrically elliptical double album told of the spiritual transformation of Rael, a Puerto Rican street kid. *Gamehendge* was likewise a kind of prog-rock conception with cinematic musical passages and a fanciful libretto.

There were nonmusical points of reference, as well. Such literary and theatrical inspirations as *The Wizard of Oz*, *Alice in Wonderland*, and the aforementioned *Chronicles of Narnia* offered surreal means for its protagonists to enter other, more fantastical worlds wherein they learn life lessons. The name Icculus in *Gamehendge* closely resembles Icarus—the character from Greek mythology who flew too close to the sun, singing his wings and falling to earth. And the name *Gamehendge* itself suggested Stonehenge, the ring of standing stones assembled in England by prehistoric Druids who were ritually bound to the earth, sun, and change in seasons.

As regards the *Gamehendge* story line, Anastasio himself offered this succinct but trenchant summary:

> There are officially eight or nine songs, maybe ten songs. Colonel Forbin, the main character, is a retired army colonel out walking his dog. He finds this imaginary door or *Alice in Wonderland* kind of thing. He falls through the door and ends up in this other world, Gamehendge.
>
> Gamehendge was originally a beautiful, serene landscape where these people were living in harmony with nature. They had this book, *The Helping Friendly Book*, that they used to guide their way of life and rituals—"The Divided Sky" and all that stuff—until this guy Wilson enters the scene. He sees how naive they are, and so he enslaves them, cuts down the trees, builds a big castle, and hides the book.
>
> The story is basically that there's a revolution brewing. They're trying to get the book back and go back to their state of peace and tranquility. There are all these characters: Tela and the Unit Monster and Errand Woolfe, which is actually the name of a friend of mine, Aaron Woolf. The song "Wilson," which was the basis for a lot of this stuff, was written by him, so I characterized him and put him in *Gamehendge*.
>
> There's also an accountant, Mr. Palmer, who's part of the revolution. He's transferring money to the revolutionaries. Wilson catches him and hangs him in the public square. There's all this stuff that goes on. Eventually they get the book back, but of course by this time they've been perverted by the concept of power. So you can never go back in the end, and the guy who led the revolution just becomes the next Wilson. That's the general story.

"Wilson" was the first song written for *Gamehendge*. With its ominous two-beat low-E intro and crowd-participation chant of "Wilson . . . Wilson," it became a concert fixture. It rises to a boil when Errand Woolfe, the hotheaded organizer behind the revolution, shouts: "Wilson, can you still have fun?"

A seemingly juvenile query, it actually suggests something deeper and more relevant to our time. That is to say, those who wield power and amass wealth but still are desperately unhappy typically do their best to make everyone else miserable and subjugate them to lives of virtual slavery, as Wilson did to the denizens of Gamehendge.

"Wilson" opened disc two of Phish's *A Live One*, culled from their fall 1994 tour. Through the breakup, they played it 203 times, more than any other *Gamehendge* song except "The Lizards." *Gamehendge* was never far from Phish's minds or set lists. Anastasio even referenced the musical at Coventry, joking before the encore that the grand finale would be a complete performance of *Gamehendge* with full orchestra.

"Wilson" was obviously an important song to Phish and especially Anastasio. Its creation predated his move to Vermont. In fact, it went all the way back to the musical clique in his Princeton schooldays. "Wilson" was originally written by Tom Marshall and Aaron Woolf. "Our whole object was to make someone laugh with music," Marshall recalled. And they wrote prolifically, drawing Anastasio into their orbit, whereupon things really got interesting.

"Aaron and I wrote 'Wilson' on a piece of paper in Latin class," Marshall recalled. "It was this bizarre set of words, and we were laughing so hard. We started singing it to all of our friends, and Aaron, almost as part of the song, would go up to people afterward and ask, 'Do you get it?'

"Everyone would smile as we sang it, but as soon as they were faced with a question like that—'Do you get it?'—the smiles would disappear and they'd go, 'Well, no, not really.' But when we sang it for Trey, he was entranced and asked us to sing it again. And when Aaron asked the inevitable, 'Do you get it?' Trey went, 'Oh yeah, I get it.' And sure enough, he did. Phish was built upon it and *Gamehendge* was built upon it. It was the seed of the whole thing."

Anastasio made "Wilson" the centerpiece of the *Gamehendge* fable, which thematically boils down to the notion of paradise lost, with Wilson as the archetypal power-mad villain. He is overthrown by Errand Woolfe, who turns out not to be the beneficent savior the Gamehendge dwellers were hoping for but a wolf in sheep's clothing. The Who's anti-authoritarian anthem, "Won't Get Fooled Again"— "Meet the new boss/Same as the old boss"—could serve as a capsule summary of *Gamehendge*'s resigned political denouement.

And so *Gamehendge* does not have a happy ending, and instead reveals a cynicism or realism (take your pick) that put off at least one other member of Phish. Bassist Mike Gordon found the *Gamehendge* finale too hopeless, and that and other reservations—mainly that he felt it belonged more to Anastasio than the entire band—ultimately relegated *Gamehendge* to the back burner.

"Trey was all excited about *Gamehendge*, and I remember there were discussions about taking it on tour," recalled soundman Paul Languedoc. "I think he wanted to do something with theatrical parts in it, too. Of course, Fish would be up for anything, but I don't think the idea went over that great with the rest of the band.

"They eventually worked the songs into the catalog and started writing new material, which I think was a better idea."

A total of seventeen songs either appeared in the original *Gamehendge* or were later added to what might be termed the world of *Gamehendge*. Anastasio's song cycle always seemed more like a work in progress than a finished product, with his senior study submission looking more like a first draft in hindsight and the *Gamehendge* concert performances more like dress rehearsals. There really has been no final form for *Gamehendge*, though the run-throughs on June 25 and July 8, 1994, suggested the following came close to a fixed running order:

1. "Kung"
2. "Llama"
3. "The Lizards"
4. "Tela"
5. "Wilson"
6. "AC/DC Bag"
7. "Colonel Forbin's Ascent"
8. "Fly Famous Mockingbird"
9. "The Sloth"
10. "McGrupp and the Watchful Hosemasters"
11. "The Divided Sky"

This lineup omits the only non-original on Anastasio's tape (Jeff Holdsworth's "Possum"), sensibly replacing it with "McGrupp and the Watchful Hosemasters," which had been an early inspiration for the project and obviously belonged on it. Moreover, two of the Game-hendge dwellers' ritual chants open and close the tale: "Kung" and "The Divided Sky." Finally, "Llama" was inserted as a communiqué from Gamehendge future that served as a lead-in to the extended recounting of its historical past. Here's how Anastasio described "Llama" in notes accompanying its lyrics on *A Picture of Nectar*: "Many years after the overthrow of Wilson, a rebel soldier crouching high on a hilltop above the war-torn forests of Gamehendge spots a group of loyalists ap-proaching from their lakeside encampment below. His trusty llama stands beside him, loaded down with a canvas pack that holds two large bazooka-type guns to the animal's sides. Near the man sits a cache of blastopast, each capable of destroying the entire hillside in an instant."

The songs that follow "Llama"—the core of the musical play, as Anastasio originally conceived it—relate the story of how this desul-tory and destructive civil war began in what had for thousands of years been a place of "peace and tranquility."

A number of other songs have ties to *Gamehendge*. "The Man Who Stepped into Yesterday" served as the instrumental music behind

Anastasio's opening narration on the senior study tape. The group performed "The Man Who Stepped into Yesterday" quite a few times, joining it with a Hebrew folk song ("Avenu Malkenu") and then reprising "The Man Who Stepped into Yesterday."

"Icculus" was a spoken tribute to the god of Gamehendge and the bible he bestowed upon its people, *The Helping Friendly Book*. A genuine rarity, it could be as amusing as it was intense. "Read the book! Read the fucking book!" shouts Anastasio in a memorably profane version from 1994. The concept and name were appropriated by fans Richard Stern and John Friedman in 1990 for their pioneering collection of Phish set lists, which they cleverly christened *The Helping Phriendly Book*. The "HPB" took on a life of its own, and eventually show reviews were added to the set lists. The voluminous work of numerous "phriendly" Phish fans, documenting set lists from 1983 to the present, now resides online at www.phish.net/hpb.

Anastasio has asserted that humor is a key to *Gamehendge*. Perhaps the funniest moment comes in "The Lizards," when the noble knight Rutherford the Brave fords a raging river, realizing too late that his suit of armor would cause him to sink and drown (thus allowing Anastasio to rhyme "sunk" and "thunk"). This necessitated a heroic rescue by a creature called the Unit Monster. As for the Lizards, they're drolly described as "a race of people practically extinct from doing things smart people don't do." "Punch You in the Eye" was written after the *Gamehendge* saga but also involves evil king Wilson, along with an unfortunate kayaker who accidentally lands on its shore. He is captured and tortured but escapes, vowing to Wilson that "someday I'll kill you till you die." The song's principal virtue, beyond further establishing Wilson's venal character, is the music: spacious, burbling rock funk that opens into a mamba featuring Page McConnell's nimble Cuban-style piano and Anastasio's Santana-esque guitar. It is a brilliant piece of music that would be the centerpiece of another band's catalog, but Phish never even recorded it.

"Harpua" is often set in Gamehendge but involves a different gallery of characters: the monstrous canine Harpua, a runaway cat named

Poster Nutbag, and a heartbroken teenager named Jimmy. The part where Trey narrates Jimmy's adventure afforded Phish all kinds of opportunities to interpolate other bands' songs, either as snippets or in their entirety, within the "Harpua" narrative. One time they performed an entire album—Pink Floyd's *Dark Side of the Moon*—inside of "Harpua."

"Axilla" was allegedly the last *Gamehendge*-related song to enter the repertoire, at least according to McConnell (speaking in *The Phish Book*). Introduced in 1992, it involves warrior mythology without directly referencing any *Gamehendge* characters, so the connection is elusive.

Just how all these stragglers fit into the larger framework of *Gamehendge* is something that Anastasio himself perhaps never quite figured out. (Which doesn't mean that he can't still do so.) This much is obvious: Extracted from the whole, "Wilson," "The Lizards," and "AC/DC Bag" were performed with great frequency, becoming standards in the group's live repertoire.

Phish performed the "Colonel Forbin's Ascent" and "Fly Famous Mockingbird" tandem often in the early nineties. Anastasio would extemporaneously weave fanciful tales from the stage, enlarging the Gamehendge myth as he expounded on Forbin's efforts to reach the great and mighty Icculus in his quest to liberate the Lizards. After 1994, "Forbin's">"Mockingbird" became rarer than mockingbirds' teeth, and its appearances were cause for celebration.

"Trey has a side to him that loves Broadway," Brad Sands noted of Gamehendge in general and "Forbin's" in particular. "'*Col. Forbin, I know why you've come here!*' To me, it's Broadway all the way."

Phish is known to have performed *Gamehendge* in its entirety just five times. Set lists are unavailable for some late-1980s gigs, so it's possible there was another performance or two. *Gamehendge* debuted at Nectar's on March 12, 1988, when the second set was given over to the song cycle. It was bookended by a cover of jazzman Charlie Mingus's "Jump Monk" and "Run Like an Antelope." This maiden performance of *Gamehendge* opened with "McGrupp and the Watchful Hosemasters," a song cowritten with lyricist Tom Marshall that, along with "Wilson," had set the whole conception rolling in Anastasio's fertile mind.

"McGrupp and the Watchful Hosemasters" began as a poem Marshall sent to Anastasio in 1985. He posted it in his UVM dorm room for a year, and it turned into something else when Anastasio began work on *Gamehendge* at Goddard. McGrupp was Colonel Forbin's dog—the one he was out walking when he fell through the time portal into Gamehendge—and the song recounts the colonel's adventures from the perspective of an observant shepherd. Though it didn't appear in the submitted version of *The Man Who Stepped into Yesterday*, "McGrupp" showed up all four times the *Gamehendge* suite was performed after its Nectar's debut, displacing "Possum" as the closing number.

The breakout of *Gamehendge* at Nectar's was the first Phish gig attended by their manager-to-be, John Paluska. He has these recollections of the performance: "I remember thinking it was a pretty bold thing to do in a little nightclub. There was a fair amount of narration, so it was asking a lot of an audience to follow, a lot to assimilate in a bar setting. It was all very new and it was impressive and almost hard to take it all in."

Curiously, *Gamehendge* wouldn't be performed again for three and a half years. They came close a few times, such as their first New York City gig (at Kenny's Castaways in Greenwich Village), a few weeks after the Nectar's *Gamehendge*. They played everything except "Tela," albeit out of order (insomuch as there is an official order). *Gamehendge* also seemed to be on their minds during a weekend stand at The Front, another Burlington venue, in October 1989. Over the course of two nights they performed every song from the saga, breaking out "Tela" for the first time in over a year and suggesting that Anastasio was still tinkering with the songs and their running sequence.

The next performance of *Gamehendge* was at the North Shore Surf Club in Olympia, Washington, on October 13, 1991. Although Anastasio had a cold that night, it was still a strong performance. Yet the omission of "The Lizards," the interpolation of "The Landlady" and "Reba" between "Wilson" and "Colonel Forbin's Ascent," and the jumbled song order indicate that perhaps Phish backed into *Gamehendge* sideways that night. Still, there was plenty of narration.

The West Coast got its second *Gamehendge* on March 22, 1993, when it popped out early in the second set at the Crest Theater in Sacramento. This mammoth set included both a complete *Gamehendge* and a "Mike's Song" trilogy. The next one emerged during a fabled 1994 show in Charleston, West Virginia. Referred to as "Game-Hoist" in fan shorthand, it found them playing a full *Gamehendge* for the first set and their latest album, *Hoist*, complete and in order, during the second set. They played to a fairly empty room that night. A special show like that was Phish's way of "punishing" fans for skipping shows in out-of-the-way places—or, looked at another way, rewarding those die-hards who did expend the extra effort to make the gig. This "you snooze, you lose" strategy, as they called it, helped inculcate the notion among the growing horde following their tours that no show was worth writing off the itinerary, lest they miss a once-in-a-lifetime event like GameHoist.

Incidentally, this Charleston show also served to ignite further such adventures by Phish, according to longtime band associate Eric Larson. Their first complete performance of one of their own albums gave them an idea that blossomed into their Halloween covers concerts.

Larson recalled: "They got talking after the show and said, 'What if we did somebody else's album? What if we did it on Halloween? That could be a surprise.' That's what started it all, that show in Charleston, and it was spontaneous. They didn't plan to do that; they just did it."

The final performance of *Gamehendge* was only two weeks after its West Virginia breakout, making for the closest consecutive performances of the epic. They reprised *Gamehendge* at Great Woods, outside Boston, during the first set of a two-night weekend stand. Apparently this one was planned in advance. Kevin Shapiro recalled telling Jon Fishman that he intended to skip Great Woods to see the Aquarium Rescue Unit. Without giving anything away, Fishman strongly suggested that Shapiro attend, intimating that they had something special planned. It turned out to be Phish's last complete performance of *Gamehendge*.

Gamehendge doubtlessly got a double airing in close proximity because Phish had begun discussing the possibility of releasing *Gamehendge* as an interactive CD-ROM. They announced plans to do so in their fan newsletter and mentioned it in interviews. Then, just as quickly, the idea was dropped.

"It was one of the few things they ever announced they would do that they didn't do," noted Shapiro.

Anastasio shelved it, having made the decision that he didn't ever want to profit from *Gamehendge*. Moreover, there was a lack of enthusiasm for the *Gamehendge* project among the other band members. No doubt the project would have taken a lot of time, effort, and expense. Given that Phish was in the process of breaking nationally, producing a *Gamehendge* CD-ROM might well have been an untenable commitment at that time.

In January 1996, Anastasio said, "*Gamehendge* is on hold. All I can think about right now is the new album" (which would turn out to be *Billy Breathes*). And it was never put back in play.

In April 2001, I spoke with him about the possibility of including one of the *Gamehendge* shows in the *Live Phish* series, which had just been announced. The band members were in the process of selecting the first six shows to release. The conversation is typical of the way forward-thinking artists tend not to obsess over or even clearly recall events in the past:

ME: Have you thought of putting out any of the *Gamehendge* shows?

ANASTASIO: Kevin's just printing them up today. I've never heard them. There's two, right? The Crest Theater . . .

ME: I think there's five. There's Nectar's in 1988, one from Olympia in '91, the Crest Theater show from Sacramento in '93, and then you did it in Charleston, West Virginia, in '94.

ANASTASIO: That's where we did *Hoist* for the second set!

ME: The GameHoist concert!

ANASTASIO: Which one do they like?

ME: Well, I like the Sacramento '93 show. You also did it at Great Woods in '94. That one I haven't heard.

ANASTASIO: I don't think that one's worth . . . [*trails off*]

ME: The '93 Sacramento *Gamehendge* is very nicely done.

ANASTASIO: That's definitely an idea.

But, alas, none of the twenty numbered volumes of LivePhish or subsequent concert discs or downloads have yet turned out to be *Gamehendge* shows.

In my opinion, *Gamehendge* remains a major piece of unfinished business. Let me draw a parallel. In 2004, Brian Wilson resurrected, recorded, and released *Smile*. This abandoned 1967 album had been intended as the Beach Boys' follow-up to *Pet Sounds*, a majestic pop opus. But the pressure got to Wilson, the Beach Boys' leader, and he let go of it as various psychological issues made it increasingly difficult for him to function. More than a quarter-century later, Wilson triumphantly re-recorded *Smile*—which turned out to be every inch the classic that pop mythology had purported—putting that ghost to rest.

Gamehendge begs for the same rite of revisitation, completion, and closure, whether Anastasio does it with Phish or as a solo project, as Wilson did with *Smile*. It deserves to take its rightful place alongside such conceptual classics as the Who's *Tommy* and *Quadrophenia*, the Pretty Things' *S.F. Sorrow*, Frank Zappa's *Joe's Garage*, the Kinks' *Preservation, Acts I and II*, and Pink Floyd's *Dark Side of the Moon* and *The Wall*.

FOUR

Growth Spurt: 1988–1992

L ate one summer evening in July 1988, Phish had a decision to
make. They'd just finished the second night of a stand at Nectar's
and were caucusing outside the club at 2 in the morning. Monday
had turned to Tuesday, and Phish had been booked—or so they
believed—to play a bunch of shows in Colorado, commencing two
days hence. At the time, Mike Gordon handled bookings, and his girlfriend (and future first wife) Cilla Foster had put him in touch with
Warren Stickney, the owner of a club-restaurant in Telluride called
the Roma Bar, where she worked. Some vague promise of a monthlong tour had been made, which got amended into the less glamorous
offer of gigging at Roma for a week for a thousand bucks. But as the
date loomed, Stickney wasn't returning Gordon's calls to confirm
arrangements, and Phish grew uneasy about traveling across the
country on blind faith.

Still, Phish was up for an adventure, and the idea of playing outside
of New England was appealing. By this point the group had been
around for nearly five years and hadn't yet extended their reach much

beyond the local circuit. Their biggest step forward thus far in 1988 had been a booking at The Front—a popular new Burlington club that was the next step up from Nectar's, in terms of size. This gave them a larger hometown venue to play at for the next three years. This was progress, but Phish hungered for more and were ready to take their show on the road.

Still, the westward jaunt "was really up in the air," recalled Paul Languedoc. "If we got out there, would the band actually be playing, or would it just be a big waste of time? Mike finally got hold of Stickney at the last possible moment, and there was a big discussion among the band members about whether we should do it. We did, just for the fun of it, I guess."

They had a vote and decided to leave then and there for Colorado. The traveling party consisted of the four members of Phish and their skeletal road crew of Languedoc and lightman Tim Rogers (who preceded Chris Kuroda). They called their pals Ninja Custodian to sub for them at Nectar's, crammed gear and bodies into their claustrophobic, plywood-walled GMC cube van (aka "The Love Den"), and, as Gordon put it, "just drove forty hours straight to Colorado." That is, until the van gave out at 10,000 feet, necessitating emergency repair by soundman Languedoc, who also served as Phish's equipment manager, all-purpose fix-it guy, and miracle worker. He built Anastasio's guitars, Gordon's basses, and the band's road cases. In fact, his invaluable expertise led to an in-joke that Languedoc had actually constructed the band members.

Phish and crew rolled into Telluride, but Telluride didn't exactly roll out the red carpet. Unbeknownst to the band, many locals were boycotting Roma for owner Stickney's alleged nonpayment of staff and musicians. As a result, perhaps six to twelve people a night would turn out to see Phish—not that there was a glut of potential customers in this ski resort during the summer season. Those who did cross the picket line, so to speak, honored the boycott by not buying food or drinks at Roma.

On a promo picture advertising the gig, the band acknowledged the possible payment predicament with these handwritten addendums: "We drove 2000 miles expecting Warren to pay us $1000," "Vermont's Most Naïve Rock Band at Roma Fri and Sat," and—with an arrow pointing to their likenesses—"Suckers."

"Despite everything, it was a blast, a great experience," contended Languedoc. Moreover, Stickney ultimately made good on the grand he owed them. Phish played seven gigs in Colorado, including five at Roma on successive weekends; one at its competitor, the Fly Me to the Moon Saloon; and one at the Aspen Mining Company. Fly Me to the Moon was directly across the street from Roma, and because this venue was kosher with Telluride's night owls, it was packed for Phish's lone gig. Two years later, they returned for an encore performance.

In 2006, Phish issued a three-disc set titled *Colorado '88* documenting their stay in the Rocky Mountain State. The cover photo is a black-and-white shot of Anastasio and Page McConnell carrying McConnell's electric keyboard across the street from one club to another. While Phish mostly played to minuscule crowds in Telluride, they made some loyal fans and, for the first time, presented their adventurous music outside of their New England comfort zone. As it turned out, Colorado would rank high on the list of states they played most often, trailing only Vermont, New York, California, and Massachusetts.

Most important, the '88 Colorado road trip galvanized Phish for the "get in the van" lifestyle of an itinerant rock band on their way up. Like all the great alternative rock bands of that time, from R.E.M. to the Minutemen, Phish paid their dues, putting in the long miles, late nights, and backbreaking work of a group hungry to be heard. City by city, they slowly built up a following. It started with Boston and Colorado and spread to Atlanta, Chicago, and Washington, D.C. College towns such as Athens, Georgia; Charlottesville, Virginia; and Chapel Hill, North Carolina, got on board early, too. Later on in the nineties, when Phish started to gain recognition, many presumed they were a suddenly successful new band, causing Jon Fishman to joke, "I guess nine years of overnights makes us an overnight success." So it was in 1988 that all four became full-time musicians, with no out-side jobs or commitments. On March 12, John Paluska, who would become their manager, saw Phish for the first time. Then a junior ma-joring in English and math at Amherst College in Massachusetts, Paluska was hanging out with his friends in the Burlington band Ninja Custodian, who took him to see Phish at Nectar's.

"I very specifically remember the guys in Ninja Custodian saying, 'They're a lot like Frank Zappa.' So I went with curious expectations, and it was a striking situation. There was something very incongruous about it to me right from the start because they were playing at this neighborhood bar for no cover on a very cramped, almost nonexist-ent stage. Yet they were so polished and so good, and they had such a depth of material.

"I've always thought of that show as a microcosm of what their thing became, in every sense, with a certain intensity and locked-in rapport between them and the audience. There was nothing casual about what was going on there. People were really into it, and I felt like probably a lot of people felt like over the years when they went to their first Phish show, which was that there was a lot of already es-tablished understanding that I didn't know anything about."

That night he approached Mike Gordon, who was their de facto business manager, and hired Phish to play a party at the co-op house, known as "The Zoo," where he was social director. It was Phish's first paying gig outside of Vermont (they made $600), and it kicked off Paluska's longtime professional relationship with them.

A childhood friend of Paluska's, Ben "Junta" Hunter, was similarly smitten when he saw Phish for the first time. Junta—pronounced pho-netically, not like the word meaning military coup leaders—was a music addict and small-gig organizer who attended Boston University. While Paluska arranged some dates for Phish in western Massachu-setts, Hunter booked a couple of wildly successful Boston shows in late 1988 at a college hangout called Molly's. He was also instrumental in arranging their breakthrough gig at Boston's premier showcase club, the Paradise.

Paluska recalled receiving a call from Page McConnell, who asked him to be their manager. He didn't know what exactly a manager did and still had a semester of college to complete, but since he was already getting them successful gigs, he said "sure." Paluska and Hunter took over Phish's business affairs, which the group had previously handled themselves. They shared an apartment in Boston and christened their management company Dionysian Productions. Hunter, who still had a year of school to finish and plans to travel afterward, eventually moved on, but Paluska helped steer their career and manage their affairs for the duration. Dionysian migrated from one Boston bedroom community to another—from Brookline to Watertown, Waltham, and Lexington—before settling down in the band's home base of Burlington in August 1995.

"He was not the stereotypical old-school manager you always hear about," said Beth Montuori Rowles, whom Paluska hired to work in the Phish office shortly after moving it to Burlington. Prior to that, Rowles worked for promoter Don Law in Boston.

Paluska guided Phish to success without making all the seemingly necessary compromises. Phish were very much a self-made band, and they negotiated their way through the music business without a screaming, heavy-handed manager having to play bad cop for them. Paluska had a quiet elegance in his demeanor, and the way he comported himself was disarming to those used to arm-twisting and raised voices.

"I guess that's just how I'm wired," said Paluska, looking back in 2009. "We just pursued a different approach. We built trust and long-term relationships with people we worked with and always had that silly, naive idea that we could actually craft arrangements with people where everybody was satisfied and felt good about things. My goal in any business dealing was not to beat somebody up or get the upper hand but to have a spirit of fairness and mutual respect."

Paluska was extremely hands-on in certain areas—routing tours, negotiating deals, working out decisions and details with the band members. Some feel that Phish's success had much to do with the working relationship between Anastasio and Paluska, who bounced around ideas all the time. The combination of the guitarist's ceaseless imagination and the manager's pragmatic execution made for a productive chemistry.

"Trey has always been extraordinarily driven and is constantly scheming," Paluska said. "He's the kind of person who's always turning ideas over in his head. That's not to say the other band members aren't as well. But I would say Trey was the catalyst, the one most actively pushing things forward and suggesting things.

"So, yeah, we spent a lot of time talking through the endless cascade of ideas that ushered forth out of him," he acknowledged with a laugh.

By all accounts, Paluska was good about delegating responsibilities to others, too, and the atmosphere in the Phish office was generally youthful, relaxed, and fun. One day his parents dropped by and joked, "Where are the adults around here?"

One of the most significant shows in Phish's career came the next year, in early 1989, when they sold out the Paradise Theater, Boston's key showcase club. The Paradise is where U2, Oasis, a post-Stooges Iggy Pop, and countless others played breakthrough gigs on their way up. The Paradise could hold 650 people, and Phish packed the club to capacity with a little help from their friends.

Much has been said about early fans' desire to spread the word by dragging friends to shows, making tapes for anyone who would listen, and proselytizing Phish at every opportunity. The faithful went the extra mile at this turning-point gig. Many made the road trip from Burlington to Boston to cheer them on. A couple of Phish's ardent early supporters, Tom Baggott and a guy known as Brother Craig, rented two Bluebird buses and packed each with forty-seven Phishheads. They also organized carpools and, by Baggott's count, sold 207 tickets to the home crowd for the Paradise show.

Since The Paradise wouldn't book Phish, Phish booked The Paradise. This was a brilliant gambit by managers Hunter and Paluska.

Arriving in carpools and busloads from back home to pack the house was the fans' contribution to Phish's upward mobility. Anastasio's mom even returned from Ireland to attend the show.

The bus ride itself was a trip, in more ways than one. "As was typical, we were all messed up the whole ride down on the bus," Baggott related. "I tipped the bus driver hundreds of dollars. I was like, 'Hear no evil, see no evil, do no evil,' and he was like, 'Fine by me.' We had a keg on the bus, and there was definitely plenty of extracurricular activity going on."

In Baggott's recollection, Phish rose to the occasion that night. "Oh, they were on fire," he said. "It was a great show." The fans performed with gusto, too, dancing with the frantic, dervish-like abandon they'd perfected over the years at Nectar's and The Front. It was quite an evening, all the way around. And it made an impact.

"I was standing right next to this dude," Baggott continued, "and he turns to someone else and says, 'You know, I wouldn't give these guys a gig, and I don't know how the hell they did it, but here they are. They sold out my club.' He was just blown away."

There were more ripples when word got around Boston that these unknowns from Vermont had packed The Paradise. And not just sold it out but left a few hundred ticketless Boston collegians standing in the street.

Beth Montuori Rowles recalled the reaction at Don Law's office the next day: "Jody Goodman, who was the club booker at the time, was like, 'Does anybody know who this band Phish is? They sold out The Paradise last night. How did that happen? I've never even heard of them before. They're from Vermont. What is this? They sold the place out!'

"All of a sudden it was like the radar's on them. The next time Phish played in Boston, the Don Law Company promoted it. They wanted a piece of it. End of story."

Interestingly, Mike Gordon—while acknowledging the Paradise show's significance—does not remember it being one of the band's more stellar performances.

"It was definitely a landmark gig, and our managers had gone to great lengths to make it seem like we were much better-known and respected than we were, with radio station ads, etc.," he acknowledged. "It was exciting, but all I remember was the music feeling not so good. Feeling like we can't really groove together, the acoustics aren't great, just sort of screechy-sounding and blaring and not fun.

In fact, the next gig, two nights later at Dartmouth College, was much better than the Paradise gig."

He felt similarly about Phish's first Boston-area gig—at Molly's, in Allston, in November 1988. "The Molly's gig was musically mediocre," he recalled. "The next night we played in upstate New York [Nardi's, in Clinton] for like ten people and it was really fun. The night after that we played a frat at Hamilton College [also in Clinton]. It wasn't anything like the exposure or landmark that playing in Boston was. But with the pressure of that gone, it was like, 'Okay, now we can let our hair down and be silly.' There was a big picture behind us of the founder of the fraternity. We'd have one big light shining on that picture as we'd play to it and make jokes about it. It was just that free-flowing feeling that can make for great jamming as well."

The success they had renting the Paradise not only opened some doors but also gave them the notion to try the same strategy in places where the doors still weren't opening very easily.

"They were having a hard time because they were so unconventional," recalled manager Paluska. "People don't realize these guys were not an easy band to pitch. They were way complicated. This was the era of grunge. In 1989 and 1990, Pearl Jam and Nirvana were breaking on the scene. It was a very different sensibility in terms of what was considered cool music, especially on a nightclub level.

"I'd send out a demo tape with 'David Bowie' and 'Golgi Apparatus' and those kinds of songs. . . . I mean, I had a lot of unreturned phone calls and very unsatisfying conversations with owners or buyers at clubs. We had to make our own breaks."

So in the early nineties they started renting venues around New England: places like the Colonial Theatre in Keene, New Hampshire; the Portsmouth Music Hall in New Hampshire; and various rooms outside Boston, such as the Somerville Theatre, the Strand (in Dorchester), and Memorial Auditorium (in Worcester). They even rented Boston's World Trade Center for one of their first big New Year's Eve shows.

"It was kind of fun, and in a way it bred this entrepreneurial spirit that led to our festivals. You can see a real direct lineage there. We were doing our own thing early on and got a taste for it. We saw the difference in how it felt to do those shows. It felt a little more like an adventure. It was our thing. We weren't playing at some club on somebody else's schedule and under somebody else's rules. We made our own rules.

"Later on, when we did our festivals, we were already in the practice and saw the benefits of doing it ourselves. We could control all the parameters and put it out there the way we wanted. There was something very satisfying about creating something out of whole cloth instead of plugging it in to some existing paradigm."

Phish began doing it themselves because many promoters weren't interested in them. But the joke was on the promoters, because Phish were doing great business every night. Moreover, by cutting out the middleman, they were able to control costs and make more money, which they plowed back into their operation.

"That was a big thing with them," noted Paluska. "They had a lot more gear and production stuff early on than most bands. They were really clear that any money that came in, they wanted to use to make their show better. Everything was in service to the show."

All this self-sufficiency emboldened Phish to continue to do things their way. In a sense, they were learning at this stage that they didn't need the music industry—or, more specifically, they didn't need to follow its rules just because it was "the way things are done." Once they were able to quit their day jobs and fully support themselves as musicians, however modestly, they realized there was no imperative to compromise.

"Within the band, there was a sense of 'Why would we want to compromise anything when we can make a good living doing exactly what we want to do?'" said Paluska. "Of course, that was the best decision they ever could've made, because people are attracted to something pure. I've always been a big believer that intent is so fundamental in people's visceral response to any art form—particularly music, since it's just a direct experience. There's no mistaking Phish's intent. There was joy and purity in what they were doing. You might not like it, but you certainly couldn't deny it."

Things started breaking for them, even in hard-to-crack New York City. The opening of the Wetlands Preserve—on Valentine's Day 1989—gave jam bands like Phish a place to play in the Big Apple. The downtown Manhattan club nurtured the fledgling jam-band scene over the next decade. It served as a launching pad for Blues Traveler and also helped the Spin Doctors, the Dave Matthews Band, and Widespread Panic gain some traction. Phish themselves played eight memorable shows there in 1989 and 1990. "Things started to build for them in New York once the Wetlands opened," manager Paluska noted. "That place was very much tailored around music like theirs. We were a natural fit and built an audience pretty quickly there."

On April 13, 1989, Chris Kuroda officially took over as Phish's lighting director. Kuroda had been a fan since first catching Phish at Goddard. Subsequently, he took guitar lessons from Anastasio and followed the band as devoutly as anyone in the crowd at Nectar's. Kuroda had been managing a place in Burlington that silk-screened T-shirts but quit to join Phish's crew. At a show in New Hampshire, the group's lightman, Chris Stecher, took a break and Kuroda filled in on "Fly Famous Mockingbird." Anastasio noticed the unusually creative coordination of lights and music, and Kuroda was bumped up to lighting director—a job he performed for the next fifteen years (and resumed in 2009, when Phish reunited).

His ability to fuse lighting with music and his uncanny sense of timing lends an added dimension to Phish shows. He became so integral that Phish had him sit in with them at band practices from time to time.

"I was hitting all the changes and trying to learn how to count the songs, which are all in wacko time signatures," Kuroda recalled. "It got to a point where they realized I was capable of keeping up with them. So we would talk about how to light certain songs— new songs they were writing that had difficult time changes." He would also "jam" with them on lights. His acumen as a lighting engineer largely came on the job, but he also went to school—learning the craft at Veralite in Dallas and Altman Stage Lighting in Yonkers, New York—during off-time. The band's move to bigger rooms necessitated greater engineering sophistication to master automated lighting and bigger rigs. He was astute enough to take into account what had happened to some of his cohorts in the Phish crew who hadn't kept abreast of changes, and he didn't make the same mistakes himself.

He believes that a certain element of synesthesia—a blurring of the senses, as in "hearing" color and "seeing" sound—comes into play at Phish concerts.

"Music affects many senses, and with lighting you can add the visual sense," he said. "More than just watching the musicians play, you see a visual mood. Color affects mood in human beings, so I'm able to enhance or augment a certain song with the right colors to create the same mood that the music itself is trying to project. You can tune in people in yet another sense, so to speak."

The same month Kuroda graduated to lights, Phish won the Rock Rumble—a battle of the bands—at The Front. They beat out some of the hipper bands about town, like the hardcore groups Screaming Broccoli and Hollywood Indians. This show was also the latest in an ongoing string of naked moments in the spotlight for their free-spirited drummer, who was lowered to the stage in the buff for his vacuum-cleaner solo. (Sadly, someone neglected to plug in the appliance.) With their cash winnings from the Rock Rumble, Phish funded the recording of "Bathtub Gin" and "Split Open and Melt," which would appear on the album *Lawn Boy*.

Meanwhile, Phish released *Junta*—their second album, if you count *The White Tape*—this same busy April. It, too, was issued in cassette form and sold at gigs. The cover illustration was drawn by Jim Pollock, the Goddard dormmate and bandmate of McConnell's. Pollock's commissioned artwork would adorn Phish T-shirts, posters, and even concert tickets throughout their career. His cartoon-like woodcuts illustrated characters and situations from Phish songs, and he also contributed cover art to the LivePhish series. It is not surprising that Anastasio has cited *Junta* as his favorite of Phish's studio albums. It was made for the innocently self-indulgent art of it, without expectations but with great care, in which the band revels in their first big burst of creativity. It contains several defining songs in Phish's repertoire, including "You Enjoy Myself," "The Divided Sky," "David Bowie," and the "Fluffhead"/"Fluff's Travels" tandem, each of which ran on record for at least ten minutes—and generally much longer in concert. "You Enjoy Myself" and "David Bowie" served as open-ended jamming vehicles, while "The Divided Sky" and "Fluffhead" were revered for their musicality and precision.

"The Divided Sky" contains some of Anastasio's most lyrical guitar work, especially a passage of thoughtful, clear-toned exposition that follows the mid-song pause. *Junta* also gave McConnell space to solo on acoustic piano on "Esther" and "Foam"—a refreshing sound on a rock album at the tail end of the synth-drenched 1980s.

Anastasio considers "You Enjoy Myself" *the* Phish song. It is by far the most-performed Phish song. For a band whose appeal had much to do with how rarely they repeated themselves, "YEM" turned up on 40 percent of their set lists. It was also the last song they played at the October 7, 2000, show that inaugurated a two-year hiatus.

As with so many early Phish songs, the words were hardly the point. In concert, "YEM" consisted of intricately composed sections that expanded into open-ended jams. A precise reading of the fixed compositional parts prepared the band members for the jams that followed, providing a kind of focus that would help ensure they wouldn't aimlessly meander. As counterintuitive as it might sound, Phish's most raging jams began with an orderly rendering of the composed sections that preceded it. This is why early compositions like "You Enjoy Myself," which followed this form, proved to be the most jam-worthy vehicles.

"'You Enjoy Myself' was the first long, written-out piece of music where there's a jam at the end," Anastasio said. "It was the first time that kind of became the thing. You're so linked up in the worked-out stuff, you're such a unit, that it gets you lined up as you're leading up to the jam."

"To get so tight in a preplanned way makes the looseness juxtapose even more," added Gordon. "I look at it that the written-out stuff is a sort of ritual, almost like a prayer session that gets my mind in gear for what's to come. Sort of like a Hassidic Jew doing a bunch of prayers and moving until he starts to reach God. There's like this legwork that has to be done, something where the prayers are already written."

There were other highlights on *Junta*, such as the playfully surreal "Fee"; the nightmarishly psychedelic "Foam"; and Mike Gordon's "Contact," the most unconventional rock song ever written about a car. The amused hosts of NPR's *Car Talk* laughingly called it the worst car song ever written.

In this period, before Tom Marshall became Anastasio's full-time writing partner, there was a rift between words and music in Phish. The lyrics might have seemed nonsensical while the music was grandly ambitious. Still, even when the playful surrealism of the words existed mainly to set the table for the music, there were shards of wisdom to be extracted here and there. Consider these cautionary lines from "Fee"— a song about an ill-fated love triangle involving a weasel, a chimpanzee, and a gospel singer—which in hindsight seem eerily predictive:

> *Oh, Fee, you're trying to live a life*
> *That's completely free*
> *You're racing with the wind,*

You're flirting with death
So have a cup of coffee
And catch your breath.

In a nutshell, these two aspects made Phish especially unique: (1) Anastasio's compositional acumen, developed under Ernie Stires and carried forward with Phish, and (2) the listening exercises Phish practiced for hours in rehearsal. They had inventive composed material to play and were also able to improvise smartly and as a collective.

Looking back on this early period Anastasio noted, "I think what made Phish unique is that there was so much composed music at the beginning. If you go back to *Junta*, it's 'Foam,' 'Divided Sky,' 'You Enjoy Myself,' 'Fluffhead.' These are long, heavily composed atonal fugues. We would play these very complicated pieces and then improvise. What I found was that the improvisation was bent because we had just coexisted in music that was very tightly composed.

"If we play a four-part fugue, with two hands on the piano playing the inner lines, me playing the melody and Mike playing the bass line, where everything's interwoven, then when we improvised, the improvisation was changing keys and going together like a snake.

"It made it unique to my ear from other bands I had jammed with. Usually you have a band kind of strumming along and one guy playing a solo. This was not really solos at all, and it really went far. At which point we liked it so much we began to do exercises and rehearse improvisation for hours. That was incredible . . . and fun."

Initially, *Junta* didn't travel much beyond Phish's immediate world as a limited cassette-only release in '89. It received its day in the sun, however, in 1992 after Phish signed to Elektra and the album was reissued as a double CD. The original work was too long to fit on a single disc but left considerable room on a second disc, so forty minutes of bonus material were added: two bits of madness taped at Nectar's ("Icculus" and "Sanity") and a lengthy extract of home jamming,

dubbed "Union Federal," pulled from one of Phish's Oh Kee Pa ceremonies. This particular one occurred in August 1989.

The Oh Kee Pa ceremony was a Native American test of endurance,
and for Phish it represented immersion into the realm of jamming
that itself tested their temporal limits as musicians. There were three
Oh Kee Pa ceremonies, at which they played for hours without stopping. Marijuana figured into the bonding ritual, and these endless
jams can be seen as precursors to the listening exercises that would
become part of band practices for a number of years. Mike Gordon
elaborated:

"Trey used to take fresh chocolate and vanilla and maple syrup
and all these natural ingredients and make four small cups of hot
chocolate that had a half-ounce of pot in them. This one time, he was
living on the river in Plainfield, Vermont, and we used to practice in
his apartment. I would do the commute to Goddard a couple times
a week. His neighbor around the corner was this Hungarian girl, and
she was cooking us this big meal—Hungarian mushroom soup and
all that.

"She said it would be ready in about two hours, so we started this
jam session and it ended up going for eight hours. She wrapped it up
for us. We never had dinner with her. We started at 3 and went to 11
at night. One of things that came up was the bass riff and the guitar
riff to 'Weekapaug Groove.'"

Over time, this means of finding riffs for songs in fragments of
jams would become commonplace for Phish. It was how much of the
music for their 1998 album, *The Story of the Ghost*, got written. The
Oh Kee Pa ceremonies and the listening exercises they'd do in band
practices are where Phish learned not just how to jam but how to
compose in the moment (and there is a difference).

Not to confuse matters (though they *are* confusing), but Anastasio
wrote a brief instrumental that he titled "The Oh Kee Pa Ceremony."
It appeared on *Lawn Boy* and had nothing to do with their ceremonial
jamming rituals. In fact, he wrote this springy little number on guitar

while riding shotgun as Chris Kuroda drove Phish back from a gig. Anastasio would look up and ask Kuroda, "How does this sound?" each time he'd come up with a new lick or section.

In the late eighties, Phish began incorporating "secret language" into their performances. These were musical cues they could play that would trigger a preplanned response. Phish's secret language was somewhat similar to Frank Zappa's hand signals in that they cued some change in the music without the audience's knowledge. One cue involved playing the chorus riff from "Up, Up and Away" (the late-1960s sunshine-pop hit by the 5th Dimension) and then hitting either a low or high note, at which point they'd ascend from the lowest notes or descend from the highest ones, respectively. A tritone down meant play at half-speed. A brief reference to the Beatles' "Get Back" meant return to the first song in a series. And so on.

At a 1992 show in Portsmouth, New Hampshire, Phish clued their audience in on the secret language and taught them cues created specifically for the fans. The best-known of these involved a snatch of *The Simpsons* theme song, at which point the crowd loudly responded "d'oh!" like Homer Simpson. Upon hearing a riff from the Byrds' "Turn! Turn! Turn!" the crowd members were expected to turn around. The point of all this seeming nonsense was to deepen the band's relationship with the audience and confound the uninitiated. The sharing of secret language encouraged audience members to become more than casual fans. They were now band-schooled and ritually involved in the enterprise, conferring a certain element of "membership" upon them while confusing newbies and non-initiates who popped into shows out of curiosity. As Ken Kesey's Merry Pranksters used to say back in the sixties, you were either on the bus or off the bus.

Phish didn't receive its first notice in the national music media until the fall of 1989, when they were accorded brief mention in *Relix*. Founded in 1973, this retro-minded fanzine existed largely to keep tabs on the activities of the Grateful Dead and other "relix" of the sixties San Francisco scene. In the nineties it would closely track the contemporary jam-band scene, too. But in 1989 there was no such scene, just a handful of bands making waves close to their respective home bases. Phish were accorded several paragraphs in the September/October 1989 issue of *Relix*.

With half a dozen years and several hundred gigs under their belt, Phish were, almost insultingly, the subject of that issue's "Too New to Be Known" column. Writer William Ruhlmann had his ear to the ground, though, observing, "The band possesses a musical flair almost beyond belief." Praising *Junta*, which had been released a half year earlier, he noted, "The underlying strength of all the material is the virtuosic musicianship and wry sense of humor that runs through it."

Indeed, humor figured heavily, especially in Phish's first decade. At a later point, when Anastasio began to worry that the gags were overshadowing the music—especially in the minds of writers and critics, who played up the jokey elements—the humor receded and the jams got longer. But making themselves and others laugh was always part of the Phish experience.

Discussing the themes that ran through Phish's career, Tom Marshall felt that "humor through music" was a key one. "'Cause it started out about making people laugh," he said. "All of the band members are incredible comedians, they really are. They're really fucking funny. I mean, I'm fairly funny, I can make people laugh, but everything out of their mouths would be worthy of writing down. And once Brad Sands [Phish's road manager] was in that mix, I couldn't get a word in edgewise and didn't want to. That's another guy who thinks on his feet.

"Those five people on one bus together were kind of overwhelming, and they loved new blood to prey on. I quickly found out anything I said that they could latch onto became fodder. Don't give them material, I guess, is the lesson I came away with. Or let them feed on someone else. It was brutal but funny as hell."

The most obvious card in the band is Jon Fishman, who's worn a dress onstage for most of the band's career (including the current reunion) and, on various occasions, would get completely naked. On the cover of *Lawn Boy*, he's shown in greenish-gray makeup—presumably caked with the filthy spew from his other instrument, the vacuum cleaner, with which he is pictured. He frequently claimed a front-and-center comic-relief spot in the set for a vacuum-cleaner solo.

Fishman's "doughnut dress" is a ghastly garment with large orange-pink circles on a bluish-purple background. In 1995, he recalled how the dress became part of the act: "I was at my friend's house and there was this pile of material they were making bags out of. There was this dress in the pile, and I was just joking around and put it on. It looked really funny and I thought, 'I'll wear this onstage tonight,' and I've ended up wearing it for like six years now."

"Without a washing," quipped McConnell.

"Now it gets washed pretty regularly," Fishman noted. Dry-cleaned, even, and neatly returned on a hanger.

At a party, Fishman was challenged to play a vacuum cleaner after claiming to have taught everyone in the band how to play their instruments. He made some ersatz squonks and bleats through the activated appliance's suction tube, and a few nights later he tried it out onstage at Nectar's. The vacuum cleaner solo became a recurring comic interlude on stages small and large across the band's career.

There were other gags: the giant hot dog that sailed the band across the Boston Garden at their New Year's Eve show in 1994; the trampolines, found at a yard sale, that Gordon and Anastasio hopped up and down on while playing at points during "You Enjoy Myself," "Mike's Song," and others; the "Big Ball Jam," during which the audience's bouncing of large rubber balls guided the band's improvisation. Even some of the songs they covered, from Fishman's warbling of charmingly acid-damaged Syd Barrett tunes and the group's faithfully hammy renditions of Deodato's "2001 (Also Sprach Zarathustra)" and the Edgar Winter Group's "Frankenstein" had comic intent.

"I think it's refreshing to see people onstage who aren't taking themselves too seriously," offered McConnell.

"The dress allows me to actually *never* take myself too seriously," Fishman said with a chuckle.

"It's a fine line between something that's funny and something that's so silly that it detracts," concluded McConnell. "I think we're always trying to push that envelope."

Pushing it to the limit was all part of the Phish experience. The recurring stage gags, the always-varying set lists, and the inventive, unpredictable jams marked Phish as a virtually unclassifiable entity on the music scene of the late 1980s and early 1990s.

"When they came up with an idea, whenever they found a new direction to go in, 100 percent focus would go that way," Chris Kuroda said of Phish's creative mind-set.

"That's Trey's personality," added Paul Languedoc. "He's very excited about what he's working on at that particular point in time. The other guys, too, but Trey's obviously a very ambitious, enthusiastic guy."

Determined to stamp themselves uniquely, Phish even began carrying their own sound and lighting equipment at a very early stage in their career. They'd always bring their own gear, and sometimes club owners would say, "Why are you bringing that crap in here? Why don't you just use what we have?"

That was the whole point: It was *their* stuff.

"We stamped ourselves with a certain uniqueness that any other band on any given night in any other club just didn't seem to have," Chris Kuroda pointed out. "Those things became incredibly important."

For instance, Phish's stage backdrops, created by Gordon's mom, were completely unique, "We always had to put the backdrop up," Languedoc recalled. "The band was insistent. They'd walk in for sound check and go, 'Where's the backdrop?' 'There's nowhere to hang it in this place.' 'Oh yeah there is.' There'd be a huddle and a meeting, and next thing you know, it was up. They'd find some way to get at least part of it up, by folding it or something, 'cause it *had* to be up."

Even some of Phish's instruments were homemade. Languedoc, in addition to being Phish's soundman and equipment manager, built guitars and basses for Anastasio and, up to a point, Gordon. Onstage, Anastasio has always held fast to a single Languedoc custom guitar, using effects pedals, rack-mounted gear, and pure technique—rather than a bunch of different guitars—to get the sounds he wants. Anastasio is, as Paul Languedoc put it, a "one-guitar man."

It's hard to overstate how important Languedoc was to Phish. Anastasio met Languedoc when he brought his Ibanez electric to Time Guitars, the Burlington shop where Languedoc worked, for repair. Anastasio sold that instrument and bought a guitar made by Languedoc, which he played for a few years. Once Languedoc began working full time for the band, he made Anastasio the first custom-built guitar to bear his own name, a prototype Languedoc hollowbody, which Anastasio played from 1987 to 1996. (Another guitar that Languedoc built for him in 1991 never saw much action.) Anastasio switched to a new Languedoc hollowbody in 1996 and played it through 2002. After Phish's hiatus, another new Languedoc model, called Alcoa, became Anastasio's preferred ax. He's held fast to his Languedocs throughout the 2009 reunion shows, too.

Over the years, Phish practiced whenever and wherever they could at their various Vermont domiciles—at the house Languedoc shared with Anastasio and Fishman on Weaver Street in Winooski, in Anastasio's apartment on the river in Plainfield, in the basement of the group house on King Street in Burlington. When Languedoc bought a house in Westford, Phish claimed the loft above the workshop he built next to it as their ultimate rehearsal space.

Phish recorded *Lawn Boy*, the follow-up to *Junta*, at Dan Archer's new studio outside Burlington. As with *Junta*, Phish packed *Lawn Boy* with songs that had become staples of their concert repertoire. These include "Reba" (the *uber* Phish song, in many a fan's mind), "Split Open and Melt," and "Bathtub Gin." For the Phish connoisseur, "Reba" had it all: zany lyrics that didn't make sense but tickled the imagination; a multipart composed section, with plenty of twists and turns; and an ending jam that carried the piece to climax with a single screaming note. Tom Marshall wrote the lyrics for three songs on *Lawn Boy*— "The Squirming Coil," "Bouncing Around the Room," and the lounge lizard–like title track—signaling the increasing role he would play as Anastasio's cowriter in the coming years.

Lawn Boy was released on the Absolute a Go Go label. Phish received a tough lesson in small-label economics after signing with the New Jersey–based outfit. There was nothing wrong with Absolute a Go Go itself, whose signings reflected the good taste of founder Brad Morrison. He created the label in 1986 and two years later signed an exclusive distribution deal with Rough Trade America, the U.S. affiliate of the upstart U.K.-based label. Throughout the 1980s, Rough Trade had been among Britain's most respected independents, launching the career of the Smiths and others on the U.K. scene's cutting edge.

In spring 1990, Absolute a Go Go released *Hot Chocolate Massage* by Tiny Lights, a likeable indie-pop band from New Jersey whose previous work had gotten buried on a major label. Phish's *Lawn Boy* came out that fall. In 1991, Rough Trade America went bankrupt, taking Absolute a Go Go (and *Lawn Boy*) down with it. (Incidentally, Rough Trade was relaunched in 2000.)

During its brief window of opportunity, the original *Lawn Boy* sold well—"To the consternation of rock critics," in Morrison's words. Morrison elaborated on this turn of events: "Phish, in particular, were hated by the music-biz establishment, who all took time out of their busy days to phone the label and tell them the record was 'shit.' As the fall leaves turned, it became obvious that the Phish record was destined to become the label's first hit. Suddenly, music impresarios all called to say that they had changed their mind. *Lawn Boy* was not 'shit,' it was now a 'fluke.'"

In the wake of the label's bankruptcy, the court seized Absolute a Go Go's master tapes. Phish bought back the rights to *Lawn Boy*, which Elektra reissued in 1992. Despite its eventual reappearance, the album's virtual vanishing act so soon after its initial release didn't help the band's momentum or inspire much faith in the music business. Incidentally, original compact discs of *Lawn Boy* on Absolute a Go Go (10,000 were made) now fetch modest collector's figures on eBay. The rarer vinyl version, of which under a thousand were pressed, now changes hands for $250 to $500.

Meanwhile, Phish were beginning to garner some solid notices in newspapers and independent media. There would always be an element of snarky, patronizing commentary. In its preview of the band's 1989 gig at a club in Poughkeepsie, for instance, the Bard College newspaper noted that "neo-hippy [*sic*] bands are trendy. . . . This is a band for Deadheads, fusion fans and light-hearted druggies." At the same time, there were growing signs that writers who didn't come bearing anti-Dead, anti-hippie, anti-jam agendas were starting to appreciate what they were hearing.

"As long as the songs are, the group never runs low on invention," wrote John Wirt in the *Richmond Times-Dispatch*. "Instead, a single song holds a rich cache of ideas."

"Fun but skillful zaniness," noted Phil Smith in a review for the *Portland Oregonian*. "The Phish style of virtuosity instinctively homes in on people's musical pleasure zones in original and endless ways."

Overseas, the *Independent* of London touted their "exuberant salad of styles."

"The music defies categorization" was a frequently repeated line, but that didn't keep writers from trying.

"We've been compared to more bands than any other band," laughed McConnell.

"It all depends on what track was playing when they [heard us]," added Anastasio.

The Grateful Dead? Santana? Frank Zappa? King Crimson? Genesis? The best answer might be all of the above—and none of the above.

By 1991, Phish were really starting to rage onstage. Kevin Shapiro, the Deadhead-turned-Phishhead who would become their archivist, caught his first Phish show in Cleveland on the fall 1991 tour and can vividly recall the experience. "I was totally blown away by the music. At the time I thought maybe it was one long song, because I didn't fully grasp the definition from one song to the next. There were short breaks, if any, between songs, and it was pretty snappy. It seemed smooth and polished. I would've called it very rehearsed. I didn't realize they played a different set every night."

Phish did realize that what they were doing from night to night was pretty special, so they started taping every show—on cassettes and then, in 1992, on digital audio tape (DAT). Plenty of other fans were taping Phish as well, with the band's blessing. The tapes were circulated and traded, and fans compared notes on shows any way they could, including an emerging online community. Phish's audience was starting to discover one another and grow in size. Typically, Phish would play somewhere for the first time and draw a fair-to-decent crowd. When they'd return, word about the last show would have gotten around and the venue would be overrun or they'd have graduated to a much larger hall. In 1991, for instance, they played a club called Biddy Milligan's in Chicago. A year later, they did two sold-out nights at the 1,400-seat Vic Theater. In 1992, they also played the prestigious Warfield Theater in San Francisco, as well as a free show in Palo Alto that drew a lot of curious Deadheads (foreshadowing a changing of the guard).

Because of the *Lawn Boy* debacle, Phish was wary of record companies. They nonetheless signed to Elektra Records in November 1991. Elektra had a long and storied history, making waves with folk artists during the early to mid-1960s (Judy Collins, Phil Ochs) and with its rock bands in the late 1960s (The Doors, Love). The label remained relevant in the New Wave era with acts like Television, Simply Red, and the Cars.

By the time Phish found their way to Elektra, the label had been absorbed into the Warner Communications conglomerate. It was still an "artist's label" but with access to major-label resources, and it seemed like a decent fit for Phish. Phish were brought to Elektra by

Sue Drew, a talent scout who recognized their potential when she saw them play New York's Marquee club on December 27, 1990. By this time, the Phish phenomenon was in full effect, and it was clear she'd be signing not just a highly creative, road-tested band, but one with a presold audience.

After the Marquee gig, she gave Phish her card; they took it and said they'd call back. They were in no hurry. For one thing, Phish wasn't entirely sure they wanted to surrender their autonomy or become bigger than they already were.

"I think we've really had that attitude since we quit our day jobs, and that's what made us a little bit different," Anastasio said in 1995. "We were just so content at that point. Never in our career have I felt this urge to get bigger. We didn't even talk much about getting signed to a record label at all."

"If anything, the talk was, we didn't want to," added Gordon. "I'd heard so many horror stories and everything," said Anastasio. "Which didn't turn out to be true. Not in our situation."

The group self-produced and recorded *A Picture of Nectar*—their first album for Elektra, released in February 1992—without any interference from the label. This was uncustomary at a time when big labels still tried to insert themselves into many aspects of a band's business: choosing producers, material, micromanaging tours, videos, marketing, and even the way a band or artist looked and dressed. But Phish were able to negotiate compromises on standard music-biz contract terms, mainly because they were completely willing *not* to sign if their demands were not met.

For example, a standard clause typically insisted that the songs submitted for an album be "commercially satisfactory" (whatever that means). Phish's lawyer had that phrase amended to "technically satisfactory," which only meant—so far as Phish construed it—that the songs had to be decently recorded.

Gordon described *A Picture of Nectar*, their Elektra debut, as "almost humorously diverse." The sixteen songs done in nearly that many styles on this album go to lengths to showcase Phish's diversity, eclecticism, and musicianship. The album also gives the lie to those who claim, based more on preconceptions than actual listening, that they "know what Phish sounds like." In any case, *A Picture of Nectar* is a solid place to start for neophytes or skeptics.

Phish recorded *A Picture of Nectar* at Burlington's White Crow Studios in late spring and early summer of 1991. Earlier that year, over at Dan Archer's studio in Winooski, they cut another album. For this one they provided musical backup for Anastasio's old pal, the Dude of Life (né Steve Pollak). As mentioned before, he'd written lyrics for several of Phish's key early compositions and joined them onstage from time to time, dressed in anything from a gas mask to a huge wig with a sparkly sequined jacket. Helping out on *Crimes of the Mind*, which was jointly credited to the Dude of Life and Phish, was a kind of thank-you for his early involvement and an attempt to help him launch a career of his own. It sat in the can until Phish's mounting popularity finally justified its release on Elektra three years later. *Crimes of the Mind* would sell a respectable 90,000 copies. So far as Phish was concerned, one of *Crimes'* songs ("Self") was musically recycled as one of the band's most high-energy originals ("Chalk Dust Torture").

Another key figure in Phish's crew entered the picture in the pivotal year of 1991: Brad Sands, a high-school swimmer turned college dropout who was looking for his niche. Sands first caught Phish at a July 1991 gig in upstate New York. Then a Deadhead, he was skeptical but left a total convert. Sands followed Phish, helping out wherever he could on the road. The operation was still informal enough to welcome such assistance, and when an opening came up, he submitted his résumé and landed the job.

At first he was Chris Kuroda's lighting assistant. In time, he became the band's road manager, sounding board, confidant, and gatekeeper. Sands developed a sixth sense about whom to let in and whom to keep out of their dressing room.

Sands eventually added even more to his plate: "I was able to grow from being road manager to being a lot more involved in the festivals, in the creative process, in the planning of the tours, that kind of thing," Sands noted. "My strength was being closest to the Phish fans. I knew what the fans liked."

He played an instrumental role in various Phish "gags" and during their New Year's Eve show in Boston on December 31, 1992, he became one of them: "The gag was me dressing up in a chicken suit for '(Fly) Famous Mockingbird' and getting hoisted above the band by a motor," he recalled, laughing.

The advent of a fan-based community in cyberspace was another turning point. It evolved along with technology, beginning as a published digest sent out to a mailing list and then an online newsgroup (the Phish.Net Usenet, whose address was rec.phish.net), and finally a Web site (www.phish.net). Now serious fans, scholars, and keepers of the keys could post set lists, analyze shows, and make plans to hook up on tour. It's hard to recall the 'Net in its infancy, when these sorts of things were novel and, given today's supersonic download speeds, almost excruciatingly slow. Yet it was an exciting new frontier, and Phish fans jumped on it. Matt Laurence, a computer designer and Phishhead living in Hamilton, Massachusetts, founded Phish.Net. Other Phishheads, such as Ellis Godard and Shelly Culbertson, found their way to it, as they began mastering computer tools and technology.

Then a student at the University of Virginia, Godard dove in headfirst. "I remember getting a newsletter in the summer of '91 that mentioned the rec.phish.net newsgroup," he elaborated. "I didn't know what that meant. I'd never heard of the Internet, and I'd never been in a computer lab on campus. So I went to the lab, and I was blown away and sucked into it immediately."

Godard edited the site's Frequently Asked Questions (FAQ) file, which then included only eleven questions and now has over six hundred. At one point, he also helped manage *The Helping Phriendly Book*, which tracks Phish's set lists. By 1992, Phish.Net served a community of roughly 50,000 music-loving computer geeks.

As the site grew, so did its offshoots. LivePhish.org, an online trading community, formed in 1994. Other Phish fans sharing common interests set up their own groups. These included the Funky Bitches (female Phish fans) and The Fellowship (a support group of non-drinking, nondrugging Phish followers, patterned after the Grateful Dead's Wharf Rats). While Phish and their music occupied the center of it all, social networks, worlds within worlds, were being created on the Internet.

The intersection of the information superhighway and the burgeoning world of Phishheads generated a tremendous amount of traffic in the early 1990s. It wasn't long before Phish.Net was third in size among online music newsgroups, behind only Bob Dylan and the Grateful Dead. In the 1990s, the Internet would further impact Phish and the music industry in an unforeseen way with the emergence of peer-to-peer sharing of music files via sites like Napster. The industry feared and fought the new technology and music fans' use of it. Phish had a different attitude toward the taping and disseminating of their music by fans, whether via cassettes or over the 'Net. They were solidly behind it. In the fall of 1993, Phish even began selling "taper tickets" by mail-order, allowing access to a special area set aside for them to erect their equipment at concerts.

"We recently premiered six songs that didn't make our new album," Anastasio told Paul A. Harris of the *St. Louis Post Dispatch* in 1992. "A bunch of people taped the show. That night, people put the titles and descriptions of those new songs on Phish.Net and how you could get a copy of the tape.

"So within days, you've got tapes of these new songs all over the country, which is exactly what we'd want. That way, we go out on this national tour, people are going to have heard of the new songs, and even *heard* the new songs, before we get to the different towns."

What would horrify most groups and record labels, Phish found acceptable and even desirable. The philosophy was that by encouraging taping and trading, they were building a committed fan base that would pay to come to shows, buy merchandise, and maybe even ante up for the occasional studio CD. The more they gave it away, the more they got back. They disapproved of for-profit bootlegging of their shows, however.

In addition to word getting around via Phish.Net, the group set up its own mailing list—launched by Trey's sister, Kristy—periodically sending out free newsletters to fans who signed up. By mid-1992, there were 14,000 Phishheads on that list. In 1994 it was renamed *The Döniac Schvice* and became a pretty big deal—especially to Jason Colton, who was given responsibility for it once he hired on with Phish's management.

In fact, the newsletter was how he found his way into the band's employ. Colton is a driven go-getter with a business head and a rock and roll heart. He heard *Junta* and was intrigued. A month later, on April 28, 1990, he attended his first Phish show, at the Strand Theater in Dorchester, Massachusetts. It just happened to be the band's first theater show, and though it was only half-full, it made an impression on him.

"I was hooked instantly," Colton recollected. "It was so unique and so cool, and after being used to seeing national touring bands, it seemed very life-sized to me. It definitely felt like a family affair in the sense that I could tell there were a lot of people who knew the band somehow."

He saw several more Phish concerts around New England in the following months. Checking out the band's newsletter, he realized that the band's management offices were located just a mile from his family's home in Newton, a Boston suburb. Before heading off to study English at the University of Wisconsin, Colton gave Paluska a call and went over to his office. He just wanted a Phish T-shirt, but the two wound up talking at length.

At the manager's suggestion, Colton said he'd try to book Phish a gig at Wisconsin. He joined the school's student concert committee on his first day and arranged for Phish to play on campus at the Great Hall on November 8, 1990. It was a sellout show that gave Phish another Midwestern beachhead, and Colton was ecstatic.

"I remember it just being a very defining moment of, 'This is what I want to do. I want to be involved with bands,'" Colton recalled. Paluska realized that Colton was shrewd, competent, and industrious, and he helped set him up in the concert business, putting him in touch with other band managers. While still in college, Colton promoted shows in Madison, Wisconsin, for artists such as Blues Traveler, Widespread Panic, and Bela Fleck.

When Phish wanted to play Madison again the next spring, Paluska told him, "Find a theater, rent the theater, do the advertising, sell the tickets, and if you lose money we'll cover you." They, of course, did not lose money, and Colton thought, "This is easy. I can do this."

He continued promoting shows in Madison, even after transferring to Stanford University, on the West Coast, where he finished his English degree. His dream had been to work for Bill Graham Presents, the concert empire built by the legendary San Francisco–based promoter, but Paluska made him a job offer first. Colton was attending the South by Southwest music conference in Austin, Texas, when the call came. With Colton's hiring, Dionysian Productions now numbered three: Paluska, Colton, and Shelly Culbertson.

After graduating with a degree in Russian from Bryn Mawr in Pennsylvania, Culbertson moved to the hippie college town of Arcata, up in the wilds of Humboldt County in northern California. Before her second Phish show—at the International Beer Garden in Arcata, on October 15, 1991—she persuaded Page McConnell to sit for an interview that she posted on Phish.Net. Interviews with Anastasio and Gordon followed a month later. In 1993, she accepted a full-time management support position with the band. Culbertson went on to develop a mail-order ticket system for fans and helped create Phish's official Web site. Colton, meanwhile, grew ever more involved with the business and marketing side of Phish's affairs—as well as with the newsletter.

At its peak, the Phish office mailed out 180,000 free four-color copies of *Döniac Schvice* each quarter to fans on the mailing list. Unlike most bands, Phish never had an official fan club. The fans had their own elaborate lines of communication. The newsletter was just a way for the band to provide them with news, show dates, and tongue-in-cheek columns by Fishman ("Fish's Forum") and Gordon ("Mike's Corner"). There was also a two-page merchandise spread that served to generate revenue through the sale of logo T-shirts and decals, compact discs, and other Phish-related swag. The *Schvice* continued publication until 2000, at which point the Internet proved a more efficient and cost-effective way to reach fans, especially since Phish had found themselves spending more than half a million dollars a year in the final years of the *Schvice*.

During the summer of 1992, Phish opened for or shared bills with a number of other acts both at home and abroad. They were one of over a hundred bands, including Nirvana, that played at the Roskilde Festival in Denmark. Except for one prior gig in Canada in 1989, Phish's jaunt to Europe in '92 represented their first shows outside the United States. On half a dozen European dates, they opened for Violent Femmes (and, on one of them, for Lou Reed as well). This limited them to single-set performances. Perhaps the experience made them more determined to forge their own way, but there were some memorable encounters. Anastasio got to make small talk with Reed before an outdoor show in Germany. As Phish headed onstage, Reed gave his fellow Yankees a pep talk: "Show 'em how to rock and roll. After all, we invented it."

Upon returning from Europe, Phish hooked up with the first H.O.R.D.E. ("Horizons of Rock Developing Everywhere") tour for four dates in the Northeast. The scene that had been nurtured at Wetlands went national with the launching of H.O.R.D.E. The idea was to take a strength-in-numbers approach to help put the jam-band scene on the map. The simple criteria, according to tour organizer John Popper, of Blues Traveler: "Good bands that played well live." Popper, who was given to bold strokes, hailed from Anastasio's hometown of Princeton, as did Chris Barron of the Spin Doctors.

The funny thing was, even when Phish were ostensibly part of a movement like H.O.R.D.E., in reality they were only tangentially connected. As if to separate themselves from the pack, Anastasio and McConnell later pointed out that Phish appeared only on the first four shows of the first H.O.R.D.E. tour, in 1992, and two dates on the '93 tour. H.O.R.D.E. continued to package jam bands for years after that, but Phish was never again among them. While they supported the all-for-one concept and benefited from the national exposure H.O.R.D.E. received, they were obviously an entity unto themselves who were meant to go it alone. Nonetheless, back in the States among the kindred spirits of H.O.R.D.E., they hammed it up at Jones Beach Amphitheater on Long Island. The group wore masks while singing their barbershop-quartet opener ("Sweet Adeline") and let Fishman rip on the vacuum cleaner toward the end.

On July 16, Phish commenced a six-week tour as Santana's opening act, which included a three-night stand at Los Angeles's Greek Theatre. At one of those dates at the Greek, they managed to squeeze only three songs into their allotted 50 minutes. Prior to the tour, the band had expressed hope that the linkup with Santana would show them how to carry their career to the next level. Carlos Santana was supportive of his opening act, coming out to jam with them for half a set in Stowe, Vermont, and inviting them out with his band every night. Stowe was a virtual hometown gig for Phish, since the ski resort lies a short distance east of Burlington.

"That was really solid," remembered Ian McLean, a fan from the early years. "'Phishtana,' when they played together at Stowe, was one of the sickest things I've ever seen."

Santana also added a new term to the Phish lexicon, derived from his words of praise for the band. The master guitarist told them that when he listened, he imagined the audience as a garden of flowers, Phish as a hose, and their music as water. From this came the term "the hose," which Phishheads thereafter used to describe an especially memorable jam.

From 1988 to 1992 were the bleary-eyed years, when Phish put in the roadwork that primed them to become the world's greatest jam band. When people talk about the golden years for Phish in concert, they most often refer to 1993 through 1995. Many of their greatest shows occurred during this time frame. Some of their greatest shows occurred outside of this time frame, too: the Clifford Ball, in 1996; Halloween 1996, in Atlanta; the New Year's runs of 1997, 1998, and 2003; and, of course, Big Cypress, where they ushered in the new millennium on a Seminole Indian reservation in south Florida. However, some longtime followers still regard the period from 1988 to 1992 as prime time to be a Phish fan, in terms of the size of the venues and sound of the band.

"I loved '91 and '92," said Jason Colton. "Something about the sonic quality and intimacy of those shows. Trey's amp and Mike's amp were both homemade, and Page on his Yamaha CP-70 [keyboard] ... There's just something so specific to that sound, before it became a bigger sound, that I just loved."

Many of Phish's most prolific years as a performing group occurred from 1989 through 1992. In those four years, they played a combined 532 times, with an annual average of 133 shows and a single-year peak of 148 (in 1990). If you add in the years 1993 (111 shows) and 1994 (125 shows), that's 768 total concerts in six years, or more than half of all shows in the twenty-two years from formation to breakup. Essentially, Phish played every third day for six years. If you additionally factor in 1988 (97 shows) and 1995 (81 shows), Phish performed 946 shows over an eight-year span—basically two-thirds of all shows in one-third of all years.

That's a lot of gigging. Twenty years on, Paul Languedoc clearly remembered that period of time—the many gigs and the long drives to them.

"For some reason they would book all these one-nighters with three hundred– to four hundred–mile drives between them," said Languedoc. "I just remember being so tired—get a hotel, sleep for three hours maybe, take a shower, drive. I remember thinking, like, 'I'll get to sleep in four days.'"

"We'd literally get there in the morning, load in, set up all day, do the show, break it down, put it in the truck, and then drive until we got to the next town at daybreak," added lighting engineer Chris Kuroda. "That kind of exhaustion.

"By the fourth or fifth day of doing this, the conversations and banter that we would have among each other at 3 in the morning as we were loading out was so nonsensical and insane. We used to make up songs about McDonald's breakfast sandwiches. It was funny. We didn't even know what we were talking about, we were so exhausted. We'd be lucid enough to look at each other and go, 'We're out of our minds.' It was sleep deprivation, but we'd have some pretty goofy times just being completely exhausted."

Kuroda recalled one stretch when they played "something like twenty-nine shows in thirty days." Upon coming home to Burlington from a grueling spell of roadwork, they would, of course, play some more. They'd finish a tour, drive all night, pull into Burlington by dawn's early light, and immediately load their gear into The Front. Then they'd go home and crash before returning to the club that night for a homecoming gig.

"It was a nice, relaxing, cool feeling," he said. "You really felt like you were home."

"We were playing places all over the country," added Languedoc, "and then would come back to Burlington and play in the same little three hundred–seat club. Nobody thought it was weird at all. Even into the 1990s."

When they weren't on the road, they were rehearsing. "*Lots* of rehearsing," recalled Languedoc. "They'd do these marathon rehearsals every day, and it's really when they got their chops down. Late eighties, early nineties. It was a very productive period for them as far as getting their catalog together."

The core members of Phish's hardworking crew during this hectic time were Kuroda, Languedoc, Pete Schall (monitor engineer), and Andrew Fischbeck (tour manager). The groundwork laid by Phish and crew during their decade-straddling growth years paved the way for the group's peak, from 1993 to 1996, where they achieved the optimum combination of creativity, maturity, and energy. And from there, the Phish phenomenon—the mystique, the audience, and the venues—just got bigger.

"Back in 1989 and 1990, Paul and I used to have this joke," said Kuroda. "You have to remember I had like four par cans then. I used to go to Paul and say, 'Yeah, someday I'm gonna walk into Madison Square Garden and say, "Mmm, I need lighting trucks #4, #8, and #12 today."' You know what I mean? *Ha ha ha. Very funny.* We'd have our little joke. And there was a moment in the late 1990s when we looked at each other and went, 'Oh my God, that came true!'"

FIVE

The Peak Years: 1993–1996

On New Year's Eve 1994, Phish sailed to new reaches of inspired lunacy. Performing in the jumbo-sized Boston Garden, they wanted to maintain some kind of connection with everyone in the crowd. They figured out a way to do just that, navigating to the farthest fan in the arena in a flying hot dog. It may have been the most brilliant of their gags.

They were brainstorming some sort of vehicle to transport them around the arena when manager John Paluska suggested "something long and cylindrical." "Like a hot dog!" suggested Fishman. What started out as a joke within Phish often became reality. In this case, designer Chris McGregor—longtime production manager of the avant-garde outfit The Residents—was enlisted to design a mobile hot dog that seated four. A side order of fries and a drink were fabricated as well. The props were rendered by McGregor and J. W. Nickel of Rocket Science, a San Francisco–based company.

Phish began their third set on New Year's Eve with "My Sweet One." They were interrupted by a voice from offstage, inquiring, "Excuse me, guys, did somebody order a hot dog?" Everyone pointed at Fishman, and a giant takeout tray appeared with the frankfurter, fries, and drink. The band boarded the hot dog, which ascended for a ride across the Garden, waving as they approached the fans farthest from the stage, as had been their initial wish while Captain Beefheart's "Tropical Hot Dog Night" played over the sound system. Then they counted down to midnight.

Thus ended 1994, one of the more phenomenal years of live Phish. They were hitting a mid-career peak. It was a time when they consistently reached for the stars and anything seemed possible. They made giant strides on the recording front with the intriguingly conceptual *Rift* (1993), the lively, accessible *Hoist* (1994), and the brooding, bottomless *Billy Breathes* (1996). They also issued the ultimate Phish primer, *A Live One* (1995), a double CD of concert highlights.

What I see as Phish's third phase, after their formative years and growth spurt, ran from 1993 through the Clifford Ball, in 1996. During this period, Phish ascended to another level. The jamming became more adventurous, the venues and audiences got bigger, and an increased revenue stream meant improved conditions on tour. For one thing, they graduated to a tour bus. Leaving the driving to others was a big relief to the band's hard-working crew, who no longer had to operate in a state of chronic sleep deprivation.

Musically, the biggest change was that they could now afford to tote a full-sized grand piano from gig to gig. It was first wheeled on-stage on February 3, 1993, in Portland, Maine, and it made a huge difference to their sound. Page McConnell shone on acoustic piano. Its more naturalistic sound jibed with Trey Anastasio's wood-toned Languedoc guitar.

Anastasio himself has noted that the group improved as McConnell's gear improved, and it was a "great leap forward" when the grand entered Phish's tour arsenal. McConnell's keyboard armory continued to expand. He brought back the Fender Rhodes on the summer 1993 tour and began adding electronic keyboards to the mix, too.

Hardly anyone has bad things to say about Phish from 1993. Band archivist Kevin Shapiro goes so far as to call it "the year Phish could do no wrong." It was the sixth year in a row they'd played one hundred–plus gigs, and the seasoning showed. The segues were seamless and inspired, and if one didn't know better one might suppose theirs was a fixed set list repeated night after night. But it wasn't. The set list changed nightly, and Anastasio was putting considerable time and effort into drawing up each night's set list.

They were carrying the improvisation farther out, too. Songs that had previously been fairly concise, such as "Bathtub Gin," became extended jam vehicles in 1993. They were also playing perfect-sized venues—large enough to represent forward progress, yet small enough to maintain some degree of intimacy.

"Phish was so creatively and musically compelling, and they were taking crazy risks," Shapiro said. "Before 1993, it had seemed to be a very practiced, concise show that flowed real fast and didn't necessarily have any huge improvisational moments. All of a sudden there were *huge* improvisational moments everywhere. You'd get some of that in 1992 and throughout the early years, but by 1993 the growth was obvious."

In 1993, they also hit a new peak as recording artists with the making of *Rift*. The majority of Phish fans generally revere the live experience and overlook the albums. Among jam-band fans in general, albums are viewed as somewhat synthetic studio artifacts. They're plainly not as organic and in-the-moment as a live performance, and fans are not present for their creation, as with concerts. There's another way to look at it, though. If a good jam-band concert is like a lengthy, articulate conversation, then a studio album should be conceived more like a series of concise, well-honed speeches. If this is true, then *Rift* is among Phish's greatest pieces of oratory, perhaps second only to *Billy Breathes*.

Rift marked a major step forward in maturity for the band and lyricist Tom Marshall. The subject matter was serious, the album cohesive, and the music exploratory and riveting. *Rift* was, in some vague sense, a musical play. In it, the protagonist is tormented by a relationship that causes a rift in his psyche. *Rift* is about feeling trapped in a situation from which there is no escape. Its sustained air of anxiety makes it a far cry from the sunny cornucopia of its predecessor, *A Picture of Nectar*.

"*Rift* was a reaction to *A Picture of Nectar*, which we thought was totally all over the place," said Anastasio. "In *Rift*, he's having a dream. The first two songs are overviews of the whole thing. Then he starts to fall asleep, and the rest is supposed to be a dream. The songs are dreamlike reflections of this rift he's experiencing in his life. 'Maze' is the first song he dreams: 'The overhead view is of me in a maze.' He can't get out, he's chasing this thing around. In 'It's Ice,' he battles with his mirror image on the ice, which is like having a fight with yourself. It goes on like that till he wakes up, 'Silent in the Morning,' and he didn't solve anything. But at least he wakes up!"

The lyrics reflected an intensely emotional period in Marshall's life, and their candor posed a challenge to Phish as musicians. When Anastasio approached the rest of the band with "Fast Enough for You," he felt some trepidation about presenting them with a relationship song. He needn't have worried; they were ready to move on to something more human-scaled and real-life.

"*Rift* was an attempt to get away from the fantasy aspect and say, 'Well, this is what's going on, let's write about it,'" Anastasio acknowledged. "The beauty of it is that we went from an extreme of fantasy kind of lyrics all the way into this depth-of-the-soul stuff, and now the whole spectrum is open to us. We can write any kind of song."

The album's artwork, a rectangular painting that extends from front to back of the CD booklet, depicts a labyrinthine dream state in deep blue tones. The painting references every song on the album (except for "The Horse") with some kind of image. The conceptual nature of the album is further reinforced inside the booklet with more lyrics and artwork, including enlarged details from the painting. The actual piece of art, which is quite large, hangs in Phish's storage facility in Burlington.

Rift was cut in Burlington at White Crow, a studio with decent gear but poor maintenance. "A complete wreck," cracked Anastasio. "All the wiring was messed up and nothing worked."

A technical glitch with the equipment resulted in recording levels being set too high—15 decibels greater than what the needles registered, in fact. They discovered this fact when they put the tapes on a normal machine for transfer as a prelude to overdubbing. They hit "play," and the levels just pinned into the red zone. "Basically, we had gone to tape hotter than we thought we had, or something like that," explained Anastasio. There were a few anxious days before they knew if the basic tracks could be salvaged. The nervous band members were asked to leave the studio so the engineers could do their work.

Rift was the first Phish album made with a name producer. At the suggestion of Elektra's Sue Drew, they picked Barry Beckett. On paper, it seemed an unusual match. For decades Beckett was a member of the Muscle Shoals Rhythm section, an Alabama-based studio band whose sessionography encompasses a galaxy of R&B, soul, rock, and folk legends, from Aretha Franklin and Wilson Pickett to Bob Dylan and Paul Simon—even Lynyrd Skynyrd. A keyboardist, Beckett was rooted in music that was earthier, more Southern and soulful, than Phish's jammy, surreal fantasias. Perhaps bringing Phish closer to terra firma was the point of his selection. If so, it didn't quite work out as intended. Phish seized the reins, insisting on working in Burlington at White Crow with a favorite engineer (Kevin Halpin), and they did not draw on or defer to Beckett's expertise as much as they might have.

Part of this was high-spirited, youthful self-certainty, and in hindsight, the group members have acknowledged that they wish it had gone differently. "The band always talks about the *Rift* album as us working with a great producer but not letting him do anything, tying his hands," Gordon said in 2004. "Because we had preconceptions about all the arrangements, all the sounds and everything, he couldn't really be that extra voice."

If the equipment glitches and muzzling Beckett weren't enough, Phish's A&R person at Elektra left in the middle of *Rift*, and the successor didn't particularly like the album. Despite it all, the album overflows with brilliant ideas and execution—particularly "Maze," with its kinetic solos from McConnell and Anastasio. On the title track, "Rift," Anastasio and McConnell alternate vocal lines, and it comes off so well one wishes they would do so more often.

Moreover, Anastasio and Beckett did connect creatively on "Weigh." "I wanted to overdub a guitar solo, and I started to get on a roll with Barry," Anastasio recalled in 1995. "It was myself, him, and this great engineer. It took five or six hours to do that guitar solo, and it was such an incredible team effort 'cause I'd come up with an idea and he'd make the littlest suggestion. 'Just bend it a little bit.' Or he'd say, 'You're playing the seventh. Try the sixth.'

"For us, the studio has not been the place where we have experiences like that. It's a bit more of a headache in the studio, and the stage is where we have these incredible musical experiences. But at that moment, I felt I was having that experience with Barry."

A few years after *Rift* came out, Phish was touring the Rock and Roll Hall of Fame in Cleveland. The band's flying hot dog—the supersized prop from their 1994 New Year's Eve show—now hangs in the museum, hoisted high overhead in the lobby's atrium. The French fries and drink are there, too, on the lower level. Acknowledging the group's presence that day, the museum staff piped *Rift* over the speakers.

"I was kind of embarrassed," Anastasio confessed. "I remember walking through and thinking, 'What the hell is this? It sure isn't rock and roll. Oh, it's me.'"

Rift, however, was hardly something be ashamed of. To the contrary, it was a challenging yet listenable work that found Phish swimming into deeper waters, thematically.

In 1994, Phish took ever bolder steps in their approach to jamming. Two of the biggest nights of their career occurred in Dallas (on May 7) and Rhode Island (on December 29).

The Dallas show was highlighted by a legendary second-set performance of "Tweezer." Originally appearing on *A Picture of Nectar*, the song was built upon a funky riff jammed into being by Gordon and Anastasio. The words—old-school Phish doggerel—were beside the point. The music provided one of the most open-ended points of entry for sustained jamming of any item in their catalog. Regarded as a concert milestone, the Dallas "Tweezerfest," as it came to be called, incorporated songs (or teases of songs) by the Rolling Stones, the Who, the James Gang, Aerosmith, the Breeders, and Prince. They also threaded two originals ("Sparkle," "Makisupa Policeman") around the towering mainstay of "Tweezer" itself—one jammy stretch of which lasted twenty-five minutes. The entire symphony-length performance went on for nearly eighty uninterrupted minutes. For an encore, Phish performed "Amazing Grace" a cappella.

"It was one of the first times we decided to blow off the set list and just keep playing through the whole set without stopping," said Gordon. "That would more often happen at jam sessions or band practices in private than onstage, but the idea that we could do it onstage and just throw caution to the wind was a memorable one for us and a monumental one, too."

On this night, Phish realized there was no limit to how far they could carry out their jamming. The "Tweezerfest" raised the bar and set the tone for the future. In Providence, at year's end, they scaled another peak, performing a free-form, half-hour-plus version of "David Bowie." This one took them out even farther.

"One thing that's different between the long 'David Bowie' from Providence and the long 'Tweezer' in Dallas is that in 'Tweezer' there are a couple radio hit–type songs we went into," Gordon explained. "A few of the really long early jams had a lot of those silly teases of radio songs or even old Phish songs, so there's a kind of lightheartedness to it that later became uncool among the band.

"But that 'Bowie' jam is different in that it doesn't segue into songs at all. It just gets more abstract. There are fewer references. It's more like songwriting on the spot, where we're trying to get to defined places we had never played before, so that if we wanted, we could piece them apart and write songs from them."

For their fifth studio album, *Hoist*—recorded in the fall of 1993 and released in March 1994—Phish outlined a reverse sort of challenge. Coming on the heels of the intricate, conceptual *Rift*, the band attempted to simplify its approach.

"The verbalized challenge was that we wanted to make a rock album," Anastasio explained. "If you think about it, we hadn't ever really tried to make a rock album. We all listen to music like that, we love music like that, so we asked each other, 'What's in your tape deck right now?' For me it was *Exile on Main St.*"

"With *Hoist*, we actually wanted record-company involvement," Gordon allowed. "We encouraged them to come and listen. We wanted guest musicians, too, so we had Alison Krauss, Tower of Power, and Bela Fleck. It was the album where we let other people get involved."

Hoist featured a bluesy shuffle ("Julius") and a pounding rocker ("Down With Disease"), with more exotic fare scattered throughout. As intended, *Hoist* turned out to be Phish's most extroverted and accessible album. They worked with producer Paul Fox, who came from a modernist, New Wave perspective, having produced such bands as 10,000 Maniacs and XTC. Phish was gung-ho about embracing this opportunity, while their more possessive fans had reservations about any angling toward the mainstream, which could only mean a bigger audience. Phish even filmed a video for "Down With Disease." It was a first—and a last.

The video didn't kick open the doors to the world of MTV or spearhead a sudden uptick in sales. In fact, its greatest exposure came from an airing on *Beavis & Butt-Head*, where the cartoon brats mocked Phish's appearance in an aquarium with comments about swimming in your own toilet. Mike Gordon directed the video, employing un-derwater imagery the band had used at their 1993 holiday shows. It blew minds at the Worcester Centrum on New Year's Eve but didn't translate quite so effectively to a small-screen rock video. As Jon Fish-man noted, that was the last time they allowed other people to override their instincts when it came to career moves.

Gordon also filmed the *Hoist* sessions, editing them down to a twenty-five-minute videotape, titled *Tracking*, that was released com-mercially. It didn't draw much more attention than the "Down With Disease" video, but his quirky home video did offer intriguing glimpses of Phish at work in the studio.

The cover image was a photograph of one of Amy Skelton's horses, Maggie, being hoisted in a sling, which is how equine veterinarians conduct certain kinds of examinations. The band had wanted to call the album *Hung Like a Horse*. In a way they did, albeit with a visual pun.

For the back-cover photo shoot, the band donned costumes plucked from a Hollywood warehouse and posed in character by the Malibu Pier. Fishman was a muscleman, Gordon convincingly resem-bled Harpo Marx, McConnell appeared as a mustachioed cad, and Anastasio dressed like a barbershop singer in a straw boater.

"We were like, 'Fishman would look funny in one of those striped bathing suits,' and it just went sort of Gay Nineties from there," said McConnell, laughing.

On the road, as if there wasn't already enough to do, the band some-times brought along musical trainers. For a week during their fall 1994 tour, it was banjoist Jeff Mosier, late of Bruce Hampton's Aquarium Rescue Unit, who coached them in bluegrass. Gordon had long been a serious bluegrass aficionado, and Fishman had penned a bluegrass number ("My Sweet One") that appeared on *Lawn Boy*. But appren-ticing in earnest with "Reverend" Mosier gave them a well-rounded overview and provided some discipline.

With Mosier's assistance, they tackled such stalwart bluegrass numbers as Bill Monroe's "I'm Blue, I'm Lonesome" and Flatt and Scruggs's "Earl's Breakdown," not to mention Mosier's own "Little Tiny Butter Biscuits." The title of that last tune emerged out of the blue from the mouth of an Alzheimer's patient Mosier worked with. From meaningless utterance to Phish's concert stage to an audience of 10,000 and out into the universe—it wasn't the first time it happened like that.

Before that, Phish apprenticed with a master of barbershop quartet who just happened to be McConnell's landlord. When McConnell said he played in a band, his landlord responded, "Oh, I'm kind of into music myself. I have a barbershop group."

Instead of chuckling to himself, as the average rock musician might have done, Page saw an opportunity for the band to further expand its horizons. "He was an international judge for barbershop for about thirty years," said McConnell. "Turned out he was able to give us lessons, and we ordered a bunch of music."

Phish took their barbershop singing pretty seriously. For a while they tried to learn a new barbershop arrangement every tour. And they worked to master the proper vocal elocution. They ordered posters from the Society for the Preservation of Barbershop Quartets in America that depicted geeky guys in sweaters and handlebar mustaches mouthing *oohs*, *eees*, and *ahs*.

"People who know would say we do bad barbershop," said McConnell. "But the fact we're doing it at all . . . It's just funny to see a band up there doing that sort of thing."

On the same fall 1994 tour where they broke into bluegrass in a big way, some of the subtle changes in Phish's evolving audience makeup could be detected. Ellis Godard, who was involved early on with Phish's online forums and went on to edit *The Phish Companion: A Guide to the Band and Their Music*, noticed something that gave him pause at a show in Alabama he attended with some friends in October 1994.

"We saw about a half-dozen people, aging hippies with long beards, frying up grilled cheese or whatever with their lap grills," said Godard. "They said they knew nothing about the band and didn't care anything for the music. They preferred the Dead's music, but they were there because the Dead scene had gotten ugly, competitive, drug-ridden, and dangerous, and this was a safer scene that had better clientele and more money. They were there to commercialize it, and they did.

"So the first turn we saw in the parking lot scene was from a couple of people trying to pay for their gas to explicit commercialization of the market. And it grew from there. You had the influx of people who also cared less about the music, who were there because there was a market and because there were drugs and things being sold in the market."

Those kinds of issues would pose more serious challenges later in the decade, but the infiltration of the lot scene with elements from outside Phish's fan base began to show at least a year before Jerry Garcia's death. Throughout 1995 it was still a pretty mellow scene and one the band members kept tabs on, to varying degrees. By mingling with the fans, they'd get an instant fix on what was on their minds, pro and con.

"Sometimes we'll actually go into the parking lot before we play and talk to people," Gordon said in 1995. "If people are thinking about something, if there's a general problem with the concert experience, then we'll know pretty quickly."

On May 16, 1995, Phish delivered on another self-imposed challenge: to debut a set of almost entirely new material. There were ten new songs (four of them covers), including the debuts of "Free" and "Theme from the Bottom." Both would be highlights of *Billy Breathes*, whose release was still well over a year off. The event was a "Voters for Choice" benefit concert in Lowell, Massachusetts. It was the band's first gig in four and a half months, and they wanted to do something special. Contrary to most artists, who would recoil at the notion of unreleased new songs circulating among fans, Phish was glad to have the tapers on hand.

"It worked out perfectly," said Anastasio, "'cause I thought we could play all these new songs and then give it a couple of weeks for the tapes to get out there."

By the time Phish kicked off its summer tour, the new songs were neither overly familiar nor completely unknown.

"Our fans like to hear us play new stuff," he noted. "I think it's different from a situation where people come to hear *the hits*."

Fans at the benefit show in Lowell even got to choose the title for one new song. From among four options tendered after they played it, the crowd shouted most loudly for "Spock's Brain." Since some Phish fans could be a little Spock-like, which is to say brainy, obsessive music geeks, this seemed entirely fitting. Phish ushered the guest of honor, feminist icon Gloria Steinem, to the stage with a version of the garage-rock anthem "Gloria."

I met Phish for the first time shortly after the show in Lowell, which inaugurated an episodic series of contacts for a *Rolling Stone* article that was two years in the making. I was invited to Burlington to hang out with the group. Interviews would come later. I flew to Burlington's small airport, grabbed a rental car, and followed an e-mailed set of directions to Paul Languedoc's modest two-story home, buried deep in the Vermont countryside, a few miles from the nearest paved road. A detached building adjacent to the house was still under construction. Languedoc's workshop occupied the first floor, where he built instruments for Phish and other clients. The upstairs alcove served as the group's rehearsal space. They paid him rent for its use, which helped subsidize its construction.

I pulled up on a crisp morning in late May to find the group gathered outside. A wiffle-ball bat rested on Gordon's shoulder. The four of them studied me with the wary look of New Englanders sizing up a stranger. The group had thus far achieved considerable success without the mainstream media, which had made virtually no effort to investigate the Phish phenomenon. So there was a certain understandable cautiousness about playing ball with periodicals like *Rolling Stone* just because they'd suddenly shown some interest.

After almost literally breaking the ice—snow was still visible atop nearby Mount Mansfield—we repaired to the rehearsal room. Cluttered and unfancy, this was where Phish spent five to seven hours a day working up material and practicing exercises of their own devising. In one corner stood a dry-erase board marked up with the set list for the "Voters for Choice" benefit they'd just played. This being a popular and prosperous rock band's workspace, one might have expected a refrigerator stocked with Vermont home brews (like Magic Hat, made in Burlington) and other goodies, but there was nothing but a box of Wheat Thins making the rounds.

They worked hard and laughed often. Phish's insistence on pushing themselves was evident at these sessions, where they spent considerable time on self-devised listening exercises. The best known was called "Including Your Own Hey." These exercises, which formed a large part of their practice regimen from 1990 through 1995, are not so easy to explain but important for understanding how Phish could maintain a seemingly telepathic chemistry in concert. The whole idea was to improve the level of collective improvisation by learning to listen to one another while jamming. They'd do this by conjuring riffs and patterns out of thin air, varying and embellishing them until they were "locked in," individually announcing their arrival with the word "hey." When they'd each included their own "hey," it was onto another round.

"'Hey' means we're locked in," explained Anastasio. "The idea is don't play anything complicated; just pick a hole and fill it." They explored different elements of music—tempo, timbre, dynamics, harmonics—within the "hey" regimen. A variation on "Including Your Own Hey," which they called "Get Out of My Hey Hole," had the cardinal rule that one musician's note could not sustain over any-one else's.

"Get the hell out of my hey hole," Anastasio barked to Fishman, and the drummer evacuated the hey hole, so far as I could tell.

"Mimicry is the lowest, most basic level of communication," ex-plained Anastasio. "These are anti-mimicry exercises—listening to each other, hearing each other, staying out of each other's way."

Another exercise found them inversely varying tempo with vol-ume. "The faster we go, the quieter we'll play," instructed McConnell. "The slower we go, the louder we'll play."

The group set up a monstrous wail on one loud, slow passage that would have frightened a Black Sabbath fan.

Yet another was "Two Plus Two," in which one musician picked another person in the band to hook up with while still listening to the other two.

They went at it like this for hours.

"This is what we spend our time doing," Anastasio said matter-of-factly. "This is our job." Years later, after the breakup, he would admit that what he missed most about Phish was band practice. I could see why; there was a tangible sense of concentration mingled with cama-raderie present in the room.

In terms of concert dividends, "It doesn't always work 100 percent of the time," Fishman noted. "But I still think those exercises really pay off, because it puts you in a state of mind where even if you are making a lot of noise and stepping on each other's toes, you're still aware of it. At least it's not like you're just blindly forging ahead."

At that point in the afternoon, Phish ran through another song for an audience of two—a captivated journalist and Languedoc's disin-terested cat. Titled "Taste," it was a complex piece of music in which they all played asymmetrical parts in different meters. The song, in a somewhat different arrangement, wound up on their next album, *Billy Breathes*. Prior to this, they'd already changed its title and lyrics, renaming it "The Fog That Surrounds" before reverting to "Taste." It was a good example of Phish's inveterate tinkering. Every song was always in the act of becoming, subject to amendment and revision.

As they worked on "Taste," it fell to Fishman to juggle four rhythms—the three other musicians', plus one of his own in 6/8 time. Afterward, Anastasio wandered over to the drums, excited because he thought he heard another implied counter-rhythm. He picked up a drumstick and tapped out the elusive fifth rhythm on a snare for Fishman, who attempted to incorporate it. They knew what they were aiming at but couldn't quite nail it.

This tangent was abandoned, but the very fact they pursued it demonstrated the group's insatiable drive to push further. They'd constantly ask themselves, explicitly or implicitly, *Is there something else we can do?* And so they'd add, subtract, and rework parts, tinkering until they were satisfied a piece was as good as they could make it. Even then, it might change at the next rehearsal, and would certainly evolve onstage. This process of continuous evolution explained why no two Phish concerts were alike.

The group, at their best, also knew how to quickly enter a creative mind-set, almost a dreamlike state of consciousness. Mostly this would start with Anastasio. As Fishman noted, "One great thing about Trey is that he always goes into that non-thinking mode, even when he's working on an intense composition. Kind of jumping up and down, walking around the room and letting it flow."

Getting out of one's own way was the idea. This goal of tapping into right-brained mode is echoed throughout music and literature. Neil Young and his producer, David Briggs, had a favorite saying: "You think, you stink." Jack Kerouac described his writing style as "spontaneous bop prosody," and he let his pencil fly without self-correction, saving any editing he might do until later. Unselfconscious expression was also the point of Ken Kesey's mid-sixties Acid Tests—a lesson learned well by the Grateful Dead, who provided the music for those unscripted happenings in their earliest days as a band.

Phish likewise aimed to create in the moment and cultivate a group mind. They also realized when it was time to stop doing the exercises.

"Early on, we did those 'Including Your Own Hey' exercises in rehearsal," said Gordon. "We were doing an 'Including Your Own Hey' exercise in sound check every day, too. And then we started to find that our jams sounded too much like the exercises, especially in the sense they were repeating patterns in two-bar or four-bar clumps. So all of our jams were starting to sound like these repeating patterns.

"I remember a point where Trey said, 'I think we should try to break out of this.' We even stopped doing the exercises and began making an effort to have the jams *not* be repetitive, where there was a specific *lack* of repetition."

After a full day given over to listening exercises and working out "Taste," a group dinner followed. It was a bit like *My Dinner with Andre* (or with four Andres). There was not a lot of idle chatter. I found them all to be lively, well-read, and serious conversationalists. Topics included the origins of myths and their place in culture throughout history; the declining role of organized religion in modern society; the work of writers and thinkers ranging from Joseph Campbell to Oswald Spengler; and the latest schools of psychological thought concerning the development of human personality from cradle to grave. Environmental issues were also discussed, with the band professing their dismay about all the nonrenewable fossil fuel that gets burned in the course of a tour by them and their fans.

"I lay awake nights wondering about things like that," confessed Anastasio.

In the annals of Phish concerts, which are dissected, analyzed, and rated by hard-core fans at Phish.Net, the Halloween '94 show in Glen Falls, New York, merited a 9.9. The only reason not to give it a perfect ten was that it started late. They didn't crank it up until 10 P.M., and because it was a three-set show, the event concluded around 3 A.M.

In addition to their usual two hours–plus of original material, Phish performed the Beatles' *White Album*—all thirty-two songs, in order, without a break.

For Phish, the motivation for undertaking such projects simply came down to "liking a challenge," Gordon explained with a shrug. Phish's Halloween shows had always been special, dating back to the Goddard College years. (Think psychedelic drugs, a gaggle of Vermont heads turned loose on a deserted college campus on All Hallows Eve . . . and Phish.) In 1994, however, they decided to up the Halloween ante by performing an album by another act in its entirety. Moreover, they let fans pick the album. The band solicited votes in their newsletter. The *White Album* won; *Sgt. Pepper's Lonely Hearts Club Band* placed a close second.

Phish mastered the bulky double album while on tour, rehearsing whenever they could steal a few hours. "We tried to learn the actual arrangements as deeply as we could get into them without doing the overdubs," Anastasio said in 1995, when Phish were getting material together for their next album, *Billy Breathes*.

"We improved as a band by it," Anastasio continued. "Several people actually said our new songs have more of a Beatles vibe. It wouldn't surprise me if that's true, because the last thing we did before writing them was to learn thirty-two Beatles songs. My philosophy is, how can you lose? It can only make you better."

Phish lived by such challenges. It was this same philosophy that inspired Phish to take musical tutors on the road, invent arcane practice exercises, and start throwing their otherworldly outdoor festivals. For much of their career, each concert was approached in the hopes of breaking new ground. Even if the end result occasionally fell short, one had to applaud the effort because the intention was always pure.

The Halloween experiment went so well they did it again a year later with a different album. In 1995, the Who's *Quadrophenia* garnered the most votes. Again, it was a double album, but with "only" seventeen songs. The performances were strong (except, perhaps, for Fishman's earnest but strained singing on "Love Reign O'er Me," a vocally demanding tune). More songs than usual were sung by McConnell, and "Drowned" lingered thereafter in Phish's live repertoire. Four years later, at a 1999 show, they jammed on "Drowned" for a half-hour. It was a rare cover tune that could launch a jam of such duration.

Phish performed the Halloween ritual twice more in the 1990s. On both those occasions they—not the fans—picked the albums. They chose Talking Heads' *Remain in Light* (in 1996, at Atlanta's Omni) and Velvet Underground's *Loaded* (in 1998, at Las Vegas's Thomas & Mack Center). In every case, learning another band's album influenced Phish's songwriting and jamming to some degree. This was especially true of Talking Heads' *Remain in Light*, whose minimalist, polyrhythmic approach became embedded into Phish's musical language.

Phish spent much time reviewing tapes of their fall 1994 concert tour to assemble something fans had been clamoring for. Many a tape-trading Phishhead desirous of soundboard fidelity had asked, "When are you going to put out a live one?" The group responded by putting out *A Live One*.

I was interviewing them at the very moment finished copies of *A Live One* were delivered to the hotel room. I mention this only because it was reminiscent of a scene in *This Is Spinal Tap*—a fact instantly noticed by Anastasio—where the group was handed copies of *Smell the Glove*, with its all-black cover. The difference was that Phish very much liked the cover of their new album. They liked everything inside the booklet for *A Live One*, too. There were tons of live shots from '94, including one of a nude Fishman onstage at the *White Album* Halloween show. Fishman's privates were just barely concealed by a flourish in the second "*h*" in Phish. One thing they didn't do, though they'd talked about it, was put a fishhook on the cover—a symbol that would have signified "The Band Formerly Known as Phish" (a sly riff on Prince's then-recent change from name to symbol).

The four of them laughed and bantered about the photo spread.

GORDON: Did you show him the hot dog?

MCCONNELL: That was last New Year's Eve in Boston Garden.

GORDON: Playing, mind you.

ANASTASIO: Wireless instruments.

FISHMAN: Kosher hot dog.

McCONNELL: That is a funny picture, Fish.

GORDON: Trampoline shot's great.

Every song on *A Live One* came from a different show, with one minor exception: McConnell's extended piano coda on "The Squirming Coil" was plucked from the same October 23 concert as "Harry Hood." (The main part of "The Squirming Coil," however, was taken from an October 9 performance.) The entire fall 1994 tour had been taped. After each show they'd make notes about songs to consider for inclusion. By tour's end, the list was well over five hundred songs long. They also polled fans online for their favorite performances. Honing it down required much listening, and at group meetings songs were crossed out or left on the master list. This process took two months, by which point they'd reduced the list to thirty. The final lineup was settled over plates of mushroom caps (baked and stuffed, not the hallucinogenic variety) during a group confab at a restaurant.

Among other things, the album revealed the extent to which Phish and their fans had bonded. The audience went beyond energizing the band with sold-out houses and applause. Now they provided cameos in key places. They chanted "Wilson" at the appropriate spot in that song, clapped three times rapidly during the pauses in "Stash," and sang while bouncing up and down to "Bouncing Around the Room." The audience had grown large but retained a group identity by means of in-jokes, knowledge of details, secret language, and concert rituals. Going to see Phish at this juncture was a bit like attending a midnight screening of *The Rocky Horror Picture Show*.

It could be argued that *A Live One* was the ultimate Phish album. Whereas the group willingly courted a larger audience with *Hoist*, there were no such concessions on *A Live One*. This was not Phish's attempt at a *Frampton Comes Alive*–type breakthrough. It was a concert compendium for hard-core fans.

Who else, pray tell, would sit through thirty-three minutes of "Tweezer"? Not only did it run longer than the typical TV sitcom, but it was also a knotty, demanding listen, even for some fans. Little about it was satisfying in a conventional sense, but it did rise to a crescendo, during which dissonant tension gave way to cathartic release. The recording came from their first concert following the *White Album* Halloween show, and the band speculated it might have been their subconscious response to the rigors of learning all those songs—a good, unstructured jam to help clean out the pipes.

Though it drew from a dozen concerts, *A Live One* was constructed to play through like an idealized evening with Phish. The two discs represented a typical show's first and second sets. Anastasio announced intermission at the end of disc one, and disc two commenced with a few seconds of typically tasty set-break music (Miles Davis's "Right Off," from *Jack Johnson*) as the band reappeared onstage to an ovation.

There was no studio-mandated succinctness here, either. The album's dozen tracks clocked in at 125 minutes. If you excluded "Montana," a two-minute excerpt from a much longer jam, the average track length was over 11 minutes. This was just as Phish fans liked it, and tough luck for mainstream listeners who'd been seduced by *Hoist*'s relative accessibility.

"That was definitely a fan-oriented album," affirmed Anastasio. "If you were really into the band, you knew what was going on. There was nothing on there for radio."

At the same time, Anastasio still held out hope that radio might someday evolve in Phish's direction. He spoke wistfully about radio when it used to be free from the constraints of outside consultants and corporate overseers like Clear Channel.

"When I grew up, I remember sitting by the radio, waiting for them to play some song I was into and waiting for hours, listening," he recalled. "So now I have this dream, and I believe it can happen. Maybe we can be part of it. That would be something I would be happy to be part of—the rebirth of radio."

In a sense, the rebirth of more organic, free-form radio did happen with the introduction of satellite radio, and there is a place for Phish on there. In fact, there's a jam-band channel on XM/Sirius. Commercial rock radio still remains out of reach, but with alternatives like satellite radio and stations that stream on the 'Net, who needs it anymore?

Apparently, there was nothing on *A Live One* for mainstream rock critics, either. *A Live One* was Phish's sixth official full-length release (not counting *The White Tape*) but only the first to be reviewed in *Rolling Stone*. Tom Moon damned the two-hour extravaganza with faint praise, hanging a tepid three stars (of a possible five) upon it. No fewer than fourteen variations on the word *noodle* appeared in the review. He called noodling "the province of spring-water hippies" and Phish "the most self-indulgent act ever to sell out Madison Square Garden."

There's an interesting technical footnote regarding *A Live One*. As Anastasio explained, "We mixed it with this new piece of gear that let us create the image of the sound coming from behind you through phase cancellation. If you sit right between the speakers on that album, you should be able to hear it. I know most people don't, but we put it on there anyway."

After *Hoist*'s failure to catch fire, Phish decided not to do anything they found disagreeable. When Elektra asked the group to make a few in-studio appearances at key radio stations to promote *A Live One*, they thought about it and replied, "We don't want to," according to Anastasio.

Gordon picked up the story: "Our manager said, 'You're right, you're making a good point. We probably would sell more records. But we don't want to do that, so we'll just have to sell less records.'"

The above-quoted conversation occurred during the second day of Phish's weekend stand at Red Rocks in June 1995. This outdoor venue, located west of Denver, was the setting for U2's 1983 *Under a Blood-Red Sky* concert video. Towering walls of ruddy sandstone surround and enfold the amphitheater. Musically, it's tailor-made for more organic and improv-oriented acts—the Allman Brothers, the Dead, Neil Young, and, of course, Phish—since the transcendent setting inspires and enhances risk-taking music. Moreover, the air is really thin, making fans a little giddy even without nitrous tanks.

Phish sold out both nights in twenty minutes. It was the third stop of their summer 1995 tour, and the mounting army of Phishheads turned out in force. Whooping. Smiling. Inhaling. Chugging. High-fiving. Exclaiming: "Man, you can practically see Kansas from here." Holding index fingers in the air—the Dead-derived plea for a single "miracle ticket"—or trying a more direct approach: "At the sound of the tone, you will give me your ticket. *Ding!*"

The little town of Morrison lies at the foot of Red Rocks. It has seen plenty of concert traffic, but Phish's traveling road show was more along the lines of an occupation. Cars, vans, and Merry Prankster–style buses claimed every available inch alongside the road. Phishheads roamed the streets or fraternized in clumps around a music source. Most didn't have the money to patronize local restaurants, even the inexpensive Mexican ones. One hapless longhair was trying to hock a pocket calculator for gas money.

Some in the milling crowd were hygienically challenged—hair matted in dreadlocks, bodies splashed with musk and patchouli to disguise the fact that it's hard to take a shower on the road when you can't afford motels. The knotty-haired tour rats you'd see scurrying around were tagged "wookies" because of their resemblance to the amusing alien hairballs in George Lucas's *Star Wars* epics. Wookies were into the total experience—the music, the travel, the drugs, and all the rituals and challenges posed by their combination—and were completely ensconced in their own world, like an army of genetically altered, if basically harmless, mutants.

Their antithesis (and nemesis) were the "custies"—coddled trust-fund recipients. They tended to be well-educated achievers from good backgrounds who didn't lack for means. They were preppy in attire and had much in common with the baseball cap–wearing frat boys commonly spotted at Dave Matthews Band concerts. (Inside the world of Deadheads, they were disparaged as "trustafarians.") Each camp abided the other with varying degrees of amusement and antipathy, and at the end of a concert each group went its separate way, the wooks to their tents and raggedy vehicles, the custies to their nice hotel rooms.

Over the course of their '95 stand at Red Rocks—my introduction and initiation into the Phish concert experience—they gave their audience ample reason for ecstasy. They performed short songs, long jams, and all manner of things in between. There were bluegrass breakdowns. Atonal fugues. Barbershop quartets. Punchy rock songs like "Suzy Greenberg." Long, dynamic pieces such as "Run Like an Antelope" and "Split Open and Melt," which built to peaks of tension and release. They played wonderfully weird covers and conducted humorous bits of onstage business.

During the second set, Fishman bounded out from behind his drum kit to sing Velvet Underground's "Lonesome Cowboy Bill," also providing a vacuum cleaner solo. As an intro and outro to his moment in the spotlight, the band instrumentally lit into the chorus of the old Argent hit "Hold Your Head Up." Why? Because Fishman particularly despised that song, and the others (especially Anastasio) loved to tease him. ("I hate that song," he said at a 1992 show. "A hateful song, indeed.") Introduced by Anastasio as "Henrietta," Fishman triumphantly received the crowd's applause.

Fishman wore his doughnut dress and goggles, which was about all there was in terms of the group's attention to wardrobe. Anastasio and Gordon dressed as casually as they would have for a band rehearsal or trip to the grocery store. Gordon's signature stage look involved rolling his pant legs halfway to his knees. Aside from that, only McConnell, with his Banana Republic–type shirts, accorded onstage attire (as opposed to costuming) the least bit of consideration. As with Pink Floyd, the real visuals were provided by the light show, and the band members were the antithesis of preening rock-star fashion plates.

I had never seen anything like this before, certainly not by a band performing to a sold-out audience at a venue the size of Red Rocks. I had never heard anything like the music they played those two nights, either. The interlude with Fishman demonstrated that the band didn't take themselves too seriously. However, they obviously took the music *very* seriously.

The shows at Red Rocks had ample musical highlights. They blazed on "Maze," with its blistering, focused solo passages, and "David Bowie" rose to a blizzard of ecstatic triplets from Anastasio's guitar. On the second night, a fine drizzle hung in the air, creating a sublime psychedelic spectacle as green and purple spotlights were absorbed into the billowy mist while the band played.

In June 1996, Phish performed for the fourth consecutive year at the scenic amphitheater. They sold out four nights in record time. The run was not without problems, however, as a purported "riot" in downtown Morrison was triggered when a car collided with a Phish fan, with the resulting brouhaha making national news. Phish would not play Red Rocks again until their reunion tour in 2009.

It was a simple question, but one that had implications the musicians likely could not have imagined at the time. In June 1995, I asked the members of Phish, "How big do you want to get?" Here is some of the dialogue that ensued:

FISH [*laughing*]: *So* big, the biggest ever!

PAGE: I think that for us, 'cause what we do is a little bit left of center, it's not going to appeal to everybody. As long as we're keeping true to ourselves, there are going to be people who love it, but it's not going to be for everybody. So I don't have a fear of [getting too big]. I really like the stage we're at now. The sheds and some of the theaters and arenas we play, I really feel like we can play to the people in those rooms.

FISH: I like the size right now, too. I don't think we've played in a room yet where we felt out of contact with everybody in the room. When we played at Madison Square Garden, Trey said, "Wow, that's a huge room. I wonder if it's gonna feel too big." When we got there, it really didn't. Because the show had this big, "all right, we're all in this together" kind of vibe. I didn't feel out of contact with people in the back, or that we couldn't occupy that space, or that the sound couldn't reach everybody well. But I do remember somebody saying that was like the edge. That was the biggest indoor room we'd ever played. That's when I realized it's just barely not too big. It's pushing the envelope. Beyond that, it's not about music anymore. It's about production.

ANASTASIO: We just had a meeting with John [Paluska, Phish's manager]. We talked about the fact we're making a concerted effort to realize that this is our career, we're going to enjoy every minute of it, and that's it. If it's not something that we enjoy, we're not going to do it anymore, because how big do you need to get? We're big enough.

At that point he cut an apple in half with a decisive snap of a knife.

What they couldn't have anticipated was the sudden death of Jerry Garcia and disbanding of the Grateful Dead in August 1995. At that point, there was nowhere else for Deadheads to go but home, and the younger ones still had plenty of partying and noodle-dancing left in them. Phish inherited not only Deadheads who were sincerely devoted to the ideals of community and music, but also the gate-crashers and parking-lot opportunists who brought a rogue element to Phish's scene. There's little question that much of this would have happened to some degree anyway, but the Dead's demise certainly accelerated the numbers and issues Phish faced after 1995.

Links between Phish and the Dead were certainly nothing new. Once Phish transitioned from an underground cult band to a story that the mainstream music press rather tardily decided was worth covering, it was the Grateful Dead to whom comparisons were reflexively drawn. The parallels were inescapable. Phish had their Jerry Garcia in Trey Anastasio, and they were a pied-piper jam band around whom a nomadic following formed. Both bands built their careers in an organic, grassroots way, flying beneath the pop-culture radar and keeping the industry from intruding as much as possible.

So was it fair to label Phish the "new Dead," or was this a spurious association promulgated by lazy journalists? The bottom line is that while it's impossible to imagine Phish without the Grateful Dead as forebears, many other musicians figured as influences upon them. Some of them—such as Carlos Santana and Frank Zappa—were arguably at least as significant as the Grateful Dead. In reality, the media certainly overplayed the Grateful Dead connection and Phish probably underplayed it, at least in their first decade.

During that first interview with Phish—two months before Garcia's death, as it turned out—I bluntly asked Anastasio: "Do associations with the Grateful Dead have any validity for you?"

He answered without hesitation.

"Oh, definitely. The Grateful Dead paved the way for what we're doing and what a lot of bands are doing now. I think even Pearl Jam wouldn't be having the same career without the Grateful Dead.

"The Grateful Dead as an American live touring act are, I think, the forebears. And it's not musical style I'm talking about, because style is style, and style is directly related to the lives that the band members have led. So whatever experiences you've had in your life are going to come out in your music.

"But conceptually, they put the music first, they put the fans first. It was a noncommercial kind of approach. And they were influenced by real American country and bluegrass bands, like Bill Monroe. That kind of thing."

While Anastasio willingly admitted to conceptual influences, he was still not acknowledging a stylistic debt to the Grateful Dead at that point. Broaching the subject was a touchy issue, since Phish did not want to find themselves in the shadow of the Grateful Dead. That said,

Mike Gordon was an unabashed Dead fan and even a Deadhead (as was, to a lesser degree, Fishman). During the same interview, Gordon said, "I'm probably the only one in the band that still tries to go to Dead concerts from time to time. . . . The fact that they're so tapped into American tradition, and mixing tradition with a real philosophy of the unknown, that's what I like."

There was a lot of automatic rejection, if not outright hostility, directed at Phish by those who viewed their scene as an extension of the Grateful Dead phenomenon. Phish started attracting regional attention in the late eighties and the first stirrings of national scrutiny in the early nineties. At that time, the indie-rock bandwagon was bouncing along and grunge would soon make its mark. Anything that smacked of "classic rock" or "hippie music" was generally reviled by indie rock's gatekeepers, and so Phish were often reflexively dismissed as the Grateful Dead redux. Phish fan Jeremy Goodwin recalled 1995 "as a time when it seemed among my friends that folks felt obliged to take a side on the Phish issue: Generally, you either loved Phish or you made fun of the people who did."

The irony was that Phish were as independent as they came.

"I wish Phish had been able to connect with a more progressive audience—somewhere between Yes and Primus rather than Widespread Panic and Aquarium Rescue Unit or whatever," said Ellis Godard of *The Phish Companion*. "We had friends who wouldn't even go see Phish until Les Claypool played with them."

Even in Burlington, in their early years, they had been the odd band out. The buzz bands on the Burlington scene, the ones expected to break out nationally, were of the New Wave or techno-pop variety. One of them, the Cuts, used a drum machine. There was a Burlington scene, but it was eclectic rather than cohesive. Phish's closest confederates were fellow nutters Ninja Custodian, the Dead-loving Joneses, and the "newgrass" band Max Creek.

During the period when Phish were emerging and the Grateful Dead receding, both bands were at best ignored and at worst lambasted by critics. Unless you read *Relix*—a periodical for Deadheads and jam-band aficionados—you'd seldom find coverage of either band in the mainstream or alternative music press. A steady trickle of younger Deadheads did begin defecting to Phish's scene in the early nineties. One of them was Kevin Shapiro, Phish's archivist.

Shapiro's Deadhead initiation came in 1989 at a show in Ann Arbor, Michigan. Next he threw in his lot for all three nights at Alpine Valley, near Milwaukee. Much of the first night's performance (July 17, 1989) was stellar enough to be released on videotape as the prophetically titled *Downhill from Here*. Then it rained torrentially for the remainder of the stand. By the end of the Alpine Valley run, Shapiro was having difficulty breathing, and his friends rushed him to a hospital. He'd contracted bronchitis, which turned into chronic asthma. "My lungs have never been the same," he noted ruefully.

This setback didn't diminish his love for the Grateful Dead. In fact, Shapiro supported himself through college by playing drums in a Dead cover band. In the fall of 1991, however, he saw Phish for the first time—at Cleveland's Agora Ballroom—and was hooked, transitioning instantly from the Grateful Dead's world to Phish's.

"When I saw Phish, it was all over for me, and I pretty much never looked back," said Shapiro. "Something about Phish—what they did and the amount of creativity that went into it—spoke to me on a deeper level."

His experience was a common one. Tom Baggott stumbled onto Phish while attending the University of Massachusetts. Up until then he'd been a tenderfoot Deadhead, turned on to them as a young teen by a woman in his neighborhood. She'd seen them as far back as the 1972 Europe tour, and she passed the music and lore on to Baggott.

"The whole Grateful Dead thing was such a mystery to me, this esoteric cult kind of thing, the mythology and symbol and ritual of it," Baggott explained. "They spoke of Jerry and everyone in the scene like it was family, but I knew it was never going to be my family because it was a whole other generation. I still went to Dead shows for the scene and the drugs and the music. It was a lot of fun and a rite of passage for me, but it was a hollow one because it was something I was hopping onto.

"When I saw Phish at Nectar's and on the UVM campus, I realized that I had discovered *my* scene and *my* rite of passage. This was my band. I realized, 'This is the nascent beginnings of something and I'm right here.' It felt so amazing and magical."

Baggott tried to turn fellow Deadheads on to Phish with mixed success.

"Phish was something we proselytized," he said. "I remember being at Dead shows and cranking Phish from a big stereo on one of my father's farm trucks. You could see the impact it was having, because people would stop and go, 'Holy shit, what's this?' I'd give 'em a plum or an apple and be like, *This is Phish!* I was one of many people who spun bootlegs and passed them around and played their music at every opportunity for crowds and new people.

"At one Dead show I had a bootleg of Phish at Johnson State College. It was a rock-heavy set with a lot of covers, and people were flipping out. They were all tweaked up on whatever and dancing, and this party was evolving around my truck. But I could also see other Deadheads reacting just as strongly in the opposite way: 'Whoa, what is this? This is just too heavy, man. I gotta go get some Jerry, brah.' Phish polarized that scene in a lot of ways."

Kevin Shapiro saw similar signs of resistance. "A lot of Deadheads felt Phish had a different kind of energy, that they were more frenetic and erratic," he explained. "Irreverent, too, in some ways. Just a lot of odd time signatures and inside jokes. With Phish, you couldn't settle into a groove and dance, particularly. Whereas at a lot of Dead shows, you really could. Sometimes the groove would stay fairly stable throughout the show. I think that their music came from a more unified place, whereas our guys had punk and reggae and New Wave and prog influences."

In addition to Shapiro, serious Deadheads could be found in Phish's crew. Lighting director Chris Kuroda, for instance, attended

252 Grateful Dead concerts. He knows the exact number, because he kept a running list of dates and venues on the inside of his copy of *Steal Your Face*, a live Dead album.

The Grateful Dead, it turns out, were indirectly responsible for introducing Kuroda to Phish. "The first time I ever saw Phish was at Goddard College on Halloween," he recalled. "They were co-billing with a band called the Joneses, which was basically a Grateful Dead cover band. That's who I went to see. I'd never heard of Phish.

"The Joneses played a Grateful Dead set, then here comes this thing Phish I'd never heard of and didn't care about. But I'm in the room when they start playing. I remember being with another friend who had never seen them before, and about forty-five minutes in we're looking at each other and going, 'Who the fuck are these guys? This is insane. I've never heard anything like this in my life.' And they were just being Phish. They were a lot wackier back then, just doing their thing. I definitely became a fan and latched on to them from the first time I saw them."

The Deadheads in the Phish crew tried to convert soundman Paul Languedoc, a Dead skeptic, by taking him to a show at Shoreline Amphitheatre, in Mountain View, California, on August 27, 1993. (Phish were playing in the area at the Greek Theater in Berkeley a day later.) Paul and Chris related the story:

> Paul: So they dragged me down and I was sitting there, and the band guys were all trying to explain to me what was happening and what was gonna happen next.
> Chris: And it was just a horrible, horrible show, the worst Grateful Dead show I'd ever seen.
> Paul: One thing I did get was the scene. I was like, Okay, I see what this is. This is just like a house party, and this is the band that's playing. People are just hanging out, and they could listen to the band or not, and the band doesn't seem to care one way or another whether people are listening or not.

CHRIS: It was especially like that in California.

PAUL: The thing that I got from watching the Grateful Dead, the sense I got about their music, was that they're all in a car going somewhere but nobody's driving, you know, and that's fine with them.

I suggested that by 1993, Jerry Garcia probably didn't want to be there, was uninterested in driving the band, and didn't particularly care whether anyone was listening.

"No, probably not," Kuroda conceded with a sigh.

"I just didn't get it," added Languedoc. "And I still think they sucked, personally. Although I respect them in a certain way."

Ellis Godard, of *The Phish Companion*, was typical of those who were enchanted by Phish's eclecticism and found the Grateful Dead to be somewhat enervated.

"I only saw three Dead shows, and it wasn't for me," Godard stated. "It was Americana, it was fine, but it was a little slow. It was sort of melancholy and morose, and I wanted something fun and energetic. I didn't wanna hear 'He's Gone' at some funeral pace, you know? I'd rather hear Phish doing 'Runaway Jim.'"

"For a lot of people, Phish was a post-Dead experience," Shapiro explained. "But for many others, Phish didn't draw on that history at all. A lot of people came to Phish from New Wave places—Talking Heads, R.E.M., more of an indie, college-music feel. I'm not saying Phish's music wasn't psychedelic. Just not in the way the Grateful Dead's was."

Jon Pareles, the *New York Times*' veteran rock critic, wrote an essay in 1996 that weighed the ways in which Phish was and wasn't like the Grateful Dead. "Its roots in the Grateful Dead are unmistakable," he wrote, "but Phish is a next-generation jam band. Like be-boppers in the wake of Charlie Parker, Phish brings its own ideas to an idiom pioneered by others. Phish is more organized, less inclined to ramble or search audibly for its next maneuver than the Grateful Dead were.

"To yield something like a Dead concert without the Grateful Dead spots, Phish maps the territory between fixed songs and haphazard jamming," he continued. "Its instrumental passages move purpose-fully from section to section. Though there's room for spontaneity, there are also long, satisfying crescendos and carefully plotted moves from consonance to dissonance and back."

Phish's staff and crew actually consulted the Grateful Dead's playbook and protocols. They contacted the Dead's organization once they started encountering similar crowd-control issues: security, drugs, bootleg merchandise, parking-lot scenes that threatened to get out of hand. They'd reference the Grateful Dead's security manual and see what they could glean from it.

"We had that mirror scene, so we had mirror issues," said Chris Kuroda. "So our people would often get advice from the Grateful Dead: How did you deal with 4 million nitrous tanks? How did you deal with people selling copyrighted art? How did you deal with those types of things and who else do you ask for advice?"

In terms of revenue, Jason Colton pointed out that Phish never were as big as the Grateful Dead: "I remember being told in 1995 that the Grateful Dead had a $22 million operation. Just merchandise! They played stadiums. We never played stadiums. For sure, Phish's touring business has been very strong, but it wasn't quite on the scale of the Grateful Dead."

The Grateful Dead played their last show on July 9, 1995, at Chicago's Soldier Field on a scorching summer day. Back in California, Garcia entered a drug-rehab facility, where he suffered a heart attack and was pronounced dead at 4:23 A.M. on August 9. He was only fifty-three.

Phish never directly hooked up with the Grateful Dead during the period—basically, from 1988 to 1995—when such a thing might have been possible. Phish was intent on carving their own niche, and the Grateful Dead were caught up in their world. Interestingly, once Phish became successful on its own terms and the Grateful Dead were de-funct, they tipped their hat to them. At Virginia Beach on August 9, 1998—the third anniversary of Garcia's death—Phish encored with

"Terrapin Station." How big was this moment? "They basically played Jerry's anthem," said Brad Sands. "It was a recognition moment, and from that point on, the Dead thing was put behind them. They could embrace it as opposed to run away from it. They could finally start to say, 'Jerry was a big influence. He was great.' All that stuff."

There would be more. In April 1999, Anastasio and McConnell participated in a three-night Phil (Lesh) and Friends stand at San Francisco's Warfield Theater, where they covered huge swaths of the Grateful Dead's repertoire and some of Phish's. Bassist Lesh and guitarist Bob Weir each sat in with Phish when they played Shoreline Amphitheatre in 1999 and 2000, respectively. Still, fans never got the ultimate thrill: a chance to see Anastasio and Garcia share a stage. Whether earthshaking music would've resulted from this historic union is a matter of conjecture. But what a photo opportunity Anastasio and Garcia onstage would've been: a dorm-room poster for the ages.

Five days after the fabled band meeting at which Anastasio announced his intention to break up Phish, he appeared on Charlie Rose's talk show. Rose asked his guest about the Grateful Dead. Anastasio went further than ever in acknowledging the influence of the Grateful Dead—and especially Jerry Garcia.

RОЅЕ: The Grateful Dead comparison. Where is it true and where is it not true?

ANASTASIO: It's not true in the sense that they are probably the greatest band in American history, just about, in terms of American bands, to me. . . . So we took as much as we could from them because they wrote a whole new framework about how you mix things up and people tour and all the great things they did. . . . You talk about having a jam-band scene—they invented it.

In the Dead's wake, the jam-band field largely and logically fell to Phish, triggering even greater growth and interest in the band. In another year they would be performing for an estimated crowd of

70,000 at the Clifford Ball—three and a half times the capacity of Madison Square Garden.

Everything started to change, not just for the band but for their fans, too. Those who had previously been on the ground floor could no longer claim Phish as their personal property. Greater numbers of fans began following Phish from gig to gig, chasing musical highs and road thrills. For some, it became a way of life, and school, job, and other responsibilities played second fiddle to "tour." (Not *the tour* or *their tour*, just *tour.*) Obviously, the clubby aura of the Nectar's days was long gone. The two to three thousand–seat theaters Phish played throughout 1993 gave way to small arenas and outdoor sheds—plus the occasional large arena in places where they were well-established— in the following years. In 1996, they undertook their first all-arena tour.

There were now obvious layers of Phish fans, arranged something like the earth itself:

- the inner core, who were there from the beginning and weren't shy about letting anyone know it
- the inner middle core, who got hip to Phish from 1988 to 1992, when they expanded beyond their Vermont home base
- the outer middle core, who gravitated toward Phish from 1993 through 1995, many of them turned on via word-of-mouth by members of the inner middle core
- the ever-expanding outer core of "newbs" who flooded to Phish after '95 for a variety of reasons: e.g., it became a hip thing to do, the music was good, the party never stopped, and Jerry Garcia was dead. They were sometimes treated with disdain by the other cliques, who blamed them for wrecking their formerly cozy scene.

During the later months of 1995, with Garcia so recently laid to rest, you could not read anything about Phish in the press without the Dead referenced close by. A glowing review in the *New York Times* of

Phish's New Year's stand, for instance, contained fifteen references to Garcia and the Grateful Dead.

These incessant comparisons didn't bother Anastasio as much as the media's invasion of his privacy in the wake of Garcia's death. He had just walked through the door of his house when he heard the news.

"One second later, the phone rang," he recalled. "The whole thing was a nightmare. People calling for statements. A lot of people were calling. I didn't even get a chance to sit down and digest the event at all, so I didn't really have anything to say."

What he said was, "Right now, I'm sad and confused."

"It took me awhile, like a couple of weeks, to think about it," he said, reflecting on Garcia's death. "The thing I've been thinking is that I learned more about music from the way he walked onstage than anything else. It wasn't necessarily what he played; it was who he was and what his intentions were.

"Intention has so much to do with it. You can hear that in music so clearly. It's not like, 'I'm such a good guitar player.' Music has nothing to do with that, you know? I read recent interviews with Sonic Youth and the Meat Puppets where they talked about how heavily they were influenced by Jerry, and they both have that same kind of thing. It's like a purity of intention."

The peak year of 1995 ended with a crescendo. They performed a four-night New Year's stand—two nights at the Worcester Centrum, followed by two nights in New York City, at Madison Square Garden. The New Year's Eve show itself has entered the hallowed hall of all-time great Phish shows.

It was quite a scene outside the Garden that wintry night. "Cash for your extra" was the mantra chanted by an army of Phishheads circling the streets. This was the group's first New Year's Eve show at this particular Garden. As usual, many ticketless Phishheads had traveled a long distance on faith, willing to gamble that a "miracle ticket" would find its way into their hands. Some paced the block with an index finger extended. Others stayed rooted to one spot, hoping the miracle would find them. As showtime approached, the chanting took on a more urgent tone:

"Who's got my extra?"

"I *need* to hear the music tonight."

Meanwhile, the cold, damp air turned the shivering fans' breath to icy fog. A bearded, gnomish fellow had hitchhiked from Georgia with empty pockets and full backpack. A young couple from upstate New York had paid a scalper's ransom, only to learn they'd been burned with counterfeits. At the last moment, I provided them all with "miracle tickets," which was truly a fun thing to do.

The startled Georgian danced a little jig and then bolted for the entrance. The elated couple proffered a group hug. Despite these happy endings, thousands more didn't get to hear the music they'd come so far on a wing and a prayer to see. And so they occupied themselves on New Year's Eve in midtown Manhattan with drum circles and acoustic-guitar strum-alongs, networking for rides or floors to crash on, and swapping fall tour tales. Those who weren't able to attend those shows no doubt heard them soon after, thanks to the ardent network of tapers, whose microphones stood on the floor of the Garden like a circle of black cornstalks, recording every note.

At the New Year's Eve 1995 show, Phish took it to the limit with a three-set, five-hour marathon. The first set was highlighted by "Colonel Forbin's Ascent" and "Fly Famous Mockingbird," from the *Gamehendge* musical. In addition to extended forays like "The Squirming Coil" and "You Enjoy Myself," the group covered the Who ("Drowned" and "Sea and Sand"), Collective Soul ("Shine"), and the Edgar Winter Group's bombastic classic-rock instrumental, "Frankenstein." They encored with one of the toughest, tightest versions of Chuck Berry's "Johnny B. Goode" I've ever heard.

After spending a fair amount of time with Phish during the year that had just ended, interviewing them and hanging out on their scene, I scribbled these thumbnail portraits of the band members:

"Mike is the analytical Phish.

"Jon is the extroverted Phish.

"Page is the reserved Phish.

"Trey is the emotional Phish."

It struck me that camaraderie was the key to Phish's success. The band members were close to one another and their families. They were close to their management company and crew. They were close, in spirit, to their fans and more willing than most to interact in person.

Mike Gordon was especially approachable. He was the band member mostly likely to hang out with fans or circulate backstage. He'd pedal his bike thorough a crowd before shows or drop into chat rooms on the Phish.Net Web site. Through 1994, he personally answered nearly every piece of fan mail sent to the band. He worried that his habit of making himself available was ego-driven, but it seemed quite the opposite.

"I think I'm overcompensating for having been unpopular in junior high," he said matter-of-factly. Gordon has a droll, deadpan sense of humor. Once, when I ran into him at a concert and the subject of my long-delayed *Rolling Stone* article came up, he broke into "The Cover of 'Rolling Stone,'" the seventies novelty hit by Dr. Hook and the Medicine Show. He knew every word. (In 2003, when Phish finally appeared on the magazine's cover, they performed that very tune.)

Personality wise, McConnell and Fishman came across as the yin and yang of Phish, especially when interviewed together. McConnell was reserved, refined, taciturn, while Fishman was boisterous, extroverted, given to fits of laughter. Yet they were definitely on the same page, finishing each other's thoughts and chiding each other in a good-natured way. The talk turned to Phish's loyal army of fans.

"I think we make ourselves more accessible than most bands," McConnell said. "On the way to the bus I'll often hang out and talk to people. Generally our fans are really respectful. They treat us as people, and we treat them with a certain amount of respect, too."

Anastasio's boundless will to create has always been the locomotive that drove Phish to the outer limits, but all four of them shared that attitude. At least some of that creative drive seemed bound up in their genes.

Of Anastasio and Gordon, manager John Paluska noted, "They took good characteristics from each of their parents. They're both very driven and organized and focused, and at the same time they've got real free spirits and creative sides."

Moreover, the group genuinely appeared to value their friendship with one another. They seemed so bonded that it would have been difficult to imagine a lineup change. Talking in 1995, they agreed.

"I would hope that if, God forbid, something were to happen . . . ," said McConnell.

"They always look at me when they say that," Fishman said, laughing. "A disaster waiting to happen!"

"I would hope that the band would just break up. I'd really hope we wouldn't try to replace anyone," McConnell continued.

"What we have right now as Phish we can never have again," asserted Fishman. "The four of us can't go out in the world and have that again, so when this ends, that's it. This is definitely a one-shot deal as far as having this kind of chemistry and the same kind of dedication."

What is it about Phish that inspires such devotion?

To fully understand the phenomenon, Phish had to be caught in concert. A typical evening with Phish consisted of two seventy-five-minute sets and an encore—roughly two and a half hours of music and an intermission.

Their magic didn't translate on MTV, which had little to offer Phish (or vice versa). Once, in 1992, the group dutifully performed for MTV's cameras, only to see brief, truncated versions of their songs used in a half-hour show called *Hangin' with MTV*. Since Phish played jams that lasted longer than the entire show, MTV wasn't the ideal medium to spread the word about the band. In their newsletter, Phish promised fans they'd never do it again.

With few exceptions, they didn't get much help from radio, either, where they were too unhip for alternative and too weird for classic rock. The myopic rock press kept its distance, too, until the late 1990s. Finally, as good as they are, Phish's albums by definition couldn't convey the excitement that transpired at a live show.

"It's a bit more of a headache in the studio," admitted Anastasio in 1995, "and the stage is where we have these incredible musical experiences."

Phish had an active repertoire of 250 songs. Anastasio made the point that he wrote material with the live show, not the recording studio, in mind. Many of Phish's best-known songs have never appeared on studio albums. So determined was Anastasio that each night's performance have its own unique pacing and energy that he'd spend hours drawing up a set list, especially in the early to mid nineties. Anastasio would study a computer printout and scrawl a tentative set list in the margin. It would be distributed and taped to the appropriate onstage spots by Brad Sands, the production assistant turned road manager. However, it was always subject to change.

"We've got enough material that we can go on tour for four weeks and not play any one song more than three or four times," Anastasio noted in the mid nineties. The Anastasio–Marshall songwriting partnership would intensify its output in the coming years, and Phish's songbag would grow even larger.

"I've got a stack of music that I bring on the road with me in case I forget some of the pieces," McConnell admitted. "Almost any of the songs that have that sort of compositional feel have been written out on staff paper."

The more popular they got, the more determined Phish grew to push the limits of live performance. In 1995, they took it even farther than they had the previous year. Some felt that the lengthier jams on the summer 1995 tour, such as the nearly hourlong "Tweezer" at Mud Island in Memphis, went on for too long with too little payoff. But no one complained about Phish's willingness to go on a musical adventure.

"I think people like us because they don't get that experience with a lot of other bands," said McConnell. "If we're really confident we're going somewhere, they're right there with us."

"It's a pretty challenging band," conceded Fishman. "All four of us have an internal desire to push our personal limits, and that ends up taking a life of its own in the group situation."

"A lot of times we'll be satisfied or dissatisfied after a set and talk about it," noted Gordon. "We started to find that the biggest problem— in some ways, the only problem—is one or several of us being in our own worlds and not trying to hook up. So 'hooking up' ends up being the biggest phrase used backstage. Are we hooking up? And what else really matters? Nothing else matters."

"If we get our egos out of the way and concentrate on communicating among ourselves, that translates into communication with the audience," said Anastasio. "If I do some kind of flashy guitar riff, I can feel an attitude of *who cares?* a little bit. Whereas if I do something very simple that hooks up with Mike or hooks up all four people, then there's this locking feeling with the audience that's uplifting."

Anastasio and Gordon discussed these transcendent moments.

"Occasionally, I'll have a real peak experience where we're playing and suddenly I realize that a lot of thoughts that would normally come into my head to distract me are gone," said Gordon.

"Losing your inhibitions is what everybody's trying to do," added Anastasio.

"If anything, it's an awareness. It's like being really aware without being analytical."

"Yeah. To get to the feeling where you couldn't play a wrong note if you tried."

"'Cause right and wrong isn't even the issue."

"Right and wrong doesn't matter, and it's just flowing through you. You're just kind of a vehicle. It's almost like Zen breathing or something. You can get to that state, and once you're in it, it just rolls along."

The year 1995 ended with what many fans consider Phish's greatest tour (fall '95), greatest month of touring (December '95), and one of their greatest single shows (New Year's Eve). The year 1996, by comparison, started out slowly and unfolded quite differently, because Phish needed time to work on a new album but also because they were beginning to feel a bit burned out.

The three-and-a-half-month trek that carried Phish through the end of 1995 had worn them out.

"At the end of our fall tour, there was this incredible feeling of having hit the wall," Anastasio said. "Everybody was tired. I still thought we were playing well, but it was like a slow-burn kind of feeling just going to dinner with everybody every night. So much of what we do is about energy, and when people are feeling tired, it's hard to put out that energy."

Although 1995 ended with a lengthy tour, Phish actually didn't play as many total gigs as they had in past years. In 1995, they played eighty-one shows—the least since 1987, when the band members were still in college or had jobs. In 1996, they played even fewer still (seventy-one shows in all). Almost every year until the breakup in 2004 yielded fewer Phish gigs than the previous one. By 1996, their priorities were changing, and they needed time off to catch their breath and reassess their position.

"It was like an era was coming to an end," Anastasio said at the time. "We realized that we had to downsize, despite the fact we were growing in terms of numbers of people who were coming to see the band. We'd spread ourselves too thin. So we started cutting back."

With the exceptions of an appearance at New Orleans's Jazz and Heritage Festival and a one-off club show in Woodstock during sessions for *Billy Breathes*, Phish took a half-year break from live shows. They wouldn't resume touring until July 1996, and even then they headed abroad for a one-month jaunt opening for Santana around Europe. America wouldn't get a Phish tour until August, with the year nearly two-thirds over, which was unheard of.

In April came the first side project that didn't involve all four members of Phish. It was an avant-garde blowing session, called *Surrender to the Air*, that had been cut almost a year earlier. It was the product of two days' worth of jam sessions involving a group of musicians handpicked by Anastasio. He claimed to have literally dreamt up the lineup of guitarist Marc Ribot; organist John Medeski; trumpeter Michael Ray, saxophonist Marshall Allen, and vibraphonist Damon R. Choice, all from Sun Ra's jazz "Arkestra"; Jon Fishman and Bob Guillotti on drums; brothers Kofi and Oteil Burbridge on flute and bass; and trombonist James Harvey.

In Anastasio's recounting, "It was a big party with microphones on and tape machines running. It's a pretty wild album. I wanted it to be symphonic in form yet jazz in language and thrash in energy."

The participants in *Surrender to the Air* reconvened for two nights' worth of live improv at New York's Academy of Music—the last shows ever played at that venue. It was a cool idea to make an avant-garde side trip with such an impressive cavalcade of musicians, though maybe not the most listenable item in the vast catalog of Phish-related projects.

Phish's chief priority for much of 1996 was cutting a new album. Two years had passed since the sessions for their last studio album (*Hoist*), and while the assembly of their concert compendium, *A Live One*, had consumed comparable time and energy to a studio project, they were itching to lay down some new music.

"Because the last one was live, it feels like we haven't done an album since *Hoist*," Anastasio said then. "And because of the whole way *Hoist* ended up going, it almost feels like we haven't made an album since *Rift*. The focus for a long time has been on touring, and we haven't been in the studio, so we're chomping at the bit."

In February 1996, Phish unplugged the phones and hibernated in a rustic barn-turned-studio next to a babbling brook in upstate New York, near Woodstock. They stayed there six weeks, working on material without a producer. The facility was called The Barn (not to be

Meat Phish: Jon Fishman, Trey Anastasio, Mike Gordon, and Page McConnell in 1987
© PHISH, INC. 1987. COURTESY OF MIKE GORDON.

Nectar's, the downtown
Burlington club where
Phish got their act together
PHOTO BY PARKE PUTERBAUGH.

"Vermont's most naive band" and crew en route to Colorado, 1988
© PHISH, INC. 1988. COURTESY OF MIKE GORDON.

Rocking the Rockies: Phish play in Aspen
© PHISH, INC. 1988. COURTESY OF MIKE GORDON.

Nothing fancy: Phish at The Front, the next step up from Nectar's

Band and fans are feeling it in Northampton, Mass.

The crowds are getting bigger: an outdoor gig in Townshend, Vt., 1990
© PHISH, INC. 1990. COURTESY OF MIKE GORDON.

The extended Phish family in the early nineties, with the band in the front row: McConnell (holding sign), Anastasio, Fishman, Gordon © PHISH, INC. 1993. PHOTO BY ALLAN DINES.

Page McConnell
© PHISH, INC. 1994.
PHOTO BY
C. TAYLOR CROTHERS.

Mike Gordon
© PHISH, INC. 1994.
PHOTO BY C. TAYLOR ROTHERS.

Trey Anastasio
© PHISH, INC. 1998. PHOTO BY SHARON FOSBROOK.

Jon Fishman
© PHISH, INC. 1994.
PHOTO BY C. TAYLOR CROTHERS.

Phish performing with Marjorie Minkin's paintings as backdrops, 1994

Jerry Seinfeld and Phish share a comedic moment backstage at a taping of *Late Night With David Letterman*

Hot dog! Phish in flight at the Boston Garden on New Year's Eve 1994

Fries and a drink—the rest of the order from New Year's Eve '94, on display with the hot dog at the Rock and Roll Hall of Fame + Museum

Garden party: sold-out Boston crowd seen through a fish-eye lens

Jumping jive: Anastasio and Gordon bounce on trampolines at Madison Square Garden

Bluegrass breakdown: Phish picks for appreciative fans at the front of the house
© PHISH, INC. 1994. PHOTO BY DANNY CLINCH.

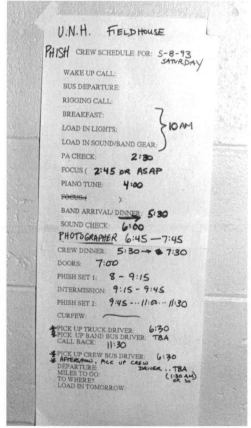

U.N.H. FIELDHOUSE

PHISH CREW SCHEDULE FOR: 5-8-93
SATURDAY

WAKE UP CALL:
BUS DEPARTURE:
RIGGING CALL:
BREAKFAST:
LOAD IN LIGHTS: } 10 AM
LOAD IN SOUND/BAND GEAR:
PA CHECK: 2:30
FOCUS (2:45 OR ASAP
PIANO TUNE: 4:00
FOCUS (   ):
BAND ARRIVAL/DINNER: 5:30
SOUND CHECK: 6:00
PHOTOGRAPHER 6:45 — 7:45
CREW DINNER: 5:30 → 7:30
DOORS: 7:00
PHISH SET 1:   8 - 9:15
INTERMISSION: 9:15 - 9:45
PHISH SET 2:   9:45 ... 11:00 ... 11:30
CURFEW: ____
PICK UP TRUCK DRIVER: 6:30
PICK UP BAND BUS DRIVER: TBA
CALL BACK: 11:30
PICK UP CREW BUS DRIVER: 6:30
AFTERSHOW, PICK UP CREW
DEPARTURE: DRIVER .. TBA
MILES TO GO: (11:30 AM)
TO WHERE?   OR ...
LOAD IN TOMORROW:

Crew schedule from a 1993 gig
© PHISH, INC. 1993. PHOTO BY ALLAN DINES.

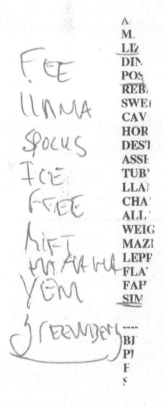

Proposed set list from 1995,
handwritten by Anastasio
PHOTO BY PARKE PUTERBAUGH.

Anastasio and Fishman head to their rehearsal space above Paul Languedoc's workshop
PHOTO BY PARKE PUTERBAUGH.

Phish rehearse Acoustic Army at Red Rocks, outside Denver, in 1995
© PHISH, INC. 1995. PHOTO BY SOFI DILLOF.

Ice-cream men Ben (Cohen) & Jerry (Greenfield) with Trey Anastasio
© PHISH, INC. 1996. PHOTO BY DANNY CLINCH.

Page McConnell at the
Clifford Ball, the first
Phish festival, in 1996
© PHISH, INC. 1996.
PHOTO BY DANNY CLINCH.

Fair weather and fine music at The Gorge, in Washington State, 1997
© PHISH, INC. 1997. PHOTO BY JEREMY STEIN.

Anastasio and McConnell at The Great Went, the first of three Phish festivals held at Loring
Air Force Base in Limestone, Maine © PHISH, INC. 1998. PHOTO BY GEOFF FOSBROOK.

The Art Tower, a pile of fan- and band-made art, would go up in flames at The Great Went, in 1997
© PHISH, INC. 1998.
PHOTO BY GEOFF FOSBROOK.

Phil and Phriend: The Grateful Dead's Phil Lesh and Phish's Trey Anastasio at San Francisco's Warfield Theatre in 1999 © PHISH, INC. 1999. PHOTO BY JAY BLAKESBERG.

Phish at Drum Logos in Fukuoka, Japan, in June 2000

Tie-dyed Phish fans sip and signify at a show in Tokyo

An illuminating thought: "Our Intent Is All for Your Delight," from Phish's 2003 It festival
© PHISH, INC. 2003. PHOTO BY BEN STECHSCHULTE.

The Tower Jam at It
© PHISH, INC. 2003. PHOTO BY BEN STECHSCHULTE.

Lightman Chris Kuroda and soundman
Paul Languedoc PHOTO BY PARKE PUTERBAUGH.

Lyricist Tom Marshall at the mysterious Rhombus, where he and Trey Anastasio wrote songs and partied as younger men PHOTO BY PARKE PUTERBAUGH.

Trey Anastasio points the way forward © PHISH, INC. 1994. PHOTO BY DAVE VANN.

confused with Anastasio's Barn Studio outside of Burlington. It was part of the Bearsville studio complex—a separate building that had been turned into a new recording space.

"The idea was to scale back and start from ground zero," Anastasio said. "With some of the other albums, I felt there were too many grandiose ideas. We were writing a lot of good music, but we tried to do too much. This time, all we wanted to do was get together and hang out. We didn't have any plans. We weren't talking much to anyone in management. It was just like, 'We're going into a barn; leave us alone.'"

The project began with "the blob." The engineer cued up a reel of tape, and the band members picked straws to see who'd play the first note. Page McConnell drew the long straw. He hit a single note on the vibes. Anastasio tapped a steel drum. Fishman played something on the piano. Gordon plucked a bass note.

"We went around in a circle," said McConnell, "playing one note at a time for about two weeks."

The exercise evolved from single notes to a turn that might involve all of them jamming for five minutes or singing something or even erasing material. Gradually, Phish built up a "blob" of music whose freewheeling, democratic construction set the tone once the group moved to actual songs.

"We'd take the blob approach, trying to have fun with all of us contributing equally and feeling free to have a more open dialogue," said McConnell. "It cleared our heads."

What they cut once they got down to serious recording was promising but needed work. Some of the songs had already been successfully road-tested but sounded disappointingly flat in their studio incarnations. Their managers worried about how to broach this difficult matter with the band, but they came to the same conclusion on their own and decided to bring in an outside producer. They tapped Steve Lillywhite, who'd produced U2's early work and, more recently, the Dave Matthews Band.

Lillywhite was an artist's producer, and he excelled at sonic atmospherics. "He has a good sense of spatial relationships," noted Anastasio. It was a good match, and with six more weeks of work in Woodstock that June, *Billy Breathes* became a stronger album.

The sessions retained their relaxed vibe. Turtle Creek flowed outside the barn where they were recording, and at quiet moments they could hear it gurgling while they were playing. Gordon drew a fascinating verbal portrait of the group's unhurried daily routine:

"We'd arrive around 3 P.M., do ten takes of a song, take a dinner break around 6:30 and watch some TV, then do a bunch more takes of a song till about 1 A.M.," he said. "It was okay because Steve Lillywhite was such a positive influence—dancing around and keeping our spirits up, which is his style. Then we'd take an hour and a half break to play ping-pong, hang out, or whatever, and resume around 2:30 or 3:00 A.M.

"By that time, I was usually laying on the couch, wondering when these guys are gonna give up. I'd get called to do a bass part, and by that time I'd be so tired that I'd just play my part without thinking too hard about it. Because we entered that subconscious zone where you're not thinking or worrying but just playing, we captured some of our best takes in the early morning hours."

Billy Breathes is relatively understated by Phish's standards, and it does exude a relaxed vibe that evokes the wee hours. Shortly before its release, Anastasio nodded along to a list of adjectives—calmer, subtler, less busy, Zen-like—that I used to describe it.

"Like there was nothing left to prove?" he said, asking and answering his own question in a way that neatly summed up the album's less-is-more aura and quiet confidence.

It was accorded a positive reception in the rock press without the usual cheap shots about the Grateful Dead and noodling. Even *Rolling Stone* gave it four stars (out of five), which amounted to a benediction of sorts.

"The album felt to me like what I had always ever really wanted, which was to hang out, stay up and record with those three guys in a barn in the woods. The whole thing was like stepping backward or forward or something."

Anastasio was quick to note that Phish were not withdrawing but recharging. "The key is putting yourself in the right frame of mind and realizing what a great thing it is we get to do, which just opens everything up," he said.

Gordon summed up Phish's outlook like this: "We always have the attitude that each moment is the most important thing we've ever done. So we try to make it work and assume it can work, that there's always that potential."

Phish had been selling out almost everywhere they played. They were now hitting outdoor sheds in the warm-weather months and arenas in the winter. As far as record sales went, they were beginning to rack up some impressive numbers. Both *Hoist* and *A Live One* went gold, denoting sales of more than half a million copies. *Billy Breathes* entered *Billboard*'s album chart at No. 7—the highest position a Phish album has achieved to date.

All the same, they still were not drawing attention in the entertainment press commensurate with their numbers and impact on the music scene. This situation both amused and frustrated the band members.

"It makes me laugh," said Anastasio. "The media's just completely missed the boat. We were chuckling about it after the Clifford Ball [their August 1996 festival]. Nobody from MTV News was there, and it was the biggest North American concert of the year. It was definitely groundbreaking. And regardless of the music, there was a real story that in an age of corporate sponsorship, this completely homegrown thing happened that was different than any other concert."

The group's low profile created a kind of paradox. By that time, nearly everyone had heard of Phish, but outside of the growing base of fanatics who followed the tours, relatively few had actually *heard* Phish. They were big but they were still kind of a mystery to mainstream music fans.

"Sometimes I wonder," Anastasio mused. "The media can't claim any responsibility for making us what we are. So maybe they have nothing to gain from covering us at this point. Maybe it's just a feeling of, 'Whoa, we really missed it on that one . . . well, we'll just talk about KISS.' Know what I mean? I mean, how many magazines have had KISS on the cover?"

The Clifford Ball came after their month in Europe and a mere nine gigs (four of them at Red Rocks) on American soil during the first weeks of August. As an aside, Phish played one of the strangest and funniest sets of their career at the Melkweg, a music club and hash bar in Amsterdam. Between sets, they availed themselves of the fully legal smoking substances, and the ensuing high made hash of the second set.

"They all went to the side of the stage and puffed for an unbelievable amount of time, like a half-hour," recounted Tom Marshall, "and then they went up and tried to play. They'd all try to start a song and go into a jam and then come out of the jam with another Phish song and go into another jam and then come out of the jam into another Phish song. They never went back and never had any idea where they were. The first set was coherent, but then they went into this wack thing. I loved it, it was great. The first time they ever came unrooted onstage, *ever*."

Officially, the Clifford Ball drew a combined crowd of 135,000 over two days, making it the most highly attended concert event in North America of 1996. In *Pollstar*'s chart of the year's top grossing touring acts, Phish placed eighteenth. That was impressive considering it was a light touring year for them and that their ticket prices were lower than those of the acts ahead of them.

Planning for the Clifford Ball had taken months, and the issues at times seemed daunting. In fact, at the last minute, the festival almost didn't happen. Promoter Dave Werlin had to pull a rabbit out of a hat to forestall cancellation by the Plattsburgh Area Revitalization Commission (PARC). Late in the game, the commission's CEO called to inform him they'd decided against hosting a concert/campout festival on their property, though they might reconsider for the following year.

"I decided to go for a Hail Mary pass and called the office of the state senator who represented the region. Although he was a Republican, he was also the chair of the New York State Finance Committee. We thought his office might understand the economic implications of tens of thousands of visitors coming to this depressed upstate community. Sure enough, his chief of staff heard us out. A couple of hours later, the PARC CEO called and asked if we could return to Plattsburgh to make another presentation, which we did, of course. And the rest is history." Backstage at the Clifford Ball, the mayor of Plattsburgh—no doubt appreciating the boost that 70,000 visitors brought to the local economy—told McConnell, "You guys have got to come back next year!"

Indeed, though they never did return to Plattsburgh, the Clifford Ball would serve as the blueprint for a series of annual festival campouts in out-of-the-way places. What Phish did would inspire such multi-band rock festivals as Bonnaroo and Coachella. In fact, many of the staff and crew who worked on Phish's festivals brought their expertise to those events and others like it. That the Clifford Ball succeeded beyond anyone's expectations served as testimony to Phish's visionary outlook and perseverance.

"I think there are solutions to all the logistical problems—any kind of problem—if you sit down and think about it long enough," said Anastasio. "So many people are just naysayers. Take Plattsburgh. As soon as we started saying, 'We're going to do this concert in Plattsburgh . . . ' 'Plattsburgh?! That's nearly in Canada. Nobody's gonna go there. There's nothing there, it's this tiny little town. What are you, crazy? Let's do it at Randall's Island, then we'll rake in the big bucks.' That's the general attitude: *Get the money.* You have to get away from that."

With this, Anastasio summed up Phish's philosophy: "Shut yourself off from the world, and just don't listen to all the people who are going to tell you what you can't do. Then just do it."

SIX

Growing Pains:
1997–2000

During the middle set on the final day of the Great Went—the second of Phish's festival campouts, held the third weekend of August 1997—the band painted abstractly on pieces of wood that had been cut into artistic designs. Two by two they took turns painting while the others played music; fans called it the "Art Jam." Throughout the weekend, Phish had solicited artwork from fans, which was collected and piled into a growing art tower. Now the musicians' own contributions were assembled jigsaw puzzle–style into one big work that was passed by the crowd out to the art tower. It was hoisted to the top of the pile, crowning the collective creation.

Then, while encoring with "Tweezer Reprise," it was all set ablaze with a giant match. The point of this act of immolation seems clear: live in the moment and don't hold on to the past, because everything—art and music included—is fleeting.

Phish continued touring, albeit at a reduced clip, in the four-year period from late 1996 through 2000. Because their tours were briefer, the special events assumed greater significance. New Year's runs and Halloween shows remained annual highlights, and the group continued along the festival path they'd blazed with the Clifford Ball, staging the Great Went (1997), Lemonwheel (1998), Big Cypress (1999), and an unnamed 1999 campout in upstate New York informally dubbed "Camp Oswego."

Then, in October 2000, they would embark upon a hiatus without specifying how long it might last (though there was little doubt they would eventually regroup). Despite all the positive spin put on the temporary breakup, it was a signal that things weren't entirely copasetic in their world. In the years leading up to the hiatus, Phish's figurative art tower started listing off-center.

Phish began to struggle with issues that included drugs, creative control, and the fiction of equal democracy. They changed their jamming style, moving in the direction of static, textural grooves that no one member might appear to dominate. Tom Marshall and Anastasio continued to generate the bulk of material, though there were semi-successful experiments in group writing in 1997 and 1998. During this period, Phish recorded a pair of albums whose differing constructions demonstrated opposite approaches to a long-simmering issue. *Story of the Ghost* (1998) bent over backward in the direction of full collaboration and group democracy, while *Farmhouse* (1999) reflected more of a unilateral vision from Anastasio. The stark differences in the assembly of those two albums was the most outwardly visible manifestation of growing pains a decade and a half into their career.

One can arguably divide Phish's career into halves: B.C. and A.C. That's before the Clifford Ball (B.C.) and after the Clifford Ball (A.C.). That August 1996 festival was a celebration and culmination of Phish's age of innocence. The Clifford Ball was the last great hurrah for what longtime fans like to call the "old Phish."

After the Clifford Ball, Phish attempted their first arena tour in fall 1996, with mixed results. Many venues were packed but not every show sold out, and some arenas were only half full. That raised a question: If Phish could play to 70,000 people in the middle of nowhere in upstate New York, why couldn't they consistently fill 15,000-seat arenas in populous urban markets around the country? The answer might have something to do with the fact that Phish still had not penetrated deeply beyond the world of Phishheads. They depended upon large numbers of fans following them from gig to gig to sell out or at least comfortably fill arenas every night. While there were enough transient Phishheads to pack large theaters and small arenas, there weren't yet ample numbers of them to consistently sell out America's enormo-domes.

One reason may be that Phish never had "the hit" that would trigger widespread interest among the general populace. The Grateful Dead's surprise Top Ten hit, "Touch of Grey," in 1987 might've been the worst thing that ever happened to them. Phish took that example under advisement and deliberately avoided handing radio an obvious hit, even though they had songs in their arsenal—"Chalk Dust Torture," "Suzy Greenberg," and "Strange Design" among them—that would've made strong contenders. Although serviced to radio, the studio version of "Chalk Dust Torture" had been slightly slowed down—ironically, to make for a more presentable tempo—rendering Anastasio's vocal more weird than listenable. "Suzy Greenberg" went unrecorded, and "Strange Design," released only as a foreign B-side, was seemingly sabotaged by a bizarre arrangement.

There was, in fact, an intention on their part to subvert potential hits. This isn't just a suspicion. In 1996, I asked Anastasio point-blank, "Are you guys ever going to get around to recording 'Suzy Greenberg'? That sounds like your great lost Top 40 single." He answered, "It's funny. I wouldn't do it, for that reason. We've had ample opportunity to record it because it was a good single, and we've chosen not to."

Perhaps they wouldn't have had a hit in any case. The infectious rocker "Down With Disease," released in 1994, failed to make *Billboard*'s Top 100 Singles chart. In a sense, Phish fell between the cracks in the nineties: too unconventional for mainstream rock radio, yet perceived as too hippie-ish and old guard for those on the indie-rock side. Like other outcasts, they found a home on Adult Album Alternative (AAA or "Triple A,") radio, a diverse, artist-driven format. You'd hear such artists as Wilco, Counting Crows, Barenaked Ladies, Indigo Girls—and Phish, for whom "Free" and "Heavy Things" fared well on the AAA charts, helping to drive album sales.

As they gained experience playing arenas, Phish segued to a more low-key jamming style. "We were discovering that since a note in an arena lasts for two seconds, we needed to experiment with playing less notes," Gordon explained. Moreover, Anastasio cut back on his efforts to drive the band's rhythm with his strumming, trusting that the rhythm section would stay locked without him and riding on top of their groove. This explains the transition from the more frenetic, full-on approach of the 1996 arena gigs to the sparser, groove-oriented sound of 1997 and beyond.

"There's so many things about climbing too fast," he said. "It takes time . . . to learn how to control a bigger room on every level: production, performance, acoustics. The way you play at a place like Red Rocks—the clarity—comes from moving into it very slowly. Trial and error, trial and error. Just like life. How often does it work out when these people skyrocket to the top and all of a sudden they're playing these arenas and it sounds like mud? Not a good thing."

Looking back, Phish professed that they felt some awkwardness on the fall 1996 arena tour. There was one unassailable peak, however: the Halloween show at Atlanta's Omni, at which they covered Talking Heads' *Remain in Light* during the second of three blazing sets. Bolstered by a two-man horn section and percussionist Karl Perazzo (on loan from Santana), Phish delved deeply into *Remain in Light*'s polyrhythmic sorcery, setting up a densely textured hailstorm of crosscutting rhythms. The groove was particularly wicked on "Crosseyed and Painless" and "The Great Curve."

Afterward, the mood backstage was triumphant and upbeat, and the band members proclaimed it their most satisfying Halloween venture to date. Still, I detected a subtle undercurrent of tension, coupled with fatigue. Anastasio, for instance, was wiped out. Slumping against a wall, he chatted amiably with well-wishers who filed past to congratulate him on a great show, but he was clearly distracted. For one thing, he clutched a golf club as if his life depended on it. When he wasn't leaning on the seven-iron like a cane, he swung it as if lining up a tee shot. He was visibly trembling with nervous energy, profound relief, utter exhaustion, and whatever other emotions might run through one's system after performing for five hours in front of 17,000 worshipful fans.

"The Halloween show is the most high-stress event of the year for these guys, by far," said Cynthia Brown, a Phish employee on the merchandise side who later married manager John Paluska.

All the same, there were murmurings of issues that went beyond the rigors of preparing to cover another band's album. The press of projects, mushrooming popularity, and loss of control that comes with getting bigger were all bearing down on them. Phish finally found itself on the media radar, and with that came an avalanche of interviews, photo sessions, and constant demands on their time. Meanwhile, the recently released *Billy Breathes* was riding a rollercoaster ride of wildly fluctuating chart numbers. It debuted at No. 7 on *Billboard*'s Top 200 album chart but dropped to No. 32 and No. 50 over the next few weeks.

The ups and downs were particularly hard on Anastasio. After all, he was the one dubbed Trey "Leadership Qualities" Anastasio by Mike Gordon in the brief band bios he penned in the Halloween "Phishbill" (a concert program designed to resemble a Broadway playbill). That had been another sore point, a subtle jab by Gordon that got under Anastasio's skin. Everyone was reportedly stressed out in the days leading up to Halloween.

"It's peaks and valleys, like any of us," said Beth Jacobson, their Elektra publicist, a few weeks after the Halloween show. "I don't think it's like, 'Oh, no, the walls are caving in.' They have their moments of getting kind of intense, but they always get their heads above water, eventually."

In Halloween's aftermath, Phish had all of one day off to rest and regroup. How would they be spending their downtime? According to Anastasio, Phish had plans to go fishing off the Georgia coast.

All the issues they had back in the States during the fall 1996 tour essentially sorted themselves out when they headed to Europe in early 1997 for their first headlining tour abroad. (They had played several headlining gigs in Europe on the July '96 tour but mainly opened for Santana.) The overseas venues they played in '97 were smaller and the crowds less adulatory. The more chilled-out vibe let them ease into the relaxed new style they were angling toward but hadn't yet solidified. Soon after returning from the continent, Anastasio summarized what happened:

"I think we were trying to change musically," he said. "It's easy to say this after the fact, but we were trying to break through to a different kind of jamming—slower, funkier, more group-oriented, and less guitar solo–oriented. We found it was a little harder to do that in the context of the American tour before that, which was our first full arena tour, ending with this big New Year's show in Boston. When we went over to Europe, playing in these little clubs, that change occurred without us even really noticing it."

Phish's European jaunts—they were there for the last half of February and returned for more dates in June—allowed them to rediscover the simple joy of playing music without worrying about how they were faring in *Pollstar* (the trade journal that tracks concert attendance and earnings) back home in the States. Phish was still largely unknown abroad. They had nothing to do with the current trends there (Britpop and electronica), and didn't care one way or the other. They had a ton of fun on their European vacations, which took them to England, Belgium, Germany, the Netherlands, France, Italy, and Denmark.

The night before a landmark gig in Hamburg, Germany, members of the group and crew got drunk at the hotel bar on a potent libation called Dr. Joe's Knockout Punch. "It had like twelve different kinds of liquors and a flaming shot of Bacardi 151 on top," Anastasio said, chuckling. "I mean, a couple of those things and you were just blind."

Anastasio ordered a round and when the drinks were placed on the table, tipsy merchandising maven Amy Skelton lifted the glass tabletop for no apparent reason, sending everything crashing to the floor in an explosion of shattering glass. The hotel manager raced over to evict them, crying, "This is a five-star hotel." They settled the $485 bill, charging it to McConnell's room (he wasn't even present) and vacating the bar to continue partying on the tour bus.

They blasted Rage Against the Machine as the bus's back lounge became a mosh pit. They opened the skylights and climbed out of them. Then the entourage lit out to carry on at some Hamburg discos. The next day they were bruised from crashing into tables and each other. The bus was pretty wrecked, too, and the table in the back lounge had been broken.

"It was just insane," Anastasio recalled. "It was somewhat out of character, but it was a great night." Moreover, it helped set the tone for the show in Hamburg by leaving them too loose and worn-out to overthink their playing. Touring Europe was a lot more low-key and depressurized anyway. Instead of five trucks and a forty-person crew, they had just one truck and a fifteen-person crew. On top of this, the group was consciously toning down its style of jamming.

"During 1996, ending with New Year's Eve, we were capping off an era of building things up to peaks a lot and blaring a lot—having there be a lot of sound and a lot of noise," Anastasio reflected. "This year, especially since we were in clubs in Europe and the whole feeling was smaller and funkier, we just got into a lot of these sparse, funky jamming grooves. Playing slow and spacious, with each note really having a purpose."

The show in Hamburg also marked the concert debut of Gordon's Modulus bass. His new ax was punchier and more penetrating, especially on the lower strings. This change in instruments would make him more of a factor in driving the jams through the end of the decade.

For all these reasons, Phish's show at the Markthalle in Hamburg on March 1, 1997, was a memorable one. They played for a crowd of 1,100, most of them Americans. This is how it went on the European tours. The audiences were largely fans from the States—exchange students or summer travelers who could afford the passage to see their heroes in smaller venues. By the group's estimate, 75 percent of the audiences in Europe were American. Still, they'd made German acquaintances while reveling in Hamburg, and a decent number of them and other curious natives turned out to see them at the Markthalle. Of all the countries in Europe, Germany came closest to catching Phish fever. "I think that Germans got it more than the British," observed management associate Jason Colton. "While they sold more tickets in the U.K. than elsewhere, the Phish culture seemed more present in Germany."

In Hamburg, they played cover songs—Talking Heads' "Cities" and ZZ Top's "Jesus Just Left Chicago"—dating back to their earliest shows as a band. They fell into funky, simmering, laid-back jams on "Taste" and "Wolfman's Brother." Humor was rampant throughout the night. They had some fun at the Doors' expense, massacring Jim Morrison's psychosexual rant in "The End." "Mike's Song" and "Weekapaug Groove" bookended the lounge-lizardly "Lawn Boy," of all things.

The group thought so highly of that evening that they culled the best parts for a CD titled *Slip Stitch and Pass*. Released in 1997, it was the follow-up to *Billy Breathes*. Unlike *A Live One*, their first concert compendium, this was a single disc extracted from just one gig. The title was a knitting term—Gordon's then-fiancée, Cilla, was trying out knitting—that effectively described the stealthy, deliberate way Phish had advanced its musical agenda while snaking its way across Europe.

Even Robert Christgau, the rock critic at the *Village Voice* for many years, had some kind words for *Slip Stitch and Pass*. He had previously bestowed a bomb symbol (indicating "a bad record whose details rarely merit further thought") upon *Billy Breathes*, without deigning to elaborate. But *Slip Stitch and Pass* earned a B+ and the headline "Look Who's Stopped Sucking" from Christgau, who wrote: "Kinda restores your faith in humanity for these guys to make like they know the difference between intelligent and pretentious."

The jacket was designed by Storm Thorgerson of Hipgnosis, the company that rendered myriad mesmerizing album covers for Pink Floyd (including *Dark Side of the Moon* and *Wish You Were Here*), Led Zeppelin (*Houses of the Holy*), and other progressive bands. For *Slip Stitch and Pass*, Thorgerson came up with an image of a guy on a beach unspooling an enormous ball of string. Phish, Europe, Hipgnosis—it all made an odd kind of sense in 1997.

In some ways, *Slip Stitch and Pass* brought Phish full circle back to their days in small clubs. Moreover, at a time when the crowds were expanding in America, the European tour and live album gave them some breathing room. In Anastasio's words, *Slip Stitch and Pass* reflected their self-acceptance:

"My realization is that you have to admit who you are. It's like, 'Be yourself, because nobody else can.' We all grew up on a block in suburbia with twenty-five other kids, playing army and waiting for the Good Humor man. Going to the mall and hanging out at the pizza place. We're these four suburban kids who grew up listening to classic-rock stations. You can hear it 'cause we're always throwing in these little quotes: the Doors, the Stones, Pink Floyd, ZZ Top, Talking Heads.

"You wonder, how did we get so popular? But it seems kind of obvious when you look at it that way, because our experiences are similar to many other people's and our music speaks to them."

Gordon made the same point about *Slip Stitch and Pass* in simpler language. "A lot of it is really just sort of fun," he said. "It's kind of letting loose. I can imagine that if people wanted to play a Phish album at a party, this would be the one."

There were notable dates in Europe during the lengthier return jaunt in June and July as well. This leg opened up in Dublin on June 13, 1997. Phish debuted thirteen new songs over the course of two nights.

This included half a dozen songs that would appear on *Story of the Ghost* (one of them, "Olivia's Pool," was reworked and retitled "Shafty") and even a trio of tunes that wouldn't show up on record until *Farmhouse*, which was three years down the road. They also broke out a memorable and never-repeated first-night encore combo of Sly and the Family Stone's "Stand" and Jimi Hendrix's "Izabella." Incidentally, the whole pile of new originals and covers, and more as well, were first tried out at a private party called "Bradstock," which was held at the home shared by crew members Brad Sands and Pete Carini.

After the European tours, Phish's approach to jamming continued to evolve, becoming more groove-oriented, ambient, and textural.

"In the late nineties, we got more into jams that would stay on one chord and not modulate as much," said Gordon. "I think there was an influence from seeing Neil Young jam in Europe and listening to James Brown a lot. Not changing so much became more important than changing a lot. Trey's guitar playing also got a little bit different. Whereas he used to play a lot of notes and do some ferocious soloing, later on he got into being more subtle and riding on top of the groove by holding out more sustaining or looping notes."

Anastasio would even stop playing guitar and bang out rhythms on a percussion setup that had become part of his rig. This phase of live Phish had its adherents, but many fans missed the livelier, more propulsive and crescendo-oriented jamming. At the same time, this more even-keeled and groove-oriented approach proved alluring to some in the Dead camp who'd theretofore found Phish too frenetic.

In the late nineties, Phish's jams more often resembled glowing embers than blazing bonfires. Still, there were exceptional shows and tours, especially the summer tours of 1997 and 1998, and there was no dearth of deserving new material. "From 1997 to 2000 was a glorious outburst of creative new Phish songs," observed Brad Sands.

"The summer '98 tour was one of the best of all time," said Eric Larson, a longtime fan and employee of the band. "They were playing very well, and every night they broke out some new cover. They had developed such a wide repertoire that you never really knew what they were going to play. That was definitely one of my favorite tours."

I would have to agree. At one show I attended—at Raleigh's Walnut Creek Amphitheatre, August 7, 1998—a hellacious late-afternoon thunderstorm blew in from one side, bringing heavy winds and downpour. Ever attuned to their surroundings, they opened with "Water in the Sky" and the Who's "Drowned" while the heavens opened up. On this same night, which later cleared up, there was also a lunar eclipse. Anastasio's sister Kristy, who lived in nearby Chapel Hill, casually mentioned that celestial occurrence to him. A lightbulb went off in his head, inspiring surreal narration during the first-set "Colonel Forbin's Ascent" that incorporated the moon's vanishing into the *Gamehendge* saga.

While the ambient grooves Phish fell into during the late nineties might sometimes become monotonous, the group often found power in repetition, tapping into the visceral, hypnotic buzz rave kids got from electronic rhythms and loops. Ecstasy, the drug of choice in that scene, was definitely on the rise at Phish shows during this time frame. When Phish played Salt Lake City's E Center, Anastasio welcomed the audience to the "*E-e-e-e-e-e* Center," and the druggy implication wasn't lost on the crowd.

"E" was one thing, but it was the arrival of white-powder drugs that started to affect their scene in troubling ways. If you were into Phish, you might have heard rumors on the fan-driven gossip mill as far back as 1997. Fishman and Gordon were reportedly just dabblers in the smorgasbord of substances that gradually became part of Phish's backstage scene. Anastasio got hooked, cleaned up, and relapsed a few times before his well-documented bust in 2006. McConnell fell somewhere in the middle.

In defense of working musicians, too little attention has been paid to the use of cocaine and similar drugs not only as a recreational high but also as a practical tool in a demanding and oftentimes exhausting occupation. The touring side of rock and roll is a grinding routine of traveling from city to city, setting up and sound checking, performing and breaking down, all the while grabbing whatever rest and sustenance one can manage while being constantly on the move. Cocaine serves an especially utilitarian function among road crews, who erect stages and equipment by day and load it all out in the dead of night. It's tough physical labor, and the hours are brutal. As rockers and roadies lose youthful resilience, cocaine combats the fatigue of their nocturnal, nomadic lifestyles. It's surely no accident that harder drugs didn't become an issue until they were in their thirties.

Humor has always figured in Phish's cosmology. In the mid to late nineties, that started to change, at least onstage. As they drew more attention, they became more self-conscious about the gags and gag songs, lest they be portrayed by the media as some kind of novelty act.

Fishman elaborated on this more serious mindset: "Trey's been on this crusade, 'I don't wanna write nonsensical stuff that's just an excuse to have singing to go with the instrumental stuff. I'm gonna get up there and sing lyrics, I want them to say something.' The biggest change is that nonsensical stuff is unacceptable. He's really turned off about singing a lot of our older things, even if there is some great music that goes with it that people wanna hear."

There was a growing sentiment that bouncing on trampolines, tossing boxes of macaroni and cheese to the audience, and having a dress-wearing drummer who played vacuum-cleaner solos might be detracting from their stature as serious musicians. Thus, in 1997, there were fewer gags, and Fishman even gave up the dress for a spell, opting for a utilitarian T-shirt and ball cap. *Classy* became the byword, while *quirky* was out of vogue. Since 1994, the band had also been elongating jams to unheard-of lengths, and by the later years of the decade all the musical exploration was crowding out the humorous bits. In some respects, life was becoming less amusing to them as growing popularity and media scrutiny brought pressures they'd not had to contend with before. And they were simply getting older, too.

"I certainly liked bringing people to shows in the early to mid nineties more than I did in the latter years," said Amy Skelton. "Because somewhere between 1995 and 1997, they started to jam more than play the funny stuff. I think they started to tire of the gags. They weren't so humorous themselves, and they were much more into playing, improv, stretching it out, going new places, and writing new music. The Big Ball Jam, the secret language, all that stuff—they got sick of it. They got sick of doing it, and they got sick of people clamoring for it, people talking about it, and articles being written about it. The focus wasn't on the music. I felt that they always kept their focus on the music, but that wasn't true of outsiders."

After returning home from Europe in early March 1997, Phish headed from Burlington back to Bearsville, where they'd recorded *Billy Breathes*, to begin work on their next record, which would eventually be called *Story of the Ghost*. They hoped to capture the new style they'd forged on the continent while their fingers were still warm.

"We'd always wanted to tape ourselves jamming and coming up with stuff, because a lot of times it feels like that's when it's most connected," said McConnell. "So we pushed the 'record' button and improvised for four days."

They repeated the scenario half a year later, holing up at Bearsville for four more days of jamming. What they took away from those sessions were forty hours of tape. McConnell volunteered to winnow the reels down to highlights, and the group used the most inspired passages as unaltered templates for songs that wound up on *Story of the Ghost*.

"We believed in the process and decided to have faith that we would make the right decisions along the way," he said.

"What you're hearing on *Story of the Ghost* is first takes, first creation, first everything," Anastasio noted at the time.

"Because it was largely recorded at the point of conception, I really do think the album sounds more like us than any album we've ever made," McConnell continued. "Parts of it are a little quieter and pull you in acoustically and introspectively, but it also has the funk and the rock stuff we're doing, and it's not overly produced."

Indeed, parts of *Story of the Ghost* weren't produced in any conventional sense at all, and it would turn out to be their most experimental album. The writing and recording of the album occurred in several bursts over the course of a year using methodologies that were unorthodox even for Phish.

Anastasio and Marshall had ensconced themselves for three-day songwriting and demoing sessions at farmhouses in the Stowe area, which yielded upward of thirty songs. Then Phish as a whole tried to get into the act of writing material together, so that the album—or at least a major portion of it—would be a true collaboration. During their working retreat with an eight-track recorder at a rented farmhouse in Stowe, Vermont, Phish added words and vocal melodies to the instrumentals McConnell had excerpted. Working from a book of lyrics by Tom Marshall, band members sang along to the instrumental tracks as inspiration struck. These farmhouse vocals, originally conceived as demos to be later recut in the studio, were preserved largely intact on the finished disc. In this fashion, the group worked up ten songs from the jam tapes. When it came time to pick songs for the album, they devised elaborate voting schemes to accommodate all four viewpoints. As a result, certain Anastasio–Marshall songs that would've made *Story of the Ghost* stronger and more cohesive, such as "Dirt," didn't make the cut. (It turned up on the next album, *Farmhouse.*)

"Some of the songs that I thought should've been on that album were voted off," said Anastasio. "Not because they weren't good songs but because it was getting weird that I was bringing so much music."

This presented a conundrum. Should the de facto bandleader, who was also a compulsive songwriter, willingly sacrifice some of his output to keep everyone happy? Or should the others, who had their own reasonable desires to be creatively involved in the music's conception, willingly step aside and be content to play songs and even parts that were almost completely mapped out on demos?

In order to exercise some of the cool stuff they were writing in front of a live audience, Phish performed a series of four shows—April 2–5, 1998—dubbed the Island Tour. The islands they played on were Long and Rhode, where they performed two shows apiece at Nassau Coliseum (in Uniondale, New York) and the Providence Civic Center. They were eager to generate some electricity and rekindle some live energy that might carry over to the studio. Ultimately, the Island Tour fired them up to finish *Story of the Ghost*.

In a few furious days later that month at Bearsville, Phish laid down twenty-nine Anastasio–Marshall songs with producer Andy Wallace. When they took stock of what they'd created, Phish found themselves with a surfeit of material: thirty-nine songs in all, from which a single disc had to be culled. It was "a necessarily painful process," noted Marshall, who initially suggested that Phish issue a double CD.

Thematically, *Story of the Ghost* hinged upon the haunting opening track, wherein Marshall confided about a friend he felt was an intermediary between him and the spirit world. Anastasio saw it in more universal terms. "Everybody's got their own ghosts," he said before the album's release. "I know what it's about for me."

The album also included "Guyute," the eight-minute epic that was the only older song on the album, having made its live debut in 1994. It was the last time one of Anastasio's intricate, multipart compositions would enter the repertoire for many years—really not until "Time Turns Elastic" turned up during the 2009 reunion. One dissonant, slalom-style passage in "Guyute" is as challenging as anything in Phish's catalog. So why did they wait four years to record it?

"The time was right," said Anastasio. "We were playing it a lot on tour, and it got to the point where it was flowing and we were inside of it. We had moved beyond the notes." Also notable was "Birds of a Feather." Spliced together by McConnell from three jam excerpts, it clearly nodded at the urgent, jittery funk of Talking Heads—not surprising, since they'd covered *Remain in Light* the previous Halloween.

"Sometimes I think the album sounds so different for us that it's about shedding the old Phish and moving on to the new Phish. I think it goes back to a line in 'Meat': 'I need a different life, I think.' It's some kind of metamorphosis, changing into something new, which has been kind of the theme for the last year. 1996 was a question-mark year—like, what is going on? Something's gotta change, gotta give. *Story of the Ghost* has something to do with the past and making it through that transition."

Was the experiment a success? The answer is yes, no, and maybe, depending on whom you talk to.

Gordon thought particularly highly of *Story of the Ghost* and the process that went into its creation. "The feeling was so collaborative and I like the way that album sounds so much that under 'Phish' on my Web site—sort of as a joke or minimizing—I only list *Story of the Ghost*," he said in 2008.

He was also quick to add, "Trey came up with all kinds of great experiments to include other people in the creativity, so I wouldn't blame him or anyone if I ended up shying away from some of it [on other albums] in the end."

A few years after *Ghost*'s release, Anastasio reflected on the process. "By the time we got to *Story of the Ghost* it started to get weird," he said in 2001. "Mike was getting a little frustrated, because I was bringing all these tunes and they were done. So then there was a feeling of, 'Well, we want to write together.' So I was like, 'All right, let's write together.' We got together in the same farmhouse me and Tom had [*laughing*], and we tried really hard to write together. It was somewhat successful and somewhat not. But it's like the point was getting lost. I got really upset, and so did Page, because I had come in with all these demos and we were like, 'We could make a great album. This is our chance.'"

Instead they wound up with an album whose whole was compromised by its various parts, which didn't mix well: the "Tom/Trey songs" (as Anastasio called them), the band-written pieces (with lyrics by Marshall), and the lengthy "Guyute" extravaganza. In hindsight, perhaps it would have been best to place the band-written songs on one album and the best of the Anastasio–Marshall copyrights on another, issuing them either as a double disc or two single ones (like Bruce Springsteen did with the simultaneously released *Human Touch* and *Lucky Town* CDs).

All the same, every song on the album turned up in Phish's concert repertoire, and many of them—particularly "Ghost," "Birds of a Feather," "The Moma Dance," and "Limb by Limb"—became live staples. With its moody, undulating groove, "Ghost" proved to be a highlight of Phish concerts for years to come.

Nine months after the release of *Story of the Ghost* came *The Siket Disc*, an instrumental album culled from their jamming sessions at Bearsville. It was issued as a Phish album, albeit with limited release, through their merchandising division. McConnell listened to, selected, and digitally edited the album's nine pieces, which bore such titles as "Quadrophonic Toppling," "Insects," and "Fish Bass." Named for engineer John Siket, *The Siket Disc* has a trance-like, Pink Floyd–meets–Brian Eno flow. There are no "songs" and it is all too brief (thirty-five minutes), but its late-night ambience is eerily captivating.

The Great Went and Lemonwheel—Phish's weekend festivals in 1997 and 1998, respectively—had much in common. Both were held in far northern Maine, in remote Aroostook County. Like the Clifford Ball, they were sited on a decommissioned Air Force base (Loring AFB, near Limestone). Though they lacked that festival's shock-of-the-new aura, both offered the uniquely surreal down-the-rabbit-hole experience Phish provided. Moreover, the art installations were even more innovative—Lemonwheel's theme, for instance, was Asian—and the sense of a community apart from the mainstream thrived in the wilds of upstate Maine.

That community ethos extended all the way to the site clean-up afterward. One of Phish employee Beth Montuori Rowles's self-assigned tasks was to go through boxes of lost-and-found materials after the festivals. The security team would send boxes of lost items to Phish's office in Burlington. Beth would don gloves and, with the help of others in the office, pick through the boxes, separating items and trying to identify their owners. They tracked down the owners of lost credit cards through the issuing bank and cell phones through the service providers. They returned as much as they could, even seemingly insignificant items with personal value, such as journals and diaries, by sleuthing for addresses, phone numbers, and other clues.

They tended to go that extra mile because that was the tone of the whole operation, from Phish's music to Dionysian Productions' management style. This attitude carried over to their work with various charities, too. In 1997, Phish established the WaterWheel Foundation. WaterWheel's original mission was loosely geared toward helping the environment, the arts, underprivileged children, and Vermont. The primary beneficiary has been Lake Champlain, the hundred-mile body of water that touches Burlington and divides Vermont from upstate New York. Over the past century, the lake has been polluted by sewage discharge and agricultural and urban runoff. Through WaterWheel, Phish has donated significant sums of money to raise public awareness, fund studies, and buy land and equipment to help control environmental degradation. Through their linkup with Ben and Jerry's via Phish Food, over $1 million in royalties has gone to the WaterWheel Foundation's Lake Champlain initiative. The foundation has also given money to Vermont nonprofits—mostly arts-related causes—and collected money on tour for designated charities in various communities.

In 1998 Phish released *Bittersweet Motel*, a band documentary about Phish, directed and produced by Todd Phillips (whose films include *Old School*, *Starsky and Hutch*, and *The Hangover*). He and his crew were given carte blanche to follow Phish around for about a year. The resulting eighty-four-minute film was a musical travelogue that tracked Phish in the U.S. from Maine (Great Went, August 1997) to

Rochester, New York (December 11, 1997). Filming carried over to 1998 for the summer tour of Europe.

Twenty-three songs are performed in whole or in part, including everything from fan favorites like "Wilson" and "The Squirming Coil" to covers of the Rolling Stones' "Loving Cup" and Elvis Presley's "Love Me Tender." The title *Bittersweet Motel* refers to an original song Anastasio and McConnell sing in the final scene. The film falls squarely in the rockumentary tradition of the Who's *The Kids Are Alright*, the Clash's *Rude Boy*, Bob Dylan's *Don't Look Back*, and—given the rock-festival footage—*Woodstock*.

It all started when Phish decided to document the Great Went. The project grew in scope from there. John Paluska called Phillips and invited him to Chicago to see a show and to meet the band. Phillips recalled thinking to himself, "'Who the fuck are these guys? How do they have money to make a movie and fly me out to Chicago?' I literally didn't know, I mean, I'd heard the name Phish but I didn't know—"

Phillips was mostly left to his own devices. "Phish told me, 'Just make the movie. Put in what you want, don't put in what you don't want.' There was never any of this thing you fear in situations with people who can exert control. You know, 'I don't look good in that shot' or 'I look weird here.' None of that bullshit. They're so open and understanding of the creative process, I guess because of the freedoms they've had.

"In a way, I think they liked the fact they were working with someone who was not a fan, because they thought, 'Oh, this guy will be a fan by the end of it.' And when I spent some time listening to the musicianship and heard how good these guys are, I became a fan. I've since been to shows we weren't filming, and I'll continue to go to them. And it's not because I'm buddies with them now but that I have a real appreciation for what they do creatively: how they don't have a set list, they're playing something different every night, and you don't know what you're going to get when you show up."

Phillips interspersed concert footage with interview snippets, backstage scenes, and other comical or illuminating glimpses of life on the road with Phish. Among other things, they discussed (and dissed) critics, made up songs on the spot, hung out on the beach, and bartered for weapons at a shop in Barcelona. During the bartering scene, Anastasio literally held a gun to Gordon's head and haggled with the shopkeeper over a whip. In one backstage scene while strumming the guitar, he made up a little funny song about McConnell on the spot.

Even when Anastasio got caught up in potentially problematic or embarrassing situations, he didn't harbor any illusions about what he was doing or hide it from the world. With the filming of *Bittersweet Motel*, perhaps he wanted the world to see exactly what was going on with the band during this period.

"It's hard having a movie made about yourselves," noted Phillips. "It can stir up weird feelings of 'What are we doing this for? Does this make sense?' The other guys were more self-conscious about it than Trey, who said, 'This is going to work. We're just going to go for it and let it go.' There's a lot of Trey in the movie because that was his attitude—you know, see what happens as opposed to avoiding it. Not that the other guys were tough to work with, but the more accessible one is, the better it's going to be. I wasn't doing an exposé, and I didn't want to bang down their doors. I wanted them to feel comfortable about it, and in that regard I would say Trey was the most comfortable."

Things were slowly threatening to get out of control, both within and without. As their scene mushroomed, Phish started to lose a grip on what was transpiring backstage and in the parking lots. By the latter half of the nineties, the lots at Phish shows were similar to the "Shakedown Street" scenes that had become institutions at Grateful Dead concerts for so many years, with vendors dealing the typical assortment of T-shirts, jewelry, food, and, of course, drugs. In fact, Phish fans also called these zones of unlicensed commerce Shakedown Street.

In terms of drugs, all the old hallucinogenic standbys (pot, acid, mushrooms) were joined by plenty of harder stuff: cocaine, heroin,

Ketamine ("Special K"), methadone, and newer knockout pharmaceuticals like Oxycontin. Plenty of nitrous oxide ("hippie crack"), too. The snake-like hissing of tanks filling balloons with nitrous was a common sound in the lot. Sucking gas from a balloon produced a brain-busting high to fans looking to get spun out of their gourds on the cheap. Ecstasy became prevalent, too, and that—combined with Phish's turn to a steadier, more grooving style of jamming—fueled the dance-party vibe.

Meanwhile, Phish's backstage scenes were starting to look more like standard rock-star bacchanals. In 1997 they set up an inner sanctum for which special passes were required. It was, unfortunately—in light of subsequent events—dubbed "the Betty Ford Clinic." It started out as a joke, with an "Alcoholic Clinic" sign hung on a backstage door at the Worcester Centrum over Thanksgiving 1997 (whose second night, incidentally, featured an hourlong "Runaway Jim," the longest song performance of Phish's career). The idea was institutionalized, so to speak, on the fall 1998 tour, when special "Betty Ford Clinic" passes were issued. The impetus was innocent enough. As Anastasio explained, the band wanted easy access to friends and loved ones like they'd had back in their club days, when all they'd had to do was step offstage and mingle.

"The Betty Ford Clinic was the party right next to the band room, which was a conscious decision," he said. "You see, once we went into arenas, we were isolated from everyone for the first time. When we were in bars, we'd come offstage and all our friends would be hanging out. In 1996 we switched into full-time arenas, and it was a really odd tour for us, because suddenly we were back there all alone. We felt like we were losing a sense of the fact we were in the middle of a huge party. We actually thought for the sake of the music, it would be much better for us to be partying, hanging around that energy, and remembering what kind of vibe was going on so we could play appropriate music to fill that void. So we started the Betty Ford Clinic. All our friends would be there, and we could come offstage—*boom!*—hang out and have a good time."

In other words, it was intended as a way of keeping them grounded in these larger new environs. However, as the partying accelerated, some friends and hangers-on wouldn't even leave the clinic to catch the show, which was another sign of shifting priorities.

One observer described it: "The focus changed. There was more interest in partying, famous guests at shows, and rich people making the scene. Post-show gatherings started to include more party drugs, booze, pills, and girls in tight dresses. Issues of access—passes, parking, private suites, poser platforms, roped-off seating—exploded into a new pecking order.

"The band carried it well, for the most part. But it was digging at them. When you start to run into and butt up against idolatry, it cuts up against what feels natural for a human being to experience. The amount of energy that is created and exchanged can become too much to handle."

Tequila, cocaine, groupies—it all sounds a lot like the mid-seventies Eagles, but it was late-nineties Phish, too. It's the stock script for practically every episode of VH1's *Behind the Music*. In 2000 Jason Colton was discussing ways to promote Phish's *Farmhouse* album with Anastasio and suggested doing something on the cable music channel.

"*Behind the Music!*" Anastasio cracked, only half-jokingly. "When you really think about it, we've had just about everything go on with us that goes on in every one of those *Behind the Music* things. We're just not as melodramatic about it, and no one ever notices."

Colton could see his point. "It's not like they haven't had serious things to wrestle with over the last few years," he noted.

If there's anything disappointing about this aspect of Phish's story, it's that they walked into the minefield of sex, drugs, and rock and roll clichés knowing better. For many years, they seemed sufficiently idealistic, intelligent, well-bred, and on guard to avoid the pitfalls. This was, after all, a group that for years had decompressed after gigs by playing chess on the tour bus. But they eventually succumbed, although no one will ever confuse Phish with Van Halen or Mötley Crüe, because they didn't wear misbehavior as a badge of honor. Besides, setting aside puritanical ethics, a certain degree of misbehavior is understandable. If ever a bunch of musical workaholics was entitled to blow off steam, it was Phish. But when all the raging started affecting health and welfare, and the forward progress of their music suffered to the extent that the band stopped practicing, one could argue that a line had been crossed. Perhaps the moral of the story is that the lure of drugs and debauchery is irresistible and that the lid to Pandora's box will pop open, as if spring-loaded, once the spoils of rock celebrity insistently present themselves.

Anastasio could see all this clearly after the fact. In an unpublished article by journalist Jesse Jarnow written well after the breakup—and just before Anastasio's 2006 drug bust—he said, "In 1996 we were all talking about how huge the scene had become, and the sense of entitlement around Phish. It's virtually impossible not to get sucked up into it yourself. I'm completely guilty of that. It never stopped. It just kept going and going and going. Same old story. It just got so big—so many people, so much money, so many expectations—that we just lost our bearings."

For more on this, listen to Anastasio's *Shine* and *Bar 17* solo albums. The lyrics aren't as overt as remarks made in interviews, but similar messages can be discerned between the lines.

Fueling the fire was the growing gaggle of hangers-on backstage and at the soundboard. Employees of Phish were allotted concert tickets and backstage passes. The newer hires especially took advantage of this perk, and the backstage areas became flooded with unfamiliar faces.

As Tom Marshall noted, "It used to be friends, family, and music geeks standing around and chatting about music or whatever. Then it became rich kids with drugs who were disappearing with the band members into the bathroom to turn them on."

As a result, "You might have two hundred, three hundred, four hundred people backstage," recalled Amy Skelton. "Not all in the band's area, but flitting about with some amount of access, and that started happening. The office got big enough in 1998, 1999, and 2000 that this crew of hangers-on got *really* big. They were also becoming older and more affluent, and they came packing. And that really affected everybody.

"That's when the drugs started getting bad. It was just sort of everywhere. 'Cause now you've got a hundred people backstage who've got plenty of money and plenty of ability to get it, whatever *it* is."

Beyond the problems drugs were causing, some of the interlopers would station themselves on the soundboard riser during the shows, causing fits for soundman Paul Languedoc, lighting director Chris Kuroda, and their assistants. They would dance, chatter, giggle, drink, and drive the crew members to distraction.

"I don't want to dwell on the negative," said Languedoc, "but there is some bitterness about this stuff, because it affected us directly. People loved to work for the band, and they'd get paid hardly anything but they could get a backstage pass and come to the shows. And that evolved into masses of people crowding everywhere and literally getting in your space during a show."

"Somebody works for Phish, and now they have a laminated access pass," added Kuroda. "Their friends are all fans of Phish. Now they have this friend who works for Phish and wants to look good in their eyes and goes, 'Yeah, I can take you on the riser. I have power now in this world.' And people really tried to push and push to get anything they could to benefit themselves. It was the give-an-inch-and-take-a-mile philosophy. It's human nature, so you can't really put people down, but there was a lot of that going on."

"For a two-or three-year period, how to deal with this problem was almost my number-one concern," said Languedoc. "It was an endless struggle."

"I remember going to office meetings when we were off tour and just pleading with people to try to be respectful," Kuroda noted. "It never worked. Just crazy." (For the record, management contests those claims.

"To say that we paid people poorly is not true at all," said Jason Colton. He added that the numbers who wound up backstage or on the sound-board riser as a result of staff ticketing policy were exaggerated.)

The same sort of thing was happening backstage, and the Phish crew found it necessary to erect walls out of road cases to keep crowds from straying into equipment areas with their drinks. Certain elements in the crew itself were becoming part of the problem, as crew members hired from outside brought their drugs (and drug habits) with them from whatever other tours they'd done.

Toward the end of the decade, the casual drugging became more compulsive, turning into what one former employee called "survival partying":

"A lot of blow, just a lot of blow, and it started to become rampant. And a lot of other stuff—pills and whatever else people had. I was concerned that somebody was going to do something really stupid on a big night out—some drug combo or whatever—and wind up dead. Either one of our dear crew members or one of the band members. At that stage, I didn't really fear for the band members. It was more crew guys. Although later, I feared for Trey."

Anastasio noted after the fact that it's difficult to cut back on partying when your employees are friends who are doing the same thing. Beyond the enabling factor, he was having to deal with employees desiring raises, money, or favors of some kind, which added stress to his already full plate. For whatever reason—most likely the close-knit family vibe within Phish's organization—he was not insulated from these pleas, and it got to be too much. Tom Marshall witnessed the toll it was taking on his friend.

"What head of what company can the lowliest person call with his personal problems?" Marshall asked. "None. Except for Phish. And Trey's the kind of guy that every single problem you put on his plate—and I'm guilty of this—every single problem, he has to solve. He's that kind of guy. And everyone knows it: 'Call Trey. Trey's gonna solve it for you.' And that's bullshit.

"Take Dave Matthews. When he's off tour, people aren't calling him saying, 'You know, I really need $15,000 more to keep my family alive. I'm not making enough and look, this guy's making this salary, and blah-blah-blah.' Dave Matthews would never get that call. Trey would get that call. He got it all the time. So this shit was weighing on him while he was trying to be a creative guy. How do you do that? How do you balance the two? I know: drugs.

"You wonder, why are these rock stars killing themselves with drugs? There's a lot of escaping that's needed when you're that big. I saw firsthand how it happened with Trey. How does the happiest guy in the world all of a sudden just be under the weather all the time and really moody and fucking touchy and not smiling and really bummed out? I guess they were smart enough to realize something needed to change and radically."

In some ways, Phish and their audience were moving in different directions. Phish had simplified and toned down their style of playing; the words "sparse" and "ambient" were often heard in conversation with the group members in 1997 and 1998. At the same time, much of the ever younger and wilder audience longed to be hosed by music and dosed by drugs as intensely as possible. But the buildups and crescendos, the displays of speed and virtuosity, weren't forthcoming from Phish as routinely in the late nineties. Between the abbreviated domestic tour schedules and escapes to Europe in 1997 and 1998, coupled with the turn to more low-key textural jamming and bass-driven "cow funk," one might infer that Phish was on some level endeavoring to tame the crowd scene.

But the scene had a momentum that wouldn't be denied. The band and their posse partied backstage while the audience raged in the parking lots. They would all come together for the music, which was probably the sanest and most rewarding part of both factions' days. As Anastasio admitted in *The Phish Book*, the stage became his sanctuary, the one place he could get away from every complicating problem or issue.

What were the parking lots like in the late nineties? Burlington-based writer Sean Gibbon described the scene in his gonzo tour diary, *Run Like an Antelope*. Disparaged by Phishheads, the book has moments of droll, objective reporting from the front lines. Perhaps Gibbon got closer to the hard truth about the ragged, itinerant lifestyles and increasingly out-of-hand lot scenes than the fans wanted to hear. Tracking the band's summer 1999 tour, he candidly unveiled the wild and sometimes seedy side of life on the road in Phish Nation.

After a gig in Camden, New Jersey, he described the late-night lot scene: "This place is out of control. Bottle rockets whizzing by, people skipping along with a balloon in each hand, screaming into the night, taking a hit of nitrous, screaming some more. Every other person looks completely crazy. Drums everywhere, people dancing on broken glass."

A week later Phish played at Oswego County Airport, outside Volney, New York. Some called the nameless two-day affair Camp Oswego. There was a second stage on which guest acts played. One aspect of Oswego that stuck in fans' minds was the heat: It was merciless and taxing, hitting a hundred degrees during the day. Even the usually unflappable Anastasio looked wiped out onstage. In the lot, nighttime offered respite from the pulverizing sun. But even though the heat was less intense, a different kind of hell manifested itself.

Sean Gibbon again: "It's ten times dirtier, nastier, meaner, scarier than your average Phish show. . . . It truly does look like a collapsed civilization—trash all around, scruffy people selling their wares and stepping over bodies as they go. . . . Some of the older Phishheads are genuinely surprised by this new wave of young kids spinning on all sorts of nasty drugs."

Most of those who were causing problems by indulging and/or trafficking in hard drugs—heroin, meth, the large-animal tranquilizer Ketamine, and various prescription painkillers—were not real Phishheads but parasites and predators looking to make money or join the party for all the wrong reasons. One benefit of staging their festivals in places so out of the way—such as remote Limestone, Maine—was that the non-fan riff-raff might be discouraged from making the trip. But there wasn't much Phish could do about this aspect of the scene on a routine run around the country except tour less or not at all (which very well may have been another point of the hiatus).

Pot, acid, and 'shrooms had long been the holy trinity of party drugs among Phishheads and Deadheads. Ecstasy and nitrous oxide raised the bar in terms of highs and health hazards. Then came the drugs that could seriously impact a user's health or even kill the rare imbiber. (There always seem to be one or two drug casualties found dead in their sleeping bags at the latter-day rock festivals.) This smorgasbord of substances, ironically, existed amid a healthy vegetarian food scene in which tour rats earned gas and ticket money by vending grilled-cheese sandwiches and veggie burritos. They also sold beer and water by the bottle and peddled homemade jewelry—whatever they could do to scrape a few bucks together.

Tom Baggott, the first-generation Phish fan who'd helped spread the word since the beginning, saw what was happening in the parking lots. By 1998 he noticed a disconnect between the drug-crazed younger kids' musical wants and Phish's less crescendo-filled jams. Baggott was working as a development agent, helping bands hone their act and find a grassroots following. One of his bands was a group out of Philadelphia whose music, he realized, would appeal to those who weren't getting spun to the extreme at Phish shows like they wanted.

"I had identified at this point an element in the Phish scene, most frequently observed in the parking lot, for whom Phish wasn't intense enough anymore," Baggott said. "This was an element that just wanted to go higher. They wanted to take the Phish crescendo and hear that the whole show. They didn't want to hear the nuances, they didn't want to hear the dynamics. They wanted to hear *intensity* the whole way through the show, and they wanted their drugs served sunny-side up— 'Supersize me, please'—and when I heard the Disco Biscuits, I was like, 'Wow, this is a band that would appeal to that part of the Phish base.'"

A "disco biscuit" is street slang for a hit of Ecstasy or quaaludes.

"That scene was all about drugs," Baggott continued. "That's what that 'Bisco' scene is all about. I didn't really fully appreciate their music until the first Camp Bisco [the Disco Biscuits' equivalent of Phish's festival campouts], when I had the opportunity to take Ecstasy and see the band for four hours, late night, a headlining set with lights. They were awesome that night."

Baggott laughed. "Not to take anything away from the Biscuits, but my grandmother would've been awesome that night on a ukulele, probably."

So there were shared or shifting allegiances happening on the jam-band scene. Some of the more restless revelers moved from Phish to Disco Biscuits, Sound Tribe Sector 9, or others in the expanding universe of trippy, trance-fusion jam bands.

Incidentally, for those who are wont to blame rock bands like Phish and Disco Biscuits for leading kids to drugs, Baggott made an interesting point: "Drugs were definitely a part of the scene," he allowed, "but that was a rite of passage that kids were going through anyway. With Phish, it wasn't that they brought people to drugs. They just gave people something to do when they were on drugs, because they were gonna do drugs anyway."

Beyond all the sideshows, there remained a sizable and deeply music-obsessed old-guard Phish community. In 1995, a group of fans published the first compendium of Phish set lists, facts and opinions. Titled *The Pharmer's Almanac: The UnoPHicial Guide to the Band*, it was followed by five ever-fatter editions. Another group of fans labored on the even more ambitious *Phish Companion: A Guide to the Band and Their Music*. Debuting in 2000 and revised in 2004, this voluminous tome details every aspect of what "phans" call "Phishtory." *The Pharmer's Almanac* was a for-profit undertaking, while *The Phish Companion* benefits the Mockingbird Foundation, a fan-created nonprofit that funds music education for kids.

If you're familiar with Phish's deep well of songs and performances, then you'll comprehend why it took several hundred con-
tributors to assemble this tome. *The Phish Companion* bagged, tagged,
collated, and commented on 22,601 song performances; 1,432 concerts; and 672 songs in the band's repertoire. Filled with facts, essays,
statistics, and insightful analyses, *The Phish Companion* is an un-
matched effort on behalf of a single band's musical legacy. Moreover,
in the spirit of sharing in the groove, all proceeds have been donated
to their own music-education charity, the Mockingbird Foundation.

The Phish Companion and the Mockingbird Foundation exemplify
the spirit of Phish's fan community. Phish thought so highly of their
endeavors that in 2003, after receiving some criticism for creating another revenue stream for themselves, the group began donating net
profits from their LivePhish downloads to the Mockingbird Foundation. (After the breakup, they scaled back, donating an unspecified
portion of the downloads' proceeds to the foundation.) So *The Phish
Companion* isn't just a document of Phish history but an essential
part of it. And to think it all started with a handful of hard-core Phish
fans who were fumbling their way around with a new technology
called the Internet way back in 1990.

As Phish gained popularity, a number of other books appeared in
the late nineties. Uber-fan Dean Budnick led the pack with his informed, conversational *The Phishing Manual: A Compendium to the
Music of Phish*. Dave Thompson, a prolific music journalist, knocked
off *Go Phish* in 1997, a breathless relating of band history largely com-
piled from clip files and fan-based Web sources. The prosaically titled
The Phish Book, an official band project jointly credited to writer
Richard Gehr and Phish, appeared a year later. Essentially an oral and
pictorial history, it was assembled by Gehr from extensive interviews
with the band here and abroad.

As odd as it may sound, Phish has always been a great cover band. For
a group as devoted to original music as Phish, the notion of drawing

from other artists might seem pointless. But it makes sense when you take several factors into account.

First, in the early days, they included covers for a purely practical reason: to have enough songs to fill a set or an evening of music while building their own repertoire. Second, Phish has never been shy about acknowledging influences. They are all musical omnivores. On the bus, in their cars, and at home they devour music from all corners, from Jimi Hendrix and the Rolling Stones to Miles Davis and Igor Stravinsky. So it makes sense that they'd pay homage to favorite songs and artists by covering them.

Third, cover songs can be approached by a rock band like Phish the way jazz musicians treat a pop standard—as a launching pad for improvisation. Finally, over the years many guest artists would sit in with them, and often they'd perform something by that artist or an iconic cover familiar to both parties.

Phish have always chosen covers wisely and well, drawing from sources both diverse and obscure. Unless it was a cast-iron rock standard like AC/DC's "Highway to Hell" or Chuck Berry's "Johnny B. Goode," Phish has always understood that a well-chosen cover reveals less-obvious influences and well-tuned ears. A number of Phish's covers became part of their basic repertoire. Several recurring ones drew from the realm of cosmic Americana they revered but weren't culturally situated to write themselves. These include Los Lobos' "When the Circus Comes to Town," Jimmy Dale Gilmore's "My Mind's Got a Mind of Its Own," Norman Blake's "Ginseng Sullivan," Josh White's "Timber (Jerry)," Del McCoury's "Beauty of My Dreams," and Bill Monroe's "Uncle Pen." In their later years they began writing strong originals "in the tradition" like "Back On the Train," "All of These Dreams," and "The Connection," and their experience of playing covers by prototypical folk, country, and blues artists had to have helped.

Given the broad range of artists they covered and the wide range of material they wrote, it's not hard to understand why Phish fans grew so loyal to them that they didn't feel the need to venture far beyond their universe of music. Phish was essentially a one-stop shop for music of all kinds. By following Phish, you'd get well-rounded exposure to all sorts of genres. Their well went so deep that there almost wasn't time to listen to anyone else, especially if attending or acquiring as many live Phish shows as possible rated as a high priority in one's life.

All this talk about cover songs is germane because Phish briefly reconsidered its relationship to outside material in the late nineties. Covers were minimized for a period in 1997, and certain classic originals were given a brief retirement, too. But then the group pointedly reembraced outside material. On the summer 1998 tour, they broke out a new cover version almost every night. They drew from an eclectic bunch of artists: the Violent Femmes ("Blister On the Sun"), Jane's Addiction ("Been Caught Stealin'"), Joe Tex ("You Better Believe It, Baby"), Marvin Gaye ("Sexual Healing"), the Beastie Boys ("Sabotage"), and Van Halen ("Running with the Devil").

Phish was willing to try anything to rejuvenate themselves at this point in their career. However, the solutions were less intuitive than they had been when the band was younger, the audience was smaller, and their business affairs were simpler. Inspiration does eventually run up against a wall of creative fatigue, and it is rare that true innovation and inspiration sustain for more than five years (if that long) in popular music. Phish has doggedly tried to swim upstream, with some success. They would manage to produce some of their most memorable music onstage (notably, Big Cypress) and in the studio (*Farmhouse*) in 1999, which was fifteen years deep into a career that was already dense with achievements. Even when there were friction and difficulties within, they still tried to act in the best interest of the music. That would never change.

Following their triumphant summer tour, October 1998 turned into an extremely busy month that found Phish becoming more deeply assimilated into the rock establishment. On October 3, they played a single set at Farm Aid on a bill that included organizers Neil Young, John Mellencamp, and Willie Nelson, plus Wilco, Brian Wilson, Hootie and the Blowfish, and more. The highlight was having Young sit in with them for a chunk of the set. At mid-month they caught up with Young again, performing at both of his Bridge School Benefits— along with R.E.M., Sarah McLachlan, and Barenaked Ladies—at Shoreline Amphitheatre in Mountain View, California.

Returning to the subject of covers, Phish played another band's album in its entirety for the fourth time on Halloween 1998. Perform- ing at Las Vegas's Thomas & Mack Center, Phish tackled the Velvet Underground's *Loaded*. This might seem an odd choice, since *Loaded* was the most accessible of the four studio albums released by Lou Reed and company during their time as a band. *Loaded* would seem to offer little opportunity for jamming or musical growth, unlike its prede- cessors. Performing the Beatles' *White Album* all the way through in 1994 helped improve Phish as songsmiths. Covering the Who's arena- rock powerhouse *Quadrophenia* in 1995 helped Phish adapt and pro- ject in larger spaces at a time when they were moving into arenas and outdoor venues. Cloaking themselves in Talking Heads' exercise in cross-cultural rhythms, *Remain in Light*, in 1997 heavily influenced Phish's music for years to come.

The Velvet Underground's *Loaded* also turned out to be the right album at the right time. Because the band had become bogged down in textures, loops, and trance-type jamming, *Loaded* offered relief in the form of song-oriented sunlight. Just as *Billy Breathes* evinced a bit of Beatles influence, *Farmhouse*—the next studio album after the Hal- loween 1998 show—exhibited some of the artful clarity and poppy accessibility of *Loaded*.

They'd covered "Sweet Jane" on their recent summer tour, and Fishman had occasionally sung "Lonesome Cowboy Bill" during his comic turn in the spotlight. As it turned out, they jammed out *Loaded* more than any other Halloween album, with "Rock and Roll" and "Lonesome Cowboy Bill" each topping ten minutes. It's been pointed out that with Anastasio's mounting affinity for groups like the Velvets and Pavement, Phish took a less perfectionist and hyper-analytical approach in concert during the late nineties. In fact, there came a point where they suspended postshow analysis altogether.

Anastasio privately revealed that Phish had actually toyed with the idea of covering *three* albums that Halloween. "We had that planned for a while," he said with a chuckle. "We talked about doing *Loaded*, *Exile on Main St.*, and *Lark's Tongue in Aspic*, or something like that." Imagine hearing Phish tackle albums by the Velvet Underground, the Rolling Stones, and King Crimson on a single night. As it turned out, Phish did have another trick up its sleeve. Two nights after the Halloween concert in Vegas, Phish played Pink Floyd's *Dark Side of the Moon* for a smallish crowd in Salt Lake City.

The motivation was poor ticket sales. Following the Halloween show, Phish had a day off before playing Salt Lake City, which was followed by two nights in Denver. Most fans drove straight from Vegas to Denver, skipping the Salt Lake show. When the band and crew got to the E Center, they noticed there were few fans in the lot. Barely one-fourth of the tickets had been sold for the 12,000-seat venue. Road manager Brad Sands and crew member Eric Larson conspired to make absent Phish fans regret this oversight.

Larson recalled what happened: "Brad and I immediately ran to Trey and said, 'There's only 3,200 people here! You've gotta hurt 'em! You've gotta get 'em good!' And he said, 'Well, what can I do?' And Brad and I looked at each other and said, "I think it's time for *Dark Side of the Moon*!' And Trey said, 'Okay, we'll do *Dark Side*. Get the band.'"

The others were pulled away from dinner and, with only ninety minutes before the start of the show, they listened to the album and ran through it once. They played the first set and went over a couple of songs backstage during set break. Then they did a full second set, concluding with "Harpua." During the part where Anastasio riffs on what "little Jimmy" is listening to on his stereo, the band launched into "Speak to Me," the first song on *Dark Side of the Moon*. Then came the second song from *Dark Side* . . . and the third . . . and so on, through the entire album.

For years, Phish fans had requested *Dark Side of the Moon*. Phish finally relented, but not on Halloween. That was a typical Phish move—ambitious, unexpected, exciting. That show quickly passed into Phish lore and helped guard against empty houses thereafter.

It was a throwback to their "you snooze, you lose" tour strategy, where a small crowd meant a big concert surprise that would leave those who'd blown off the show cursing the decision.

"There were probably 3,200 cell-phone signals coming out of the arena when they struck that first note," Larson said with a laugh. "And then, of course, the fans thought they were just getting one Pink Floyd song. And then when they went into the second song people said, '*Oh, my God. They're gonna give us the whole album?!*'"

"Brad and I were climbing off the bus in Denver," Larson recalled, "and some kids asked, 'What'd they do last night?' We just looked at them and went, 'Ohhh . . . You didn't go?' 'No, we came right from Vegas.' We said, 'Ooh, bad move. Not good.' We wrote it down and handed them the list. They looked at it and then looked at this one kid and said, '*It's your fault we skipped that show!*' I'm sure there was a lot of that going on, a lot of finger-pointing at somebody who was trying to cut some miles off the road."

Larson still marvels about that night: "To be able in about ninety minutes' time to listen and learn a whole album and then come out and perform it? I mean, *please.*"

The year 1998 ended strongly with a Thanksgiving stand at Hampton Coliseum (in Hampton, Virginia) and an unprecedented four-night, one-venue New Year's run at Madison Square Garden. Since Phish's first gig there in 1995, Hampton had became a favorite venue. There were no skyboxes or big-arena affectations at Hampton, which had an old-school vibe and plenty of musical ghosts in its past. The Grateful Dead, for instance, played a legendary show there in 1989 where they broke out "Dark Star" for the first time in five years. Phish's two nights at Hampton went so well that they released the whole of it as *Hampton Comes Alive.* The six-CD box earned a Grammy nomination for packaging, made *Billboard*'s album chart (unusual for a box set), and attained gold status (indicating 500,000 units sold) from the RIAA.

The new year started off slowly, insofar as band activities were concerned. Phish didn't even play their first concert of 1999 until June 30. In hindsight, this looks like mini-hiatus. (There was, incidentally, a pre-tour dress rehearsal at Trey's Barn Studio on June 24, an affair dubbed "Carreystock" because of the presence of comedian Jim Carrey.) During those six months sans Phish, Anastasio formed a solo band with an outside rhythm section while Gordon threw himself into his first feature film. Starring Col. Bruce Hampton, it was titled *Outside Out*. He claims to have invested five thousand hours in its making. Gordon's left-of-center project related "the story of a boy, and a guitar, and his desire to be a true artist."

Phish convened for an abbreviated summer 1999 tour that concluded with four shows in three days at the Fuji Rock festival in Japan. The band was given its own stage, dubbed "Fields of Heaven" by the promoters. Then came a monthlong fall tour, followed by recording sessions for *Farmhouse*. They hit the road again in December, culminating with the live event known as Big Cypress, the millennium concert in the Florida Everglades, at year's end.

With the notable exception of Big Cypress, these weren't the best of times for Phish. Anastasio reflected on the reasons in a 2004 interview with Anthony DeCurtis in *Guitar World*: "In 1994, every night, I would rush back to the hotel and work for six hours on the next night's set—literally. But I couldn't maintain that. And once I stopped doing that, what people saw—maybe in like '99—was a sloppier Phish."

Eschewing the experimental strategies that went into *Story of the Ghost*, Phish assembled the more accessible *Farmhouse*. The recording of *Farmhouse* occupied much of fall 1999. Big Cypress further fired up Phish when they reentered the studio for mixing and overdubbing in January 2000. Phish felt truly at home in the studio, because now they literally *were* at home. *Farmhouse* was recorded at the Barn, a refurbished 150-year-old barn that Anastasio had hauled to the top of a mountain not far from Burlington. By the time of *Farmhouse*, two other albums had already been recorded there. One was by mandolin-ist Jamie Masefield's Jazz Mandolin Project. (Masefield was another Vermont native and one-time pupil of Ernie Stires.) Over the years, Anastasio and Fishman were intermittently involved with Masefield's group. The other project was *One Man's Trash*, an Anastasio solo CD of experimental snippets that was sold through the band's mail-order division.

The Barn was baptized and ready when Phish came in to record *Farmhouse*. Having their own studio gave Phish accessibility at any hour and allowed them to work in a more casual environment with-out an expensive hourly charge. In fact, much of the time the sessions took on the tone of a spirited happening, if not an actual party. A snippet of the bantering that went on around the soundboard was recorded on the sly and tacked on as a coda to "Twist."

"It's got a great vibe," McConnell said of the Barn. "We recorded this album much more quickly as a result of being relaxed about it."

That homey, pressure-free atmosphere resulted in some of the most cohesive studio playing of their career. These were rock-solid songs built around grooves of varying flavors and tempos. They ranged from the shuffling railroad rhythm of "Back on the Train" to the exuberant bounce of "Gotta Jibboo," from the bottom-heavy funk of "Sand" to the blithe, bopping "Heavy Things." There are moments of delicacy and lyricism, too, such as the ruminative, sweetly melodic "Bug" and the orchestrations that weave in and out of "Dirt." *Farm-house* also included two instrumentals: "The Inlaw Josie Wales," a piece of acoustic "newgrass" augmented by Bela Fleck on banjo and Jerry Douglas on dobro, and "First Tube," a first take recorded on the first day of tracking for the album.

"We were coming right off a tour, got a bunch of people all around us, and had a big party," Anastasio enthused at the time. "We were having a breakthrough in terms of musical solidity and simplicity. There was a feeling, too, that we're settling into our own groove as people and as musicians."

Behind the scenes, Anastasio acted to dispense with Phish's "democracy bureaucracy" that had crippled *Story of the Ghost*. He asked his bandmates to let him produce the album without collective oversight, and they agreed. Anastasio's co-producer was Bryce Goggin (Pavement, Lemonheads), while John Siket—a regular at Phish's sessions since *Billy Breathes*—worked the board and brought an eclectic assortment of tube amps, vintage mikes, and old gear. The trio were mainly responsible for the making of *Farmhouse*.

"With this album, Trey said he needed to be able to stretch out and make decisions without having to check with everybody," Gordon said at the time. "With music, learning to get your ego out of the way makes it better, so in a sense surrendering the democratic process was a way for us to do that. As a result, we were better able to be ourselves, to do our thing and jam and have a loose attitude and come up with good-sounding songs."

"Nobody was threatened by the fact that I had all these arrangements in my head," Anastasio asserted. "I had written all these songs and had a pretty clear vision of how I wanted them to sound. The other guys let me step forward, and they were cool about it."

That's not to say there weren't bruised feelings.

"There was one point when I definitely felt jealous, because there was a creative process going on I wasn't part of," Gordon admitted. "But the stuff sounded good. And then Trey came up and said, 'I really want to thank you for letting me do this, because I was in a mental rut.' The fact that he said that made me feel that it was the right thing that we did."

Eight years after its release, Gordon elaborated on his true feelings about the album. "*Farmhouse* was one I felt very not involved with. I didn't have any songs on it and we had given it to Trey to produce, which often Trey was doing anyway. But beyond that, maybe it was the headspace I was in at the time. I was really going through hard times on my own and I just felt very distanced. So I don't think I ended up with as much a feeling of ownership."

By pointed contrast with *Story of the Ghost*, there were no group-written songs. Those few that weren't Anastasio–Marshall collaborations grew out of the solo tour Anastasio undertook with bassist Tony Markellis and drummer Russ Lawton in the spring of 1999.

At the time Anastasio said, "Phish is going to be around for a long time, and there will be plenty of opportunities for each member to take the reins." But the band would announce its hiatus soon after *Farmhouse*'s release, and no reins would be taken by other band members on the albums recorded thereafter. That statement was typical of Anastasio, who always tried to put the best face on things. Behind the scenes, things were not going so well, and he took over the album because they weren't interacting much offstage.

"That was honestly part of the reason Phish had to take a break," he said during the hiatus. "If you think about that *Farmhouse* album, what was weird about it was that I got together with Russ and Tony, and there was this creative outburst. We wrote all these tunes, and the ones we didn't write, we arranged. So that's 'Heavy Things,' 'First Tube,' 'Gotta Jibboo,' and 'Sand'—half the *Farmhouse* album—in like a weekend. And then the next couple of weekends I got together with Tom and wrote 'Farmhouse,' 'Bug,' and other songs on *Farmhouse*. I played all the instruments and Tom wrote all the lyrics and did vocals. So I had drum parts and bass parts and everything.

"When we got together to record *Farmhouse*, it just had been so intense with Phish for so long that we weren't really doing anything together anymore except for the live playing. They weren't even there, basically, for that album. I mean barely at all. Basically Mike and Fish played the exact bass lines and drum parts that either Russ and Tony or I had played, and then left. You can hear on the Tom/Trey album [*Trampled by Lambs and Pecked by the Dove*, an album of Anastasio–Marshall demos released via mail-order in late 2000] that those songs are virtually identical. And then normally Page would've been more involved, but he had his baby right then, so he couldn't be there, either. So even some of the piano parts I played.

"I really like the album and everything, but I felt like we needed to—you know what I mean—something weird was going on."

In the midst of this, Big Cypress reestablished Phish as a band still capable of groundbreaking magical strokes. Arguably *the* all-time Phish concert, Big Cypress was a rock and roll landmark. With a gross of over $11 million, it was the biggest money-making event in America on New Year's Eve 1999. The parameters were different from its festival predecessors. Instead of the typical late-summer gathering, Big Cypress took place as December 1999 gave way to January 2000. Instead of northernmost New England, the event was held on a Seminole Indian reservation in the Florida Everglades.

Originally, the plan was to hold it in Hawaii, but that proved impossible for legal and logistical reasons. They wound up looking for another warm-weather locale in the lower forty-eight states, and Florida seemed an obvious place to base their search. Florida had the advantages of being on the East Coast, easily accessible to the heaviest concentration of Phishheads, and generally temperate weather in late December. They visited five Seminole reservations, picked one, and went to visit Chief Billie—who was on the Big Cypress reservation that day—to ask permission and work out details. After laying eyes on Big Cypress, they thought it would be the most amazing site of all for the festival. Figuring it couldn't hurt to ask, they did just that.

"Why not?" said Chief Billie. And the rest is history.

Promoter Dave Werlin termed Big Cypress "the holy grail of festivals. This was probably the ultimate Phish experience from every point of view."

Like a lot of the group's brightest ideas, it started out as a "what if?" kind of joke, a crazy idea that assumed a life of its own. The idea dated back a number of years to the band's notion of staging a long gig (or "LG," as they took to calling it). Beth Montuori Rowles recalled how Anastasio related the original idea to her. It went like this:

"What would happen if we told the audience they couldn't go home that night? We'd ask them all to fold up all the chairs, and we would provide mattresses. There would be oranges and bananas, snacks people could eat, and doughnuts and coffee in the morning. Basically tell everybody they could make one phone call to let people know they were not coming home that night. Everybody would stay and the band would play all night long."

Big Cypress became that all-night slumber party. It was the most labor-intensive of Phish's festivals. Roads were cut, a stage was built, and a pool was dug backstage for the band and those on their voluminous guest list. The biggest hassle was traffic. The arrival of Phishheads resulted in a twelve-hour jam along Alligator Alley that had nothing to do with music. Once the crowd had assembled, Big Cypress revealed itself as *the* place to be as the clock ticked down to the new millennium. Though Big Cypress and the Clifford Ball were the twin peaks of Phish's career, there were some obvious differences between them. By the time of Big Cypress, Phish and its crowd were four years further down the experiential road than they had been at the Clifford Ball. The drugs were harder, outside elements in the scene more visible, and the party vibe more unbridled and extreme.

In advance of the year 2000, people all over the world were concerned about planes falling out of the sky, computers crashing, and other disasters related to the "Y2K" phenomenon. Some were made so paranoid they thought that time itself would stop. These cosmic jitters were in the air as 1999 rolled to a close, and this no doubt contributed to the aura of footloose revelry. Yet this weekend gathering of 80,000 Phishheads in the Everglades played out without catastrophe.

"At that point, we used to stay up all night all the time anyway, so it really wasn't a question of being tired," added Brad Sands. "But even people I know who are pretty straight-edged stayed up the whole night. The audience was definitely there the whole time. That was amazing."

"It was over the top, beyond anybody's comprehension," said band masseur and videographer Eric Larson. "We stayed up four nights in a row. You wanted to be up, 'cause it was so exciting."

Big Cypress culminated in what many—Phish among them—consider their greatest single set of music. "The Show," as fans call the nearly eight-hour performance, began about twenty-five minutes before midnight with a witty bit of theater. "Father Time" appeared onstage, pedaling an exercise bike that powered a clock. But the old gent's energy flagged and he collapsed, stopping the clock just shy of midnight.

Phish came to the rescue, arriving on a swamp boat that exploded to reveal the same mobile hot dog that had ferried them around the Boston Garden five years earlier. Onstage they revived Father Time by feeding him "meatsticks" so he could power the clock to the midnight hour. At that point, logically enough, Phish began their marathon performance with "Meatstick." This was all very amusing, but in the process of moving props offstage a cable got run over and ruptured, causing a short in the lighting system and short-circuiting Chris Kuroda's evening as well.

"I actually lit from midnight to 8 A.M. on about a third of the lighting rig," Kuroda recalled. "I was very frustrated and spent most of the time trying to get it working with technicians changing cables and running around back there. It never came back, so my personal experience of Big Cypress was kind of a nightmare. But whenever I talk about that, I always make a point of expressing that I know how special it was. My little bubble on that night was not that great, while tens of thousands of other people's bubbles were incredible."

Indeed. Paul Languedoc consciously kept the volume down to a reasonable level to keep the audience from getting exhausted from eight hours of loud music. After a certain point, the group ran on adrenaline, as all self-consciousness slipped away and the music played *them*.

"Big Cypress, which was the biggest show ever, felt like it had some of the best jamming ever," said Gordon. "That eight-hour set was so much a pinnacle for all of us. We just jammed free-form and let the year 2000 come in as the sun reflected across Page's grand piano at 7:30 in the morning. It just felt like we were playing in someone's living room, even though it was 80,000 people."

As Phish left the stage after performing for nearly eight hours, road manager Brad Sands asked, "Do you want to do an encore?" They looked at him like he'd lost his mind.

Fan-chronicler Jeremy Goodwin summarized the whole amazing night in these words: "We had just seen the peak of rock musical accomplishment in the twentieth century. They had just jumped through an enormous hoop for us, and I felt 100 percent satiated. I never needed to see this band play again. What more could I possibly expect them to do for me?"

That turned out to be a question that Phish posed themselves. How could they possibly top Big Cypress? What more was there for them to do? Their big summer-into-fall tour of 2000 was not bad, mind you, just anticlimactic. There was the notable exception of a seven-show Japanese tour in mid-June, which let the band return to its roots by escaping large crowds and untenable expectations. They were also dealing with the reality of fraying relationships, having lived for a decade and a half in incredibly close quarters—not just on buses, stages, and hotel rooms, but inside each other's heads.

At the same time, Phish was now a big-time rock band. Both *Story of the Ghost* and *Farmhouse* had entered the album charts in the Top Ten. From 1996 through 1999, Phish's total concert grosses came to $93.1 million. They sold a lot of ice cream, too: The Ben and Jerry's flavor Phish Food, introduced in February 1997, was the company's third most popular, with 3.5 million gallons sold annually. Finally drawing the attention of the mass media, Phish made the cover of *Entertainment Weekly* (for the week of August 4, 2000), and that issue had not one but four different covers, each bearing the face of a band member gurgling in water, like—ha-ha!—fish.

Behind the scenes, music was no longer the shared, all-consuming occupation it had been. For years they'd been committed to a four-way marriage with Phish, touring and practicing obsessively. Now familial links were impinging on those fraternal bonds. All of them had gotten married in the nineties—Anastasio to Sue Statesir, Gordon to Cilla Foster, McConnell to Sofi Dillof, Fishman (briefly) to Pam Tengiris—although among the group members' first marriages, only Anastasio's would last.

Marriage, divorce, and kids further altered the interpersonal land-scape among the band members. They were no longer footloose twentysomethings who could pledge their allegiance entirely to Phish. Those legendary daylong rehearsals, where they'd work on collective improvisation and musical group-think, were in the past. According to Anastasio, they virtually stopped practicing after 1998, except at concert sound checks. While families and outside projects figured more into their lives, they were also starting to fret among themselves about the burgeoning office staff. The increasing overhead brought with it pressure to tour even if they didn't feel up to it—and in the wake of their marathon triumph at Big Cypress, there was a certain amount of band ennui and "what's the point?"

Though their operation never grew anywhere near as top-heavy as the Grateful Dead's (which surpassed three hundred employees), Phish's payroll numbered just over forty. However, the perception from within the band, particularly from McConnell's and Anastasio's perspective, was that the office had become an albatross. The band members didn't always recognize all those in their employ when they dropped by their combination office and warehouse space on Pine Street in Burlington. If Phish wished to suspend touring for a while, they still had fiduciary obligations to their employees. The only al-ternative was to downsize.

Yet from the start it had been Phish's desire to keep as much as possible in-house, including merchandise. Early on they'd tried farm-ing work to outside companies, but the products lacked the stamp of uniqueness Phish wanted on everything that bore their name. They enjoyed coming up with ideas and having the artists and staff on hand to actualize them. When done in-house, they could go from an idea someone might've had over coffee one morning to reality in a matter of days. That is in contrast to wrangling with slow-moving outside entities that likely didn't grasp the Phish aesthetic.

"There were some tensions once their business had grown so large that there was a lot to keep track of, to the degree they wanted to en-gage with and have people accountable to them for things," Paluska allowed. "It's hard to juggle that as an artist, so there were times when they wished things were simpler. In the case of merchandising, you can do it yourself and do it well, or there's a market that's going to get filled by somebody else. I always wanted the business to be run as well as possible, and we were really into doing things ourselves, and they were into that, too. But sometimes the realities of doing that felt like a lot to them. All of the business stuff could be oppressive at times. There were certainly plenty of tensions and complexities in juggling the artistic and business stuff over the years, and at some level I think that's just unavoidable."

The bottom line is that one can't have a lean payroll and receive the benefits of in-house merchandising, art, ticketing, and management staffs, not to mention a loyal and dedicated road crew. But the idea that the group, exhausted after working steadily since 1985, couldn't take time off because they had to meet a sizable monthly payroll engendered a slow-burning paranoia among them about the office. In the sense that the staff were paying their own way—each worker added value to the bottom line over and above salary and benefits—the office issue was something of a scapegoat. The notion that Phish were burdened by excessive staffing might have been more perception than reality, but any and all issues at that time were to some degree magnified by drugs and fatigue.

And so they took a hiatus to address that and other matters weighing upon them at the time.

Anastasio announced the impending hiatus onstage in Las Vegas on September 30, 2000 (his thirty-sixth birthday). All kinds of reasons were given, but it boiled down to these things: They were exhausted; they needed a break from each other and from the bus and backstage bacchanals; and they intended to streamline the office staff. They also wanted to play with other people and work on solo projects.

Drugs were never overtly mentioned as a reason for the hiatus, but after the resumption Anastasio stated it plainly to writer Anthony DeCurtis in a 2003 *Relix* interview: "Nobody ever talks about this around Phish, but drugs had infiltrated our world—and me. I don't want to point my finger at that, because the problems had started a long time before. It was about losing myself, losing track of who I really am."

This open-ended break held forth the possibility they might never regroup, an option feared by fans who'd grown accustomed to organizing their lives around Phish tours. Many Phishheads had spent much of the previous decade living from tour to tour, and now the plug was indefinitely pulled on their main source of pleasure and personal identity. They'd either have to find another band to follow or give up the game until Phish returned.

Phish performed their last show before the hiatus—or "the first last show," as it's since been called—on October 7, 2000, at Shoreline Amphitheatre in Mountain View, California. It was a memorable concert, highlighted by a great "Mike's Song" trilogy and a sublime jam on "Bathtub Gin" that, in some indefinable way, got to the core of all that was good about Phish and what both sides, band and fans, would miss when they were gone. They encored, fittingly, with "You Enjoy Myself."

After Phish left the stage, the crew members were introduced and received standing ovations from appreciative Phishheads. Paul Languedoc played the Beatles' "Let It Be" as they cleared the stage. Many tears were shed.

Meanwhile, the band huddled by themselves, silently honoring the moment and taking stock of what they'd accomplished over the past seventeen years. Brad Sands stood sentry outside. Not even close relatives were admitted as they reflected on how far they'd come together, not knowing how long they might be apart.

SEVEN

Hiatus, Resumption, Breakup: 2001–2007

In the wee hours of August 3, 2003, Phish took over the control tower at a U.S. military installation. They staged this bloodless coup at It—the actual name of the event—which was the sixth Phish festival and their first since Big Cypress, three and a half years earlier. (Unsurprisingly, sensing a vacuum and opportunity, Bonnaroo—the Phish-inspired mother of all latter-day rock festivals—debuted in 2002, during their hiatus.) In a nutshell, It was mud-plagued but musically and conceptually solid, and it had one particularly remarkable moment: the Tower Jam.

The group borrowed a line from William Shakespeare for the occasion. These words were inscribed into an illuminated arch beneath which festivalgoers passed as they entered the site: "Our Intent Is All for Your Delight." They got the wording slightly wrong. The exact quote, lifted from Shakespeare's *Twelfth Night*, was this: "Our *True* Intent Is All for Your Delight." Phish made good on that statement of intent.

"I just loved that line as the mantra for the festival," said Jason Colton. "It's like, 'We are creating this magic for you.' Trey often talked about the concept of completely reimagining a concert environment, thinking about everything through the eyes of a fan. What can you do, how can you create a space for the fans' sake? That stuck with me because it really was a philosophy to go by—to check everything you're doing and think about how it's going to affect the fans and their experience. That overlying philosophy was an exciting goal to shoot for."

There was much at It to delight, confound, and blow the minds of festivalgoers. Burlington artists Lars Fisk and Scott Campbell designed an installation called Sunk City, filling a recessed spot in the landscape with a partially submerged skyline. The installation looked like a future archaeological site filled with the listing remnants of a collapsed urban civilization. Ten thousand rolls of masking tape were used to wrap trees in a patch of forest, like some project that artists Christo and Jeanne-Claude might've dreamed up on a bad trip. Roaming through the masking-tape forest were performance artists attired as squirrels and other bizarre characters (imagine perambulating the masking-tape forest while tripping). The water tower bore Groucho Marx's likeness, and a giant statue of a burger-toting Big Boy—the fast-food icon whose uplifted arm held aloft a plate, which one could stand on—perched at the edge of Sunk City. It was an extreme recontextualization of familiar cultural icons, delightfully disorienting and appropriately surreal.

Even with the wealth of sideshows, sights, and displays, nothing was more mind-blowing than the Tower Jam, which started at 2 A.M. For the next hour, Phish jammed free-form in a shimmering, ambient-techno fusion style on the roof of the control tower. That wasn't the half of it. Chris Kuroda lit the structure with his phantasmagoric palette. Strobe lights encircled the tower, which was also bathed in green and red spotlights. Pink fireworks and circling blue lights lit up an adjoining field. A trio of dancer-gymnasts rappelled along the sides of the tower like giant gravity-defying spiders as Phish played and lights danced.

"The coolest manmade psychedelic installation of all time," ventured archivist Kevin Shapiro.

"One of the most creative, over-the-top 'gags' ever devised by the band and crew," agreed promoter Dave Werlin.

Even fans who thought they'd seen it all rated the Tower Jam as a special moment. Overall, it and It were something of a last hurrah—the undisputed high points of the rather brief reunion that followed Phish's hiatus.

After staging Big Cypress, Phish spent much of the first decade of the twenty-first century out of commission. To summarize, they went on hiatus in 2000, regrouped in 2002, toured heavily in 2003, and broke up "for good" in 2004.

But the members of Phish did not rest on their laurels. The amount of musical output from them actually multiplied because instead of one band, there were now several bands and side projects.

During the hiatus, Trey Anastasio ramped up the activities of his solo band and also formed Oysterhead, a supergroup of sorts, with Primus's Les Claypool and the Police's Stewart Copeland. In an inspired pairing of two like minds, Mike Gordon formed a duo with guitarist Leo Kottke. He also released his first solo album (*Inside In*) and second film (*Rising Low*). Page McConnell became a bandleader, forming Vida Blue with a sterling rhythm section. Jon Fishman drummed for the Burlington-based outfits Pork Tornado and the Jazz Mandolin Project.

After two years apart, Phish regrouped. They quickly cut a new studio album (*Round Room*) and returned to the stage with a New Year's Eve show at Madison Square Garden. They toured throughout 2003, a year that included a lot of ups (an amazing summer tour, climaxing with the It festival) and a few downs (more of the problems that had caused them to declare a hiatus).

Barely fifteen months after the New Year's Eve reunion show, Anastasio declared "we're through" with a note on the band's Web site. There was a final album (*Undermind*), a short summer tour, and Phish's muddy, messy farewell festival outside Coventry, Vermont, which wrapped things up on a sour note in August 2004. In its wake, Phish disbanded, Dionysian Productions dissolved, and virtually all crew, staff, and employees were dismissed.

Then it was back to solo careers for Anastasio, Gordon, McConnell, and Fishman, and an acceleration of archival concert releases. The Phish family dispersed professionally and geographically, moving on to other careers or absorbed elsewhere in the music industry. Certain key figures—Brad Sands, Chris Kuroda, Paul Languedoc— kept working intermittently with Anastasio, though things weren't quite the same as his personal situation fluctuated and, ultimately, deteriorated.

No one saw any of this coming when Phish entered their hiatus in October 2000. The dictionary definition of *hiatus* is "any gap or interruption," and in this sense there was discontinuity in the career of Phish. But the hiatus did not mean there was any sort of musical stoppage or lightening of the workload at the Phish office. To the contrary, the staff found themselves attending to four careers, each of which involved albums, tours, and detailed planning. "We were super busy during hiatus because they started doing their side stuff *and* we downsized in staff at the same time," said Beth Montuori Rowles. "So instead of one band we had four or even five bands, depending on what day it was and what Trey was doing."

She laughed at the notion that Phish's staff had nothing to do for two years. "People were like, 'You work for the band, but what do you do? I thought they broke up. How can you still have a job?' I would say, 'You have no idea how much these guys put out and how much caretaking it takes and how much administration it requires.'"

In other words, it may have been a hiatus, but it was hardly a vacation. The band members were as busy as ever. As soon as the hiatus commenced, Anastasio—for whom "downtime" is not part of his vocabulary—got right to work on a long-cherished project: a symphonic version of "Guyute," the ambitious, extended centerpiece of

Story of the Ghost. Parts of it sound like a Celtic jig, and no wonder: Anastasio composed it in Ireland. "The first day of the hiatus, I started working on orchestrating 'Guyute,'" he said. "I came home from that Shoreline Amphitheatre show, woke up the next morning, pulled out the manuscript paper, sat down at the piano, and started writing. And I was pretty much working all day for months. At least four months."

"Guyute" would take on a life of its own in this decade. First it was scored for and performed by the Vermont Youth Orchestra. Then Anastasio recorded it with an orchestra in Seattle. That version became the highlight of *Seis de Mayo*, his all-instrumental solo album (released in April 2004). Finally, he conducted the Nashville Symphony Orchestra in a live performance of "Guyute" on the final night of the 2004 Bonnaroo festival.

That was just the beginning. Anastasio maintained a grueling workload from the hiatus to the reunion and on through the breakup right up until his 2006 drug bust. His recorded output in that six-year period included seven solo albums (*Trey Anastasio, Plasma, Seis de Mayo, Shine, Bar 17, 18 Steps,* and *Horseshoe Curve*), two Phish studio albums (*Round Room, Undermind*), and a studio album with Oysterhead (*The Grand Pecking Order*). There were tours with Phish, Oysterhead, and his ever-evolving solo band ("Trey Band," in fan parlance), which grew from three to eleven pieces. He played on Dave Matthews's 2004 solo album (*Some Devil*) and tour, which was the hardworking singer-guitarist's own version of a hiatus from the ridiculously popular jam band that bore his name.

Early in the hiatus, Anastasio cast his lot with Oysterhead. The Oysterhead story began when Claypool was approached in 2000 by New Orleans–based Superfly Productions to organize one of their "Superjams"—interesting and even improbable combinations of musicians brought together for a night of jamming. Claypool recruited Anastasio, with whom he'd played a few times—most memorably at a 1996 Phish gig in Las Vegas, where he and Primus guitarist Larry LaLonde sat in for a wild, extended "Harpua" encore—and Stewart Copeland, the former drummer for the Police who'd been doing film sound-tracks in Los Angeles since that band's breakup. They played a single sold-out show at New Orleans' Saenger Theater on May 4, 2000. That was supposed to be all there was to it, but they got the bug to pursue their promising chemistry, and Oysterhead took on a life of its own, leading to an album and tour.

"I play with a lot of people, as does Trey, and I've never felt that kind of chemistry before," said Claypool.

This trio represented the convergence of, as Anastasio put it, "three alpha dogs." Their neo-psychedelic album, *The Grand Pecking Order*, mushroomed (pun intended) at Anastasio's Barn Studio (or "tree fort," as Claypool called it). Anastasio and Claypool knocked around song ideas. They had a big jar of 'shrooms, which contributed to the trippy, black-humored vibe of an album that, thematically, examines how the world works in a time of military-industrial complexes, global terror-ism, and tyrants who subjugate the masses. Anastasio and Claypool must have had their ears to the ground, because they tapped into this unsettling zeitgeist mere months before the terrorist attacks of 9/11.

It was during the Oysterhead sessions that Claypool nicknamed Anas-tasio "Johnny Flip-Flop." It was a kind of compliment that recognized his willingness to compromise or change course. He would willingly try options and did his best to keep people happy. A seemingly ad-mirable character trait, Anastasio's accommodating nature ultimately helped drive him over the edge. Even he owned up to it. Speaking to *Rolling Stone*'s Will Dana about the Phish organization in 2001, Anas-tasio allowed, "I always feel like, because of my role in this thing, a kind of responsibility. I want everybody to be happy."

Shortly after recording *The Grand Pecking Order*, Claypool had this to say about working with Anastasio: "He's a very well-rounded player. He's very intuitive. He's Mr. Happy Pants, too. His personality, he's just a good positive-energy kind of guy. He's got a good sense of humor, and he's a pleasure to play with."

Tony Markellis, who played bass on Anastasio's solo projects from 1998 through 2004, also saw this side of Anastasio.

"He's a very generous friend and employer," said Markellis. "As long as I've known him, he's gone out of his way to help those around him. If you need something, he'll give it to you. I'd call him up or he'd call me up, and he'd say, 'Hey, what are you doing?' and I'd say, 'Well, kinda sitting around trying to figure out how to pay the bills.' And he'd say, 'Well, let's go on a tour.' I mean, literally it would go from maybe I couldn't figure out how to pay this month's bills to a week from then there'd be a tour planned, just because the spark of, 'Someone I play with needs some money. Let's do something.'"

A groove-oriented bassist with a long résumé, Markellis also got a bird's-eye view of Anastasio's relentless creativity. He confirmed the perception of Anastasio as someone whose brain is in constant motion.

"As far as I can tell, his mind never stops working," said Markellis. "It never stops creating. And it just seems to be sparking at all times. I really don't know if he ever has a moment's relaxation. I certainly saw it when we were onstage. We'd even be backstage waiting to go out for an encore and he would say, 'Here, I want to teach you a new song.' And he would teach us a new song for the *encore*, as we're waiting to go onstage! I don't know how he does it. I can't imagine what it's like to be inside his head."

The barrage of work from Anastasio during the hiatus included his first major-label solo album, the self-titled *Trey Anastasio* (released in 2002). It was a way for him to score for horns, to explore aspects of harmony more deeply in a larger group setting, and to delve into African, Cuban, and Caribbean rhythms. He even incorporated a seventeen-piece orchestra into a few of the numbers. He spoke of the band with an excitement that he hadn't exhibited about Phish in quite a while.

"I'm trying to make music that uses what's good about improvisation—which is the spontaneous moments—while getting to a point where not even ten seconds go by that there isn't some elegant or unique moment happening," said Anastasio. "This band is an idea I've been carrying around in my head since before I did *Surrender to the Air*. If you look at it, interestingly, it's virtually the same band. Not the same people, but the same array of instruments: two drummers, organ, bass, guitar, and a horn section with flute, alto sax, trombone. And now, with these tours and this album, this is a much more fully realized version of that, I would say."

Markellis saw how Anastasio's work with the solo bands, in which he was the unquestioned leader, gave him some freedom from Phish's sometimes stifling group democracy.

"Trey was one of four nominally equal partners in Phish, although that could be argued," said Markellis. "Most of the decision-making really was more him than any of the others, probably because of the nature of his personality and the way his brain works. Where another person might come up with an idea or a suggestion a week, he's got a hundred of them a day, and of those hundred, at least fifty of them are probably pretty good.

"So just by sheer volume of output, he's gonna be the leader of a group like that by default. But in the case of the trio and all those other groups I was involved with, there was no question that it wasn't a democracy. Yes, he wanted our input, but he was the boss and we were there to do what he wanted us to do. So I think for him it was an opportunity to mentally breathe in a way that he hadn't been able to in the context of Phish."

"He's a very sentimental guy," Markellis added. "One funny thing I noticed was that he's not good at goodbyes. At the end of a tour, everyone would be saying, 'See you next time' or whatever, and he was nowhere to be found. He doesn't care for saying goodbye to people, even temporarily."

Mike Gordon was also productive during the hiatus, making a documentary film, *Rising Low*, about bassists and bass playing.

Rising Low had a threefold purpose. First, it was an homage to Allen Woody, bassist with the Allman Brothers Band and Gov't Mule, which he co-founded with Allman's guitarist Warren Haynes. Woody was found dead of heart failure—with drug use a contributing cause—in a hotel room near New York's LaGuardia Airport on August 25, 2000. Second, the film documented recording sessions during which Gov't Mule's surviving members—Haynes and drummer Matt Abts—cut two albums' worth of new music using twenty-five guest bassists from across the musical spectrum. Released in two volumes as *The Deep End*, the albums and Gordon's accompanying documentary were a sendoff to Woody and a way for Gov't Mule to carry on without him.

Finally, Gordon delved into the roles, styles, and psychologies of those players who hold down the low end. He covered a lot of ground in what is probably the "straightest" project he's ever undertaken. Yet in his inimitable way, *Rising Low* managed to combine documentary insight with offbeat perspective. Gordon even managed to incorporate a fictional bassist, Joey Arkenstat, into the narrative, getting well-known bass players to cite him as an influence.

In those years, Gordon also struck up a productive musical partnership with a fellow eccentric, twelve-string guitarist extraordinaire Leo Kottke, which resulted in two albums of subtly twisted musical genius, *Clone* and *Sixty Six Steps*. They were Kottke's first collaborations with another musician on full-length albums. Gordon had sent the guitarist a tape of one of Kottke's songs ("The Driving of the Year Nail"), over which Gordon had dubbed a bass line. Kottke could see the potential for collaboration, and they clicked.

Kottke described their improbable fit: "By the arranging rules, Mike and I shouldn't be able to play together because he plays the bass more like a lead instrument, especially with me, and when I play the guitar, I hog the bass job. I'm playing a lot of the twos and the threes and roots and stuff, and I'm always stepping on bass players' toes. I drive 'em nuts, and they drive me nuts.

"So you get a guy who plays the bass like a horn, who's much busier than most bass players, and it should just be a collision, but it's not at all. It continues to startle me how much we can play without getting in each other's way."

Page McConnell, who was "the quiet Phish" much like George Harrison had been "the quiet Beatle," surprised everyone by also forming a band. He called it Vida Blue, after a major-league hall-of-fame pitcher. He recruited an A+ rhythm section: bassist Oteil Burbridge (of the Aquarium Rescue Unit and the Allman Brothers Band) and drummer Russell Batiste (who joined a reformed Meters in the 1980s and hails from one of New Orleans's great musical families).

"I saw the Allman Brothers and the Meters within about two weeks of each other," said McConnell. "It just all came together for me then, and I started making calls."

Vida Blue's self-titled first album was, in fact, cut in New Orleans, with sessions commencing just three days after the terrorist attacks of September 11, 2001.

The second Vida Blue album, *The Illustrated Band*—whose title punned on novelist Ray Bradbury's science-fiction classic *The Illustrated Man*—appeared two years later. This one was made in Miami with the Spam All-Stars—a five-piece band with a deejay and a Latin, dance-oriented groove. It was almost completely improvised and pushed into areas both contemporary and experimental, making it the hippest and most urbane of all of Phish's side projects.

Another project that might seem unlikely from the soft-spoken keyboardist: he sponsored a demolition-derby team, for which long-time friend and Phish fan Ian McLean was the driver. They called it Team Vida Blue.

"Not that many people know that side of Page," said McLean, laughing. "He was the financier. We would find a car and fix it all up, and then I would drive it in the local demolition derby. That was wicked fun. We had great bonding and a huge time doing that. Maybe at some point we'll do it again, fire up Team Vida Blue and smash more cars up."

Meanwhile, Jon Fishman served as drummer for Pork Tornado, a group of Burlington all-stars who were the ultimate Vermont bar band. Among its members was guitarist Dan Archer, at whose studio

Phish had recorded *Lawn Boy* years earlier. Working titles for the album give the irreverent flavor of the enterprise: *Kiss My Black Ass*, *Naughty Pooping Pig*, *Plain Cardboard Cover*. After the record company weighed in, they simply called it *Pork Tornado*. It is a wildly fun and amusingly unkempt piece of music that touches on everything from R&B and funk to country and novelty tunes. "It's a freak show," said Fishman upon *Pork Tornado*'s release in 2002. "It's just the weirdest group of people. It's a constant source of entertainment for me. The mix of people is as eclectic as the music. That is why I'm in that band. Every time I go back to it and we're partying or working on something or whatever, it's always a laugh a minute."

You wouldn't expect anything less of a project with Fishman at the center. He also drummed with the Jazz Mandolin Project, which he's done on and off for years, most recently in 2009.

Amid this flurry of activity by the individual members, the group also launched the LivePhish series. If the fans couldn't see Phish for however long they were away, at least they could purchase these live soundboard recordings of choice gigs.

The first batch of six LivePhish releases launched in September 2001. Another half-dozen followed in 2002. The next set comprised all four Halloween shows at which they covered other bands' albums. Gordon selected four more, including a couple of shows from 1994—May 7 in Dallas and December 29 in Providence—that were such obvious milestones, it was surprising they hadn't been released during the first round.

Despite plans for a semiannual barrage of LivePhish releases, the series stopped at twenty. After the initial runs sold out, the deluxe packaging—silver-foil covers adorned with unique Jim Pollock illustrations and plastic double-folded CD housings—were scrapped. That was a good thing, as the plastic partially liquefied and leeched onto the CDs—well, my copies anyway. They're available as downloads at livephish.com, and can be ordered online as physical CDs, too.

During the rollout of the LivePhish series, I was asked to do a number of interviews with key associates who performed important non-musical roles. One of them was Dominic Placco, Phish's bus driver. I was curious to see if his impressions jibed with mine on one matter in particular. I'd always been impressed by the fact that even when there were issues or conflicts, the members of Phish still displayed mutual respect. They never spoke ill of one another publicly or, in my experience, privately. They put friendship on an equal footing with music. If anyone was in a position to witness how Phish truly interacted during the long hours offstage, it was Placco. And so I put the question to him.

He's an interesting fellow—a musician himself who'd been part of NRBQ's Whole Wheat Horns. In fact, that beloved cult band wouldn't have existed without Placco, who brought members of different bands together to form NRBQ. Placco started working with Phish in 1994 and didn't stop until they did. He's driven for Anastasio's solo tours, too. He has even restored cars for the band members: a Chevy Camaro for Anastasio and a Buick Riviera for Fishman. He got to know them all pretty well, and he saw the partying and their private lives. In fact, his bus became Phish's preferred place to blow it out.

"Phish was pretty wild, to the point they would play the stereo loud and just get going," said Placco. "Most of the time, if we were staying overnight somewhere, they would just come down to the bus and spend the night hanging out. That was distracting in a good way. It didn't bother me. It was a little weird that you'd go down in the middle of the night and the bus was going wild. It made it a little hard sometimes to take care of the bus, but I didn't mind."

Beyond that, he commented on the bonds between them. "To me, they're the most together group I ever worked with," Placco continued. "It's like they think alike, they do everything alike. They're worried about one another, and they think about one another: 'Is this affecting you? If it is, let's change it.' *Nobody* does that. No group does that. Other groups make it seem like they're together, but Phish really is together. I really appreciated the way they treated one another."

I asked for thumbnail impressions of each member, and Placco offered these overviews: "Mike is probably the craziest one, 'cause he's just so different. Trey is just a straight-ahead guy, man. Jon is one of the most honest people in the world. He can't help being so honest that it gets him in trouble. Page is just a great person, a super-nice person.

"As far as I'm concerned, there's not a bad one in the bunch."

Phish ended their hiatus almost exactly two years after their last show. They made the decision to reassemble at a band meeting in Lake Placid (a lakeside resort not far from Burlington). Upon regrouping at the Barn for rehearsals, the music started to flow and an album of new material basically recorded itself.

"It was all new and fresh, and that's what we wanted," said Anastasio soon after these posthiatus sessions. "It was a lot of things. For one, it felt like no time had gone by at all and at the same time it felt as if lots of time had gone by. The thing that struck me was that lots of life had gone by and still there was continuity to it."

Phish went into the studio to rehearse new material for their reunion shows and left, barely two weeks later, with a finished album. They called it *Round Room*. The title track was a Mike Gordon song (a first), and the cover was a piece of art—a round room, in fact—by Burlington artist Lars Fisk. The album itself was an aural documentary of Phish performing new songs almost as quickly as they learned them. When they realized good things were happening, they contacted producer Bryce Goggin and hustled him up to the Barn to run the machines. The idea was to catch the songs on the fly, and *Round Room* wasn't so much produced as it was, simply, recorded.

The group considered about thirty songs—upward of twenty from Anastasio and Tom Marshall, close to ten from Gordon, and even a contender from McConnell—and winnowed down the album to an even dozen. Most were cut during a few charmed nights in September after two weeks of rehearsal. Though they initially regarded them as demos, the recordings sounded so fresh that the group didn't think that further work would improve them. The mantra became "don't fix, don't tamper."

"There was something nice about hearing the first time we played together in two years captured on tape," said Anastasio. "There is a lot of emotion involved, to my ear."

"To make an album so close to the moment of conception was pretty cool," added Gordon. "Because we were still discovering the songs, I think our sense of wonder comes out. It doesn't surprise me that there would be good stuff in that moment."

Round Room included five big jams—"Pebbles and Marbles," "Walls of the Cave," "Waves," "46 Days," and "Seven Below"—which was unique for a Phish studio album. Those lengthier pieces had a raw, elemental feeling to them, like leaning into a gale or being pelted with sea spray. One of the songs, "Walls of the Cave," has an interest-ing story.

"I wrote 'Walls of the Cave' shortly after 9/11 happened," Marshall allowed, "but I was really writing a song for my son, like 'Here's some-thing that will endure for you when I'm gone.' It's a semi-morbid song. Right away when Trey heard it, he said, 'Oh, this is about the World Trade Center,' and I sort of pooh-poohed it: 'Nah, it's a song for Brody [Marshall's son],' and Trey was like, 'Okay.'

"But then everyone instantly keyed in on the World Trade Center and found lyrics like, 'When it fell, you caught my heart before it hit the ground.' Lots of people took it piece by piece, and I realized that maybe I did subliminally write it about that. But the fact that 'Walls of the Cave' and 'World Trade Center' have the letters *WTC* in com-mon was just luck, though no one believes it. That kind of thing has been happening more and more."

McConnell savored the challenge of learning so many new songs whose length and complexity harked back to Phish's early years.

"We were trying to learn this huge volume of material, and I love that," he exclaimed. "I absolutely love rehearsal and learning new songs. Just working my brain in that way again was so much fun."

There were some memorable shorter songs on the album, too. "Anything But Me" and "All of These Dreams" were in the more introverted and ballad-oriented vein that Anastasio and Marshall had been mining in recent years.

The band's innate sense of communication survived their time apart. For instance, when Fishman played a straight-ahead beat while learning "Thunderhead," Anastasio interjected some cryptic instructions.

"It's not supposed to be on the ground, it's in the air," Anastasio said.

"Oh, it's floating, it's in the air," replied Fishman. "Oh, okay."

"We just know what we mean by that," Fishman continued, laughing. "It's so weird. I guess that's what happens when you've been playing with people for seventeen years."

For the rehearsal and recording of *Round Room*, the group isolated itself from everyone, including crew and management.

"They weren't pushing us away," manager John Paluska said at the time. "They were more like, 'We just need to go be the four of us like we were back in 1984 when nobody cared.'"

They claimed they were ready to walk away from the reunion, if it wasn't working.

"I'd gotten to the point where I thought Phish is a really special thing, and if it's meant to keep going, it will," Fishman said. "By the time we got to the studio, we were all in that state of mind: 'Hey, if it doesn't work out we can go home in three hours, so let's see what happens.'"

What happened was "Pebbles and Marbles"—the ten-minute epic that opens the album. It all unfolded quickly from there. Whatever else one might say about *Round Room*, it was Phish's least labored studio project. For a band that had always thrived on spontaneity in performance, achieving a similar breakthrough in the studio counted for something.

At the time, Anastasio noted that despite all the ballyhoo and drama over the hiatus, *Round Room* appeared only two years after *Farmhouse*.

"Let's say we hadn't taken the hiatus," Anastasio said with a chuckle. "When you look at it, we probably aren't that far off the normal schedule of releasing another Phish album. Someday, it's not even going to look like we took a hiatus!"

Indeed, if they hadn't uttered the word "hiatus" and just went quietly inactive for a while, their absence wouldn't have drawn all the attention it did. A mere two years' downtime between albums and tours would actually qualify as an accelerated schedule by many musicians' standards. *Round Room* nonetheless fared poorly on the charts, reaching only No. 46, and was disparaged by fans and critics. Perhaps fans were punishing them for not touring. Critics never really did get Phish, so their disapproval was nothing new. Admittedly, a few songs on *Round Room* did seem unfinished or in need of further work, but the album as a whole had a spontaneous freshness and sounded like nothing else in Phish's catalog.

"We went away and came back recharged, which was the goal," said McConnell soon after the *Round Room* sessions. "We're back, simple as that."

But in hindsight, it wasn't quite that simple. Looking back in 2005, Anastasio admitted that Phish came back too soon and not for all the right reasons. His attitude toward *Round Room* also evolved away from the positive words he spoke upon its release.

"Throughout the hiatus, we still had an organization that required hundreds of thousands of dollars a month," he said. "It was totally overblown. So basically what we had during the hiatus was a lot of people, from my standpoint, saying, 'When are you going to get back together? We need the money.' If you go back and listen to *Round Room*, it just sounds exhausted, like four exhausted people."

If you pay attention to the earliest shows of the reunion, you might well draw the same conclusions: that they were still tired and not ready to come back, that the core problems that led them to take two years off had not been worked out during the interim.

The New Year's Eve show at Madison Square Garden that welcomed in 2003 was a case in point. The performance wasn't as noteworthy as the event itself—Phish's much-anticipated return from a two-year hiatus. It was an entertaining show, and one highlight was the supposed appearance of actor Tom Hanks, his presence triggering the band's use of a scene from his then-current movie *Cast Away*. In the film, Hanks is marooned on a desert island with only a volleyball for companionship. The manufacturer's name, Wilson, is stamped on the ball in big letters. A chunk of Hanks's deranged monologue, directed at Wilson, provided an inspired lead-in to Phish's song of the same name. The group purported to bring Hanks to the stage, where he blurted the "blat-boom" line when "Wilson" kicked in again. The crowd was fooled; in actuality, it was Page McConnell's brother Steve, who closely resembles the actor. It wasn't just the crowd that got pranked; some news media picked up the story of Hanks's guest spot at Phish's reunion show and reported it as fact. It was good to see that Phish's prankster instincts were as sharp as ever.

However, during the three-night run that followed at their beloved Hampton Coliseum, they seemed rusty, and fans worried that Phish was still unwell. Anastasio appeared addled on the second night. Brad Sands brought coffee onstage to help straighten him out. However humorous the gesture, it was also a bit disconcerting. During the second set, the band had to restart "You Enjoy Myself" after botching the intro.

"We're gonna start again," a peeved Anastasio told the crowd, "because we've practiced it and we know it so fucking well, and I'm really ashamed of the fact that, after two and a half years off, that's the best we can do. So please, let us play it again."

That early stumble proved to be more of an aberration, as 2003 turned out to be one of Phish's strongest later touring years, featuring some of the most solid performances and adventurous set lists since the mid-nineties. The playing was especially inspired on the summer tour, which has been referred to as the "sober tour." The group—and

Anastasio in particular—made a conscious effort to walk a straight line and avoid enabling one another. Anastasio swore off everything (even caffeine!) and practiced yoga and meditation in hotel rooms. "That tour, for Trey, it was basically doing yoga and working out. He was having me find yoga people in every place," said Brad Sands.

In part, the tour strategy came from Neil Young. They noticed Young would "do a runner" after shows: that is, get offstage, into a car and out of there. For a band that was trying to reform itself, it seemed like a great idea: instead of succumbing to backstage temptations, just get shuttled to the hotel or point the bus out of town. It made for a memorable summer tour, and for the band's year-ending four-night stand in Miami, Anastasio still practiced yoga and did a nightly runner up to West Palm Beach after the shows.

"Everyone was making a conscious effort to turn the tide," recalled Brad Sands. "I think you could hear it in the music."

In 2003 Phish played loads of new songs, brought back some long-neglected items—especially the uber-rarity "Destiny Unbound," whose one-time unveiling after 11 years absence shocked Phishheads—and attacked old favorites with renewed vigor. There were many remarkable nights on that tour, including their two-night stand at Palo Alto's Shoreline Amphitheatre (July 8, 9), which featured some amazing playing; a show in Pittsburgh that had plenty of breakouts and rarities (July 29); and a performance in Utah (July 15) with a riveting half-hour jam on "Mr. Completely" and a playful segment that wove in and out of Gordon's mock hardcore song "Big Black Furry Creature from Mars."

Phish's It festival ended the standout summer 2003 tour on a high note. It was a big event, drawing 60,000 fans to the remote reaches of caribou country. Musically, Phish continued pushing the envelope, looking for fresh combinations of new and old material. A ninety-minute PBS documentary of the event aired a year later. It was filmed in high definition and mixed by Elliot Scheiner, who'd worked with Steely Dan. Issued as a double DVD, *It* included four hours worth of music and extras. It's a fine documentary package that leads one to conclude how much better it might have been had Phish ended things there instead of Coventry.

At that point, Phish seemed right where they needed to be and were playing as well as any reasonable fan could hope for twenty years into their career.

After the hiatus, the group took LivePhish a step further, offering downloads of shows within forty-eight hours of each performance. They did this from their December 31, 2002, reunion concert at Madison Square Garden through their bow-out at Coventry in August 2004. Fans could purchase full-resolution digital downloads of individual shows or entire tours. An individual show cost $9.99 in the MP3 format—not bad for three hours and three discs, on average. They've continued the practice since reuniting in 2009.

"Phish broke all kinds of ground throughout their career, but the live download thing was a huge innovation," said archivist Kevin Shapiro. "It was a generous step for them to agree that you'll get it and you'll get all of it, uncut, from the soundboard. Paul [Languedoc] had an incredible touch recording the live shows, but they're still revealing and unforgiving, and a loud bad note in the room becomes a *really* loud bad note on a soundboard tape. I always thought we should reserve the right to say no on some given show. But I think it demonstrated great trust on their part of their own output."

The LivePhish downloads also brought change to the industry by streamlining the bureaucratic licensing process for songs by other artists. Because Phish typically performs at least a few covers per show—in whole or, during a jam, in part—they needed licenses for those songs before they could put them up for sale in the digital realm. Every song they covered required a license from its publisher, and any given song might have multiple publishers.

"I can't tell you how difficult it was to license all of that stuff, because nobody else was doing it," said Beth Montuori Rowles. "It was impossible to get a digital license because they hadn't yet set rates for digital downloads. So when you went to these large publishers to get a license for a digital download, first of all, the federal copyright act mandates a thirty-day notice, and obviously we were violating that term since we were putting up shows within forty-eight hours.

"No one was saying no to us, but nobody was saying yes, either. It was like you couldn't obtain the license because they didn't know how to write it or how much to charge for it. And to get it through these big publishers' business-affairs departments was ridiculous. So we couldn't actually get physical licenses, but we were getting letters saying, basically, 'Do this and we'll figure it out after the fact.' Of course, we wouldn't be getting a letter like that from every single publisher, so we just had to move forward."

The tide started to turn when Harry Fox, a company that handles licensing for multiple publishing companies, began offering instant live licenses for shows released within seventy-two hours.

"When they made that available," Rowles continued, "I went to them and said, 'Okay, now we're starting to talk. Not all the terms meet our needs, but we're actually going in the right direction.' We were one of the first companies to get involved in this digital realm of licensing that excludes the thirty-day notice. Honestly, I think it took us two years to get the first licenses going. So the band's always been on that really innovative cusp."

Even on Phish's musically triumphant summer 2003 tour, there were signs of chinks in the armor, at least from a business perspective. Attendance on the summer tour was down from what it had been prior to the hiatus. In 2000, their last previous touring year, Phish sold out 95.5 percent of capacity. They took in $39 million from 54 concerts, for an average per-show gross of $722,222.22—not a bad haul for a band that didn't gouge fans with ticket prices. In 2003, Phish played to 90.8 percent of capacity. That's only a 5 percent drop, but it was indicative of a trend.

Did that mean Phish's audience had stopped growing? Had some Phish fans aged past the point where they'd suffer the inconveniences of the road to traipse around on tour? Did some fans not return to the fold posthiatus? Was Phish's latter-day style of playing not as captivating to longtime fans? Did the modest decline in ticket sales reflect a more general music-biz trend as listeners retreated to more "virtual" hideouts, like computers and iPods? Or was it simply the economy? The answer no doubt resided in some combination of all those factors, although Phish's manager, John Paluska, felt one was particularly significant.

"I think the biggest factor is our economy," manager John Paluska told *Billboard*. "It made people more selective. Instead of going to a few shows, they might go to one."

"We weren't selling quite as many tickets," acknowledged lighting engineer Chris Kuroda. "Everyone has his or her own reason why they're not buying a ticket anymore, from being grown up and working to support a wife and kid to they're just not into it anymore to it's not as good as it used to be."

Phish turned twenty on December 2, 2003. They celebrated that milestone anniversary with a concert at Boston's Fleet Center on that date. A career-spanning film montage, assembled by Mike Gordon and engineer/editor Jared Slomoff, played in the arena at intermission.

They closed out 2003 with a four-show New Year's stand at the American Airlines Arena in Miami, sounding much stronger than they had at the same point a year earlier, when they broke the hiatus. On occasion, they still wrestled with some of the more challenging passages in songs like "Reba," but the jams were fluid and the vibe playful and upbeat throughout the run.

They were joined on the third night by George Clinton and the P-Funk All-Stars for a second-set jam. The irrepressible Clinton exclaimed, "Y'all ready to funk up this place tonight? Phish with a P! That's funky to me, y'all! We got a little P with us, too! P-Funk, y'all!" The stage filled with costumed funkateers and a twenty-minute "P-Funk Medley" ensued. The sight of two seminal American jam bands sharing a stage made for an unforgettable moment of music history. The cherry on this funky sundae was that George Clinton got an arena full of white suburban Phish fans to chant, "We need the funk! Gotta have the funk!" in unison (more or less).

For New Year's Eve, Phish had devised another great gag. A local high-school marching band emerged one by one from a Mini Cooper that had been lowered onto the stage over a trapdoor. As the clock struck midnight, the band joined Phish in a medley of Kool & the Gang's "Jungle Boogie," the traditional "Auld Lang Syne," and Black Sabbath's "Iron Man." There was an odd bit of luck in that the band hailed from Palmetto Senior High School, so their uniforms were prominently emblazoned with a "P." The three-set show careened to a close with Fishman singing "Feel the Heat" from the *Boogie Nights* soundtrack, performed because this arena was home court for the NBA's Miami Heat.

Phish ended the year by raising the temperature, but their world would turn a good deal colder in 2004.

There weren't more than a handful of outright bad Phish gigs one could point to as evidence of waning inspiration, poor execution, and drug problems. Not everyone liked the turn toward ambient jamming and "cow funk" in 1997 and 1998, but the shows were inspired and well-played. The years 1999 and 2000 were off but not awful—just unspectacular, for the most part, by Phish's standards. The concerts at which the shit really did hit the fan (or fans) were their three nights in Las Vegas in April 2004 (overindulgence in Sin City) and Coventry (their calamitous festival finale). Although 2004 was a largely gloomy year for Phish and Phishheads, even it had some red-letter shows—such as their two-night runs at Brooklyn's KeySpan Park and the Saratoga Performing Arts Center. *Undermind*, Phish's tenth studio album, was also born during the season of travail that led to their breakup.

As with *Round Room*, it mixed brief, well-crafted songs with lengthier, more complex pieces, but it was an altogether tighter and more produced record. After working with Bryce Goggin and John Siket for years, Phish decided to try someone new. They turned to

Tchad Blake, who's worked with Tom Waits and Los Lobos. They liked his experimental bent, penchant for found sounds, and ability to create evocative musical atmospheres.

"We were looking for a producer who was compatible and yet came in with his own opinions," said McConnell. "It was good to bring in someone with a different sensibility and perspective, some fresh ideas and fresh ears."

Undermind came together during a month of sessions at the Barn. Unusually for them, the album was cut mostly by the light of day. "We made a daytime album that has a fresh afternoon feel," noted Gordon. "There's a peaceful kind of sound that comes about when we're working in the afternoon and are able to look out over the mountains."

Taking a cue from Blake's kitchen-sink approach, Gordon played five different basses on the album. McConnell laid down multiple keyboard parts—including Hammond organ, Yamaha synthesizer, and Fender Rhodes—to create sculptural textures. Fishman brought in old, beat-up cymbals and hi-hats at Blake's request. Anastasio got to stretch out on "A Song I Heard the Ocean Sing," a slab of moody, ornate psychedelia. *Undermind* was the first album to feature songs by all four members of Phish. The album closed with "Grind," a piece of barbershop quartet on the subject of teeth. They submitted it to Joe Lilles—one of the foremost barbershop arrangers—to write an arrangement geared to their vocal ranges.

The album's undisputed pinnacle is "The Connection." A burnished gem, it is a song so simple, tuneful, and eloquent that you could swear it's always been there.

"When Trey brought in the demo for 'The Connection,' I thought it was one of the most beautiful songs I'd ever heard," recalled Fishman. "To be able to write one song in your life with that level of simplicity and depth is a great thing. My respect for Trey and Tom as a songwriting team went through the roof. It was a sense of, 'This is really a sign of growth. Look at what this is developing into . . . and I get to contribute to this? What an opportunity!'"

"We're all happy with the album," said McConnell. "We did a lot of the vocals live, and the three of us would stand around and sing together. I really enjoyed that, and we were able to capture some nice moments."

"The whole project was easy and fun and creative, like a big celebration," said Gordon. "I feel our albums keep getting somewhat more accessible, yet at the same time they sound more unique to us.

"I'm feeling so good about Phish and what these experiences in our lives are leading to musically and lyrically," he continued. "I know we've been in a band for twenty years, but it still feels like it's ripening. With *Undermind*, I feel that it's really starting to take wing in a whole new way."

Three and a half weeks after Fishman, Gordon, and McConnell made those upbeat and hopeful statements, Anastasio broke up the band.

All the while, gossipy fans dished and deconstructed every perceived flub and rumor of substance abuse on their various online forums—Phantasy Tour, Jambase, Phish.Net. Contrarily, some heard, saw, and spoke no evil, attacking anyone who dared point out deficiencies. Music writer Jesse Jarnow posted reviews of all three nights at the Thomas & Mack Center in Las Vegas on jambands.com. Jarnow was a longtime Phishhead, and his criticisms of that run were both constructive and critical.

The three-night Vegas run of April 15–17, 2004, comprised the only shows Phish played that spring, so there was keen anticipation. Of the first night, Jarnow wrote: "The band seemed disoriented onstage during their first set, nervous even, guitarist Trey Anastasio puttering around between songs, back slightly hunched. . . . The second set was better, if a little more bizarre, [although] Anastasio continued to blow cues. . . . By two hours into the show, one could very easily wonder about what excites the band these days."

Of the middle night of the run, he wrote, "Last night was a fantastic Phish show, more than making up for the uneven performance of the opener." But the third night raised another red flag: "Everything was frayed during Phish's last night in Las Vegas. The band's old songs, once a source of puzzlebox beauty and underscored by their seamless playing, revealed their all-too-intricate constructions as the quartet once again blew transitions ('You Enjoy Myself') and forgot verses ('Tweezer'). The band's newer songs, the numbers they should be able to play in their sleep, also fell prey to disheartening sloppiness."

He remarked on the band's "collectively decaying memory." Perhaps that was a consequence of playing so infrequently and rehearsing less. Booking a handful of nights in Las Vegas was no way to keep a band like Phish on its toes. Jarnow's severest judgment: "Whatever the hell's going on, Phish can't continue to play like they did on the first and last nights in Las Vegas and expect to be taken seriously."

As if to affirm the perception that something was amiss, there was an unnerving interview with Anastasio on the second DVD of the *It* documentary. It was filmed right after the Las Vegas run in 2004, and the wear and tear his lifestyle was taking was evident. He looked pale as a ghost as he enthused hoarsely about the band's "new beginnings."

Jarnow's honest assessments nudged Anastasio to the tipping point. He read the reviews, listened to the soundboards of those shows, and then called a band meeting. To his bandmates' surprise, he came to break up the band—for good this time. The rest of the band didn't see Anastasio's decision coming. They thought he might have in mind some major downsizing of their office and warehouse staff. The meeting took place at Gordon's house on May 21. Gordon told *Rolling Stone*'s Will Dana that Anastasio started crying and said, "I can't do this anymore."

Anastasio posted an announcement on Phish.com on May 25, 2004, five weeks after the Vegas gigs. It sent shockwaves through the fan world. Signed only by Anastasio, it was unambiguous in its finality. It read as follows:

> Last Friday night, I got together with Mike, Page and Fishman to talk openly about the strong feelings I've been having that Phish has run

its course and that we should end it now while it's still on a high note. Once we started talking, it quickly became apparent that the other guys' feelings, while not all the same as mine, were similar in many ways—most importantly, that we all love and respect Phish and the Phish audience far too much to stand by and allow it to drag on beyond the point of vibrancy and health. We don't want to become caricatures of ourselves, or worse yet, a nostalgia act. By the end of the meeting, we realized that after almost twenty-one years together we were faced with the opportunity to graciously step away in unison, as a group, united in our friendship and our feelings of gratitude.

So Coventry will be the final Phish show. We are proud and thrilled that it will be in our home state of Vermont. We're also excited for the June and August shows, our last tour together. For the sake of clarity, I should say that this is not like the hiatus, which was our last attempt to revitalize ourselves. We're done. It's been an amazing and incredible journey. We thank you all for the love and support that you've shown us.

—Trey Anastasio

Page McConnell eventually added his own note of assent and explanation. Fishman kept quiet. Gordon made no secret of opposing the breakup. He argued for staying together on the basis that longevity was preferable to demise. For that, Phishheads accorded him hero status.

Because of his reviews, Jarnow was saddled with the reputation of being "the guy who broke up Phish" within a certain unforgiving corner of the fan world. He got a subtle earful from Mike Gordon, too. A month after the breakup announcement, following the first show of the summer tour—an awesome performance at KeySpan Park, on Coney Island, that was released on DVD—Mike Gordon pulled Jarnow aside in the Betty Ford Clinic and told him, "Just so you know, your reviews came up at our end-of-band meeting. No hard feelings, though."

Once he made up his mind, Anastasio was capable of following through with an assertive finality. For example, Gordon told *Rolling Stone* that Anastasio got rid of his CD collection and set fire to his television set. He was given to such bold strokes, and his handling of Phish was no different.

"I have to see this [disbanding Phish] as one of those things," Gordon noted.

I didn't see it coming in the conversations I had with McConnell, Gordon, and Fishman for the *Undermind* album bio. Perhaps I should've gotten a clue when Anastasio demurred on his interview, as it was the first time that had happened. But Anastasio was a very busy man with a lot on his plate, so that was understandable.

I did speak with him on May 19—two days before the meeting at Gordon's where he pulled the plug—about his upcoming performances at Bonnaroo. I was writing an article about Anastasio for the festival program. He was scheduled to play as a guitarist in Dave Matthews's solo band; as conductor of the Nashville Symphony Orchestra in a program of his compositions; and as the leader of his horn-filled solo band. He was juggling a daunting set of tasks, and the pressure must have been considerable.

He said little that would have led me to believe he was poised to end Phish. In hindsight, the only comment he made that might offer a clue to his weary and overwhelmed mindset came as he praised David Byrne, who was also appearing at Bonnaroo.

"There's hardly a day that goes by that I don't find myself laughing about some David Byrne lyric in the context of my life," Anastasio said. "It happens so often. It just happened recently. He's right on the money. Like 'No Compassion': 'So many people . . . I'm not interested.'"

After the breakup, Anastasio mused freely about his reasons for disbanding Phish. There were many such reasons, some of them extramusical, but in retrospect the fact that they'd gotten away from the band practices that were so fundamental toward bonding them loomed large.

"I often liked band practice better than the . . . " he said, trailing off.

"Performances themselves?" I offered.

"Yeah. My memory of band practice is the thing I'll miss the most. And maybe that's part of the reason why . . . We don't practice anymore. We haven't practiced . . . We can't."

"I don't think the music was as good after Big Cypress, from 2000 through to the end," said Amy Skelton. "Certainly, the last show before the hiatus had some really incredible moments. But those years weren't that amazing. And I wasn't jaded. I still loved the band most of the time, but I remember standing in the room many times, listening and saying 'yeah,' but I wasn't sucked in. My hair wasn't standing on end at the top note of one of the best songs. They were sort of going through the motions. It was decent, but it wasn't transcendent. There were a lot less of those moments in those years. And some shows, I didn't get it at all."

Not coincidentally, those were the years when Phish stopped practicing and instituted a "no analysis" rule for their live shows. The escalation of drug use and backstage scenes was also a cause or symptom. All of these things eroded the intense self-scrutiny and disciplined, goal-oriented strategy that had made them so unique for many years.

Even after the hiatus, the organization the band felt financially obliged to support remained something of an obsession, the elephant in the room.

"I don't know if you ever went to the Phish office, but it was pretty big," Anastasio said in 2005, after it had all gone away. "I mean, as long as it was going to keep going, it was as big as it needed to be. It's very hard and I felt so guilty about all the people losing their jobs and everything. I still do. There's still people floating around Burlington kind of trying to work for Phish. . . . But, I mean, people were unhealthy. Things had gotten really gross in a certain way, and now they're not."

Chris Kuroda elaborated on how consuming life working for Phish had become. "Phish was 365 days a year whether you were on tour or not," said Kuroda. "It became all-consuming of all of us. We were just living this Phish thing day in and day out, being consumed by it in an unhealthy way. Personally, I came to realize I'd lost my identity. I thought my identity was there when my identity as an individual was something completely different."

Anastasio felt especially weighted down, rightly or wrongly, by the organization. In a far-ranging interview that ran in *Guitar World* in August 2004—the month of Coventry and Phish's breakup—he identified "owning a merchandise company" as being among the things that most bugged him.

"I love the people who work on it," he elaborated, "but every time I walk in there, I really get kind of ill. There's boxes and boxes of posters, and a feeling of the selling of us. I'm not going to be sad when that goes away."

Of course, there was another side to the story.

"When the band reflects on the beast that the office became, half of that weight was mail-order, although it was the easiest half to farm out," noted Amy Skelton. "You can always farm out merchandising. There are lots of merchandise companies in the country. But they'd been down that road, and they didn't like it. It wasn't smart, it wasn't responsive to their needs, it wasn't necessarily respectful of their artistic taste. So that's why everything slowly went in-house and stayed there."

"My feeling was that Phish could have had the best of both worlds with a better plan after they broke up the first time," noted Brad Sands, referring to their failure to resolve in-house staffing issues to their satisfaction during the 2000–2002 hiatus.

Leaving the band members out of it for a moment, the crew and the office staff each thought the other had gotten too big. The crew-office dynamic can be contentious in any band organization, and Phish's situation was no different.

Paul Languedoc, for instance, had much to say about the office staff:

"I was the equipment manager for what eventually became a four thousand–square-foot warehouse of equipment. I had Pete Carini as an assistant, although he eventually became the guy at the Barn [Anastasio's studio]. I've always felt like if I did things the way the office did things, I'd have a staff of twelve people and we'd have to get a bigger space because we'd be creating more stuff.

"I've always personally liked things to be small and efficient. But what happened at the office was that it was John [Paluska] and Shelly [Culbertson] at first, and then John hired his girlfriend [Cynthia] to take care of the merchandise. So she was in charge of the merchandise department, and then she'd hire somebody else. They'd hire friends, and then *they'd* hire *their* friends to be assistants, and eventually they'd split off this little department. They just kept hiring people, and they kept hiring their friends."

Skelton made a counterargument in defense of the office:

"There was never any dead weight," she said. "Everybody who ever worked at the office wore a lot of hats and produced a lot of work. There weren't that many full-time employees. The only dead weight was that Phish still had to pay a lot of crew. In most of the rest of the rock world there are *some* crew that get paid year-round, of course, but many of them are road crew—you hire them [temporarily] for a tour, and you're done. That's why they're called *road* crew.

"So that was the only dead weight. But we never hired one person, one-*half* a person, more than we needed to get the job done. We were exceptionally frugal with people in mail-order, and the Dionysian Productions side stayed pretty static through the whole time. Once it got to a certain size, it stayed right there. And that was the size we needed to get the job done. It couldn't have been any smaller.

"We had tickets in-house, merch in-house. Doing all of our own management. It was all in-house, and you just couldn't do it with any less people."

Phish themselves created and nurtured this monster, which perhaps wasn't really such a monster. Had the organization, in fact, grown too big?

If Phish were annually playing half as many shows as before, maybe yes. But if they were now adding four (or five) solo and side-band careers to the mix, maybe no. Moreover, if one or more members was looking for something to blame escalating drug use and intergroup tensions on . . . well, the office made a convenient scapegoat.

"It was something to fixate on when there were a lot of other problems," Skelton noted. "It *was* kind of a scapegoat, an issue that was easy to point at, while the other ones were a little harder to talk about."

It's an old story: Drugs are used to escape problems, and then they *become* the main problem. Anastasio knew this to be true, and he'd discuss it with Skelton, who by 2000 was walking a straighter path while watching, with growing concern, what was going on all around her.

"Trey and I had a lot of heart-to-hearts in those years," said Skelton, "and we had them because he was hooked and he wanted to talk to somebody about it."

Eric Larson, among the earliest Phish fans, was on the band's payroll as a massage therapist and chiropractor. When asked how he, as a health-care professional, approached Phish about substance-abuse issues, he had this to say:

"As the health-care guy I have to make suggestions," he said. "You can't make demands of anybody. So I tried to intervene where I thought it was reasonable to intervene and make suggestions, knowing full well that people are going to do what they're going to do. I think I had some limited effect. Certainly, overall, in terms of diet and posture and exercise and fasting and all those things, I think I gave them much over the years.

"When you get into a scene where there's drugs and alcohol, everybody's got to make their own decisions. It really has to come from the person. No one else can dictate or tell you how to behave. So I think for all of us it got disturbing, and that certainly contributed to them wanting to take a break. I did the best that I could and tried not to be involved in the whole situation anyway. Just being on tour, the whole thing was a big party. Moderation's a tough thing on the road. And if you last, you eventually learn some degree of moderation. That's the only way it *can* last, right?"

Larson left the Phish organization in 2003, while Skelton moved to Nova Scotia with her family after the breakup.

"It was a different time for Phish at that point," said Skelton. "There was a lot less energy trickling down, and the writing was kind of on the wall."

So why do groups break up?

For one thing, talent, creativity, and leadership are not equally allocated. Within any musical group there will inevitably be imbalances, leading to bruised egos, factionalism, and disproportionate compensation to he (or she) who is prolific and also writes the songs that resonate most with the audience and best represent the band.

Phish wrestled with this dilemma as rationally as they could, allowing deep friendship, good intentions, and institutional democracy to smooth over the rough spots as much as possible. But it was still an issue that simmered beneath the surface.

Inevitably, somebody's got to lead. Back in 1972, David Bowie took Ian Hunter of Mott the Hoople aside when that group was foundering and told him, "Somebody's gotta play God." Within Phish, Anastasio was the undeniable leader, by virtue of his inexhaustible store of energy, enthusiasm, and ideas. He naturally has a "take control" type of personality—not in a heavy-handed way but as a consequence of the music that continually flows from him. He can't help himself and shouldn't have to try. Trey Anastasio is a force of nature, pure and simple.

Yet the other members are abundantly gifted and have been bandleaders in their own right. Within Phish, however, none of the other musicians generated the type or profusion or type of material that defined the group from day one. That has always been Anastasio's role, and it made him the driving force in the band.

To use a metaphor, think of a band as a car. Cars may have four tires (which make contact with the road, per a beloved Mike Gordon song), but they do not have four steering wheels. There is only one wheel and can be only one driver. That's not to say the others are just along for the ride. They can be navigators, too. They can even spell the driver and take the wheel themselves from time to time.

To extend the metaphor, Anastasio willingly relinquished the wheel at various points to keep his fellow travelers happy. He did it during *Story of the Ghost* and the more ambient, sparse, and funky phases of live Phish in the late nineties. In terms of administrative decision-making, Phish outwardly functioned as a democracy, with each member getting a vote and each capable of nixing any decision. The four of them had to be in unanimous agreement before moving forward on such things as producers, tour plans, big events, album covers, and whatever else came up in their increasingly complex career.

Even management had a say in the voting, as the Phish organization bent over backward not to be a typical top-down hierarchy. This was an office that didn't even assign formal job titles. Eventually, this led to what they called the "democracy bureaucracy." At that point, Anastasio declared "enough" and assumed a unilateral role in recording *Farmhouse* in 1999. After the breakup, Anastasio claimed that twenty-four band members and employees had to be polled about the minor design issue of enclosing the band's name in a box for the cover of their 2004 album, *Undermind*.

Phish brought a lot of the headaches that plagued them in later years upon themselves. They wanted in-house management, merchandising, ticketing, etc. It's a key reason they operated so effectively outside of the mainstream and were able to imprint their personality upon every aspect of their career. But it did involve them in micromanaging everything from T-shirt designs to staff salaries—matters the average musician does not have to contend with all or even any of the time. And that took its toll.

Phish's concern about staff size—combined with mounting drug issues and the simple fact that Phish needed a break from each other after seventeen years of constant work—led to their two-year hiatus. However, those unresolved issues came back to haunt them posthiatus. In addition, tensions between McConnell and Anastasio intensified—especially on McConnell's side, when he perceived that Anastasio's drug use affected his playing and, therefore, their shows.

McConnell outwardly maintained professionalism and self-discipline. Anastasio's less responsible behavior, coupled with his oversight of the band, caused McConnell's resentment to simmer. McConnell's issues with management went so far that he actually had Dionysian Productions audited.

Despite his reserved manner—no one in the band quite comported himself with McConnell's well-heeled politesse—he could exhibit a steely, unsentimental resolve when push came to shove. Some thought of him as the "ice man," and even he referred (in *The Phish Book*) to "the dreaded 'call from Page' you don't want to get when you're in the Phish organization."

After the disastrous breakup year of 2004, McConnell reportedly didn't speak to Anastasio for a long time. "He holds a lot inside, and he was bitter about things for a long time." said former Phish employee Amy Skelton. "I think he's come to terms with a lot of that. It took him some time to decompress and relax and see everything for what it was. But he was steaming mad for quite some time—at the office, at John [Paluska], at Trey, at Mike. He was unhappy. And towards the end, particularly with Trey, those two butted heads a lot."

After the breakup, Anastasio made a curious remark that set Phishheads' antennas waving: "The truth of the matter is, somebody should call Page and talk to him," he told Tim Donnelly in a *Relix* interview. "He wanted to stop as much as I did. He had serious issues that date back to *Billy Breathes*."

There is some ambiguity in the remark. Phishheads, rightly or wrongly, took "serious issues" to mean drugs, while in the context of the interview, Anastasio might well have been referring to Page's problems with the organization.

Mike Gordon also had his issues, which he dealt with in a more passive-aggressive manner. Once he realized his contributions wouldn't be accorded equal time, he quietly redirected his songwriting energies into other endeavors.

"When I started to see that my songs weren't going to be used on albums or when I didn't have the confidence to bring songs to band practice and push them through," Gordon reflected in 2008, "I decided I would start making movies, which was another thing I wanted to do anyway. I spent four years on my first movie when I could've been writing songs for Phish. The point being that I found a creative outlet where I could work fourteen hours a day, which I like to do. Whereas with Phish I couldn't really do that.

"Phish was an incredible collaboration," he allowed. "It was a collaboration with a clear leader and a lot of intelligence and creativity with all the people involved. For me, in a way, I haven't always been mature enough to use my incredible creative drive in the collaboration."

He noted that jamming, the live experience, was inherently more participatory and satisfying. In terms of generating new material at rehearsals or putting the albums together, Gordon felt less involved in the process.

"We were great at making decisions and steering our career and talking openly and being disciplined and having a sense of vision to see it to incredible heights," he continued. "But for me the piece that was missing was sort of a creative—not indulgence, but when you're fully immersed in something. So my task now is to try to mature to the point where I can be as creative in collaboration [with Phish] as I've been on my own," he concluded.

The point is not to blame McConnell for rocking the boat or Gordon for finding other boats to sail, because their issues were largely valid ones. McConnell, for instance, had some understandable frustrations about being in a group that was fronted by an increasingly dysfunctional leader in its later years.

It's a familiar story: mounting drug use, natural imbalances in power, and years of living in close quarters fuel grievances to the breaking point. There's also simply a natural cycle, a rise and fall, in the lifespan of every organic entity, including (and especially) rock groups. After twenty years, it wasn't surprising that internal issues would tear the fabric binding Phish together.

In contemplating the career arc of musical entities—especially dynamic and gifted ones like Phish—I'm reminded of passages from Oswald Spengler's *The Decline of the West*, in which he employs biological metaphors to describe the life cycles of great cultures throughout history. A rock band like Phish, which attracted an entire community to it, giving rise to a unique set of beliefs and lifestyle, is a subculture to which the same principles apply. Spengler wrote of the "majestic wave cycles" by which cultures swell and swamp the ordinary with their creative power. He also foretells their inevitable demise:

> A culture is born in the moment when a great soul awakens out of the proto-spirituality of ever-childish humanity, and detaches itself, a form from the formless. . . . It dies when this soul has actualized the full sum of its possibilities. . . . But its living existence . . . is an inner passionate struggle to maintain the idea against the powers of chaos without and the unconscious muttering deep down within. It is not only the artist who struggles against the existence of the material and the stifling of the idea within him. Every culture stands in a deeply symbolical, almost in a mystical, relationship to the Extended, the space, in which and through it strives to actualize itself. The aim once attained—the idea, the entire content of inner possibilities, fulfilled and made externally actual—the culture suddenly hardens, it mortifies, its blood congeals, its force breaks down.

Ergo, Phish at Coventry, if you want to apply the theories of a controversial German historian to a troubled twenty-first-century rock festival. And why not? The inevitability of Spengler's worldview is not incompatible with Trey Anastasio's outcome in the make-believe world of *Gamehendge*.

To this day, the mere mention of Coventry is enough to strike fear in the hearts of Phish fans. It was the finale from hell. Anastasio was in poor shape, and this mud- and muck-filled weekend did not make an ideal exit scenario for spirits already dampened by the knowledge that this was the last hurrah. Among some Phishheads, Anastasio had become a villain for bringing an end to the good times and community that had formed around Phish. Some at Coventry wore T-shirts that read "BeTREYed" and "Trey Is Wilson" (Wilson being the evil overlord of *Gamehendge* who confiscates and withholds the source of the protagonists' way of life).

One of the art installations inadvertently expressed the out-of-kilter aspect of the scene within and without in its topsy-turvy later stages. Trees had been dug up and replanted upside-down, with their roots in the air. They looked kind of cool, with the root-system canopies resembling the tops of palm trees. But it was a bit like karma stood on its head: the opposite of the way things ought to be, upside-down, out of sync, and unhealthy. One fan posted this note on the Phantasy Tour Web site: "At Coventry, I don't know how many times I heard, 'Got your coke . . . got your meth . . . got your Oxys.'"

Summing up the scene, another disgruntled blogger described Coventry as "a mass of 70,000 screaming fans getting their final look at a bunch of dorks who took about half of their disposable incomes."

If the rain-soaked and mud-caked Phishheads were having a hard time at Coventry, it wasn't much more comfortable in the areas set aside for friends, family, and hangers-on, either. The thousands of them on Phish's VIP guest list couldn't be accommodated in the VIP parking and camping area, which had flooded. Between the rain and bad vibes, many guests left early or bagged Coventry altogether. Much of the planning had been designed to accommodate the small city of guests in the pampered manner to which they'd grown accustomed. Afterward, Anastasio estimated the bloated guest list at 3,500. Others say less. Some say it was more.

Coventry almost didn't happen at all. The Vermont State Police felt strongly that it should be canceled. Phish's management puzzled over how to handle the situation as it worsened by the minute.

"It's one of those events that when it's happening in real time, it's so surreal," recalled manager Paluska. "It's kind of like you're in triage, doing the absolute best you can but it's so far beyond controlling. It was like a mini Hurricane Katrina: Everything was happening too fast, coming apart at the seams and falling apart."

Fortunately, Sgt. Bruce Melendy of the Vermont State Police—who was roused from bed and sent up to Coventry at 4 A.M. to help sort out the mess—could clearly see that canceling the festival on the day it was supposed to begin would have been the worst thing they could have done, stranding 30,000 people in a mudhole and possibly sparking a riot. In addition, though this didn't figure into his thinking, shutting it down wouldn't have been fair to the tens of thousands of people who'd traveled from all over the world and were already there.

The compromise solution was to let the festival go on with the 30,000 who were there and to close the highways, forcing the 30,000 who were still trying to get in to turn around and go home. It didn't quite work out like that. The Phishheads marched down the highway to the festival site. The sun came out, and the show went on.

Acknowledging Gordon's loyal opposition to their breakup, Phish opened the first set on the final night at Coventry with "Mike's Song." About the best thing you can say about the sets they played that weekend was that they got through them. The biggest buzz had to do with speculation over what song they'd finish with. Given that this was ostensibly a breakup and not a hiatus, it would be the last song these four musicians ever played together, for all the audience knew. The final number was, in fact, "The Curtain (With)," a compositionally and improvisationally inspiring early song and a fitting one with which to drop the curtain. Among its lyrics: "Please me have no regrets."

In a conversation held almost exactly a year later, Anastasio recalled the experience of playing at Coventry: "Leading to it was so confusing and so dark, and Coventry itself was such a nightmare. It was emotional, but it was not like we were at our finest. I certainly wasn't."

As soon as the festival ended, his wife, Sue, spirited him and their daughters to the airport, where they jetted off for a recuperative ten-day family trip to Bermuda.

"I didn't want to be around for the aftermath," he said. "When we got to Bermuda, I slept for like a week. And that was it."

"It was a very hard way to end," acknowledged Paluska. "Really hard. It was tough for that to be our final act."

Coventry was just one bad—well, disastrous—gig in the twenty-one-year lifespan of a group that had performed 1,400-plus shows that were good to great to off-the-charts. To put it all in perspective—and by "all," I mean the scene in toto: the community of band, crew, staff, and fans—I'd like to relate a story about the quixotic journey of a Phishhead. If it were presented in song-lyric form, it might be titled "The Ballad of Mike Meanwell." It was an amazing odyssey related by Beth Montuori Rowles, who has worked for Phish since 1995.

One day Phish's office staff received an inquiry from the father of a Phishhead who had died in a fiery car crash close to home. The father knew how much Phish had meant to his son, whose name was Mike Meanwell. The father asked a favor of the organization in his memory: Could they put a tin with a few of his ashes onstage at a show?

Rowles picks up the story:

I said, "Sure, I can do that, that's pretty easy." I was thinking, "I can put his ashes in my pocket and walk onto the side of the stage." The father sent me one of those little stash tins that we sell—which was kind of funny, 'cause I don't think he actually realized what it was used for—with some of the kid's ashes in it. So I went to several shows on that last tour, and I basically told the crew guys I had this kid's ashes with me. And we had them on the soundboard. We had them on the monitor board. At one show—I think it was Great Woods— Brian Brown [Anastasio's guitar tech] took the ashes and touched them to each of Trey's guitars. There were things like that that went on during that whole tour.

I had him in my backpack the whole time at Coventry, and every single time [*pauses*] . . . It was really difficult on a lot of levels for the people employed by the band, because they were about to move on. We knew people were going to move and exodus from Vermont like crazy. These were the people you spent every day with, so it was really hard. And every time I started thinking about how horrible it was, I would think about Mike Meanwell and think, "This really isn't all that bad. This could be so much worse. This is just life moving on; this is what happens. It happens all the time. We'll get through this. It could be so much worse, 'cause here's Mike sitting in my backpack." And it really helped me. I tell you, it really helped me.

After the whole thing was over, I got back in touch with his father, told him what we'd done, and asked, "Do you want me to send the ashes back?" He said, "No, you can dispose of them however you see fit." So we went out one night—me and my husband, David; Kevin Shapiro; and Jared Slomoff, who works for the band—and we all read Phish lyrics that were meaningful to the situation. We had a little ceremony and cast the ashes into Lake Champlain, right off Burlington.

The machine was winding down, and Coventry was where it came to rest. In a sense, the ensuing breakup actually turned out to be the *real* hiatus, in terms of addressing unresolved issues of physical health, interpersonal relations, and business arrangements.

In the immediate aftermath of Coventry, virtually everyone was let go. Former Phish employees recall the frequent going-away parties over the next year as many of them found it necessary to leave Vermont to look for work. The organization that had taken two decades to build was now dismantled with haste, like the art tower that got torched at the Great Went.

Mike Gordon subsequently rethought his opinion of the breakup. "As most people know I was the one who was clearly against breaking up when we did it, and I even have a picture of Trey wearing the 'Mike Says No' T-shirt," he said in April 2008. "The fans kind of liked me for that and at first were giving Trey a hard time for being the biggest instigator of the breakup. But I think over time they've seen that it had to see its course. And with me, I've found it in some ways the easiest, the breakup.

"My Phish career is incredibly—I can't say enough about how rich a career it had been, in terms of the depth of experiences that I never imagined a human could even go through. I thought that I had the best job in America that a person could have because (a) to be a rock star, sort of, but (b) to be in a jam band where you can actually have fun with the music and improvise, and then (c) to be the bass player, where I can be subconscious about it and not have to do soloing and stuff just seemed incredible."

At the end of 2004, even though the band had broken up and Dionysian Productions had dissolved, Phish held their annual Christmas party at a restaurant called The Waiting Room in Burlington. The band, management, and local crew guys all came.

"It was really fun," recalled Megan Criss, the office manager. "And we all took a group picture. I don't remember it feeling like a farewell party."

Over the next few years, the Phish family scattered and found their way into other areas of the music industry. For instance, Chris Kuroda has been lighting director for artists as varied as the Black Crowes, R. Kelly, and Aerosmith, while Brad Sands has road-managed Gov't Mule, The Police, Les Claypool, and Anastasio's pre-bust solo tours. Meanwhile, Phish's office dwindled to a skeleton staff and then just one skeleton. At one point, the only person whose checks read "Phish Inc." was Kevin Shapiro, their archivist.

Manager John Paluska watched the end arrive with a mixture of sadness and acceptance.

"I learned a lesson in 1996, after the Clifford Ball," he recollected. "It was such a high and such an amazing experience. But as soon as it was over, it didn't exist anymore, it was gone. I remember walking around the day after everybody was gone, and it was just a bunch of garbage and a lot of cleanup and petty hassles that had to get resolved, and that was such a downer after such an amazing event.

"Once I made my peace with all that, I realized, 'You know what? It's all about process.' It was a great life lesson. The process of creating that festival was amazing, and then when it's over you move on to the next thing. You don't dwell on it, you don't try to hold on to it. You just let it slip through, because it doesn't exist anyway. I guess it's a Buddhist perspective, which is very appealing to me these days.

"So by the time the office had closed, I'd reached a place of seeing things that way—that it had been an amazing ride, and everything has an end, and the end is a new beginning to something else. We had reached the point where people were tired. It was sad to see all the intangible value that the office collectively represented taken apart, because so much work went into creating the relationships and the way it functioned. But it was time for something new."

Meanwhile, the larger jam-band scene went into remission as well. None of Phish's musical peers—Widespread Panic, String Cheese Incident, Umphrey's McGee, moe.—filled the void after their demise. String Cheese Incident disbanded, too. There were even deaths in the jam-band world. Widespread lost one of its founding members, guitarist Michael Hauser, to pancreatic cancer. Blues Traveler lost bassist Bobby Sheehan to a drug overdose. The commercial peak of the jam-band phenomenon, in terms of CD sales and airplay, came in 1994 when Blues Traveler's "Run-Around" and the album it appeared on, *Four*, both reached No. 8 on the singles and album charts. *Four* wound up selling more than 6 million copies, making it the best-selling album by a second-generation jam band. That's not to say success in the jam-band world was defined by CD sales and chart positions. Concert tickets were the bottom line, but even on the road there was stagnation and retrenchment. A dozen years after the first H.O.R.D.E. tour put the jam-band world on the map, the scene was starting to play itself out.

For one thing, there were too many festivals. Following in Phish's wake, nearly every jam band had its own festival. Disco Biscuits had Camp Bisco, moe. had their annual "moedown," and Yonder Mountain String Band (for whom Jon Fishman would guest on drums after Phish's breakup) had the Northwest String Summit. It was simply too much.

Unlike the Grateful Dead (with "Touch of Grey") or Blues Traveler (with "Run-Around"), Phish didn't have the spike of a hit single that led to multi-platinum album sales. Their best-selling albums, *Hoist* and *A Live One*, sold around 650,000 copies. After the breakup, some in and around Phish felt that Elektra could have done better with the band.

Jon Fishman said as much in interviews, insinuating that Elektra didn't really get the band or its audience. Jason Colton expressed mixed feelings: "Elektra had some people at the very top who never understood the band at all. Some of their ideas were so absurdly off-base we thought they were kidding. Fortunately, there were key people for the majority of the band's time there that completely got it and made the process feel more like a partnership than a struggle."

Mike Gordon took a charitable view of Elektra.

"I always felt good about that relationship," he said. "We never sold 3 million copies of an album, and you could always argue that maybe some other record company would've found some way to do it. But probably not. We were doing our own thing.

"I don't personally remember getting too much pressure," he continued. "I don't really ever remember Elektra saying 'You have to be a certain way.' If we had just said, 'Well, we're never going to get a major label because we're afraid of what it might take away from our integrity' and 'Our path is on our own,' then we would've missed out on our exposure. We were already so isolated that just to be tied in with the industry was good. I'm not a genius on any of this, but I would say Elektra was really good."

After the breakup, the group founded their own label: JEMP Records (as in *J*on, *E*rnest, *M*ike, and *P*age), named after the logo on their panel truck circa 1991–1993. Ernest, of course, is Ernest Joseph Anastasio III, better known as Trey. JEMP was registered in November 2005 and began appearing on LivePhish and other archival releases. Their latest album, *Joy*, appeared on JEMP, too.

After Anastasio posted his unequivocal breakup announcement in May 2004, he expressed second thoughts on a few occasions. After a stellar second set on June 19 at the Saratoga Performing Arts Center (in Saratoga Springs, New York), he told Gordon, "If we could play like this every night, I would play forever!" In a *Guitar World* interview, he allowed that Phish could regroup as a new band with a new repertoire and a new name—like "Phowl."

Eight months after Coventry, Anastasio and Gordon shared a stage in New Orleans, performing Hank Williams Jr.'s "Old Habits" ("old habits like you are hard to break") and other songs. Half a year after that, in November 2005, McConnell sat in with Anastasio on some Phish songs at a solo-band show. ("Halfway there," remarked Anastasio.) Later that same month, Anastasio, Gordon, and Fishman played "The Divided Sky" onstage. That one was "nearly there."

In 2005, Anastasio released a new album (*Shine*) on a new label (Columbia). Everything about his situation seemed new. His career was now being handled by Coran Capshaw—manager of the Dave Matthews Band and others—whose Red Light Management is headquartered in Charlottesville, Virginia. Capshaw has had his hands in all sorts of music-related ventures: Bonnaroo (which he started), ATO Records (whose artists included Gomez, My Morning Jacket, and Gov't Mule), and the Music Today merchandise and fan-club company (which he sold to Live Nation). With his hands in all those kinds of pies and sterling track record with Dave Matthews, Capshaw seemed a logical choice as manager for Anastasio after the disbanding of Phish and dissolution of Dionysian Productions.

"I knew Coran when Dave Matthews was playing in clubs," Anastasio elaborated. "Coran was at the Clifford Ball and Coventry. He's been around the whole time. He's a great guy but he's also the only person who could've stepped in at this point in time with the sense of history." Incidentally, Jason Colton—Paluska's right-hand man at Dionysian Productions—moved to Red Light, where he works with Anastasio, Fishman, and Gordon as solo artists and is again involved with Phish.

The recording of *Shine* started out as a fiasco. Originally Anastasio was working with Bryce Goggin, a veteran of numerous Phish and Anastasio solo projects who had to drop out when his wife had a baby. That's when he was paired with Rick Beato (who's produced such acts as Shinedown and I-9). "I proceeded to spend about four months and piles of money and piles of time away from home working with a guy who essentially turned out to be, as far as I'm concerned, like a nut," said Anastasio. "It was really bizarre." Beato also assembled 70-Volt Parade, an ill-fated backing band for Anastasio.

On the second go-round, *Shine* came together smoothly under the direction of Brendan O'Brien, who is among the top producers in the country, having worked with everyone from Pearl Jam to Bruce Springsteen. But then this seemingly jinxed record wound up being saddled, as were half a dozen other albums released at the same time, with a draconian new form of "copyright protection." It contained a dreaded "rootkit"—a program similar to viruses or spyware that creates security vulnerabilities. Rootkits can be used by hackers to take over a computer and use its resources (though this was not Sony's intention). When a first-pressing CD of *Shine* was inserted into a home computer or laptop, Sony's rootkit installed itself. There was a hue and cry in the national media when this came to light. Blasted with bad publicity, Columbia Records' parent company, Sony, offered free online software that removed the offending program. The label also replaced consumers' copies with new discs that were free of copyright control. Fallout from the rootkit controversy no doubt impacted sales of *Shine*, and even though the problem was fixed, the moment was lost.

This was a shame because *Shine* was an inspired piece of work. The inspiration was largely the ending and aftermath of Phish, during which Anastasio claimed a lot of anger was directed at him by former employees and Phishheads. In fact, he refers to it as the "anger period."

For the first time in many years, Anastasio did not collaborate with Tom Marshall. He wrote all the lyrics on *Shine* himself. Why?

"I had a lot I wanted to say," Anastasio explained, "'cause everybody around me was just acting like the fucking world was gonna come to an end. I can't tell you how many Phish fans were saying, 'I'm never gonna hear good music again.'"

Some of the songs came directly out of unpleasant encounters with disgruntled former employees.

"'Black' was actually a response to a particular conversation I had with one person," Anastasio said. "I was having a lot of them at the time, 'cause people were mad so they were taking this chance, you know—'Okay, now you're letting me go. Well, I've been wanting to say this to you for the last ten years anyway, you fucking asshole'— stuff like that. A lot of people worked for us up in Burlington. I had this one conversation with somebody that was just really harsh. Something somebody was unloading on me, which I was getting about twenty of those a day. I just went home and it was just like *boom*, wrote the whole thing."

His musings returned him to the band's origins. "It was just some people from Burlington, but something started to happen that was really beautiful," said Anastasio. "I loved to watch the expressions on people's faces as they got really lit up. I saw there really is a connection to the light. It all sounds kinda New Agey or something, but I've experienced it enough times to believe that it's actually true. Now as soon as you start thinking you can't change because you've figured

out a way to connect to that light, so you gotta keep doing that—
that's it, you're dead.

"What's really hard to explain to people that once you find a connection to the light, clinging to it is not the answer and in a lifetime it's exactly the opposite from the answer. There's a poem by William Blake
that I love, and it goes, 'He who binds himself to a joy / Does the winged
life destroy / But he who kisses it as it flies / Lives in eternity's sunrise.'"

Two years into the breakup, more sharing of stages fueled talk and whet-
ted Phishheads' appetite for a reunion. In July 2006, for instance, everyone but Jon Fishman congregated onstage in Vermont for a cover of
"Who Are You?" by the Who. That fall, Anastasio made statements like
"We're not necessarily done," and he had the whole band over to his
house for dinner. It was the first time in over two years—since Coventry, in fact—that all four of them had been in the same room.

And then . . . he got busted.

Anastasio was stopped at 3:30 A.M. on December 15, 2006, while driving through the village of Whitehall, New York, near the Vermont state
line. The officer noticed that Anastasio was driving erratically on U.S. 4
north. Presumably, he was heading home to Richmond, Vermont, eighty
miles away. (He divided his time between there and an apartment on
the upper East Side of Manhattan, where his wife and daughters were
living.) He failed a field sobriety test. The arresting officer found three
prescription drugs—Vicodin, Percocet, and Xanax, for which he had no
prescription, in his late-model Audi. Heroin was also found in the car.

Anastasio told Whitehall's chief of police, "You know what? I've
got a drug problem, and I've got to take care of it. Everything happens
for a reason."

"He's a real nice guy," said the gendarme.

Rolling Stone referred to the booking photo taken of Anastasio that
night as "the most bemused mug shot ever." This image soon turned
up on T-shirts, amusing some of the more twisted members of Phish
nation.

"I feel terrible about what happened last night, and I am deeply sorry for any embarrassment I have caused my friends, family, and fans," Anastasio said in a brief prepared statement.

Leading up to the bust, there had been signs, once again, that all was not well. For instance, an odd exchange appeared in *Rolling Stone* a few months before the bust.

AUSTIN SCAGGS: What secrets have you learned for survival on the road?

TREY: I'm starting to get it figured out now. There are a few simple rules. Don't spend all your time freebasing cocaine—that's gonna make your tour a lot shorter. It was getting ridiculous there for a while, and it was showing. So on the last tour, I reeled it in. And get at least five hours of sleep every third night.

Perhaps this statement was less an amusing exaggeration than the reckless truth (and even, on some level, a cry for help).

I asked Phish's former manager, John Paluska—now living in northern California and working for the Biomimicry Ventures Group—if he was surprised to learn about Anastasio's bust with such a dangerous pharmacopeia two years after the band's breakup.

"No."

A long pause followed before he resumed.

"Trey's personality is not particularly well-suited to fame," said Paluska. "I don't mean that in a negative way at all. He's such a warm and giving person. He didn't like to disappoint people, and he often assumed that he might be. I remember him saying at Coventry something to the effect that 'I feel like I'm letting everybody down. I walk onstage, I feel like I'm letting those people down. I walk around backstage, and I feel like I'm pulling the plug on this thing and everybody, you know. . . . '

"That was how he saw it. Over time, imagine the pressure of that, the intensity of that. I think I can make a generalization that those kinds of outcomes are just symptoms. They just illustrate how much mental strain goes with being in the position that those guys are. It's very difficult. The notion of being able to check out and get a break from it starts to look very appealing as the pressure builds. And then it's a slippery slope."

At a court hearing on January 3, 2007, Anastasio pleaded not guilty to possession of a controlled substance and driving while intoxicated. Because of the quantity of drugs involved, the district attorney convened a grand jury, which returned seven charges against him: one count of felony drug possession, two counts of felony driving under the influence of alcohol and drugs, three misdemeanor charges of drug possession, and a traffic infraction. He faced up to fourteen years in prison if convicted on all counts.

Four months later he signed a plea agreement in Judge Kelly S. McKeighan's drug-treatment court in Fort Edward, New York. On a morning in mid-April—Friday the 13th, as fate would have it—Anastasio pleaded guilty to fifth-degree attempted criminal possession of a controlled substance. In return he was required to undergo a drug-treatment program for twelve to fifteen months.

Drug treatment required weekly court appearances, along with drug counseling and community service. He was required to move within an hour of Fort Edward for the first three months for random drug testing. The Glen Falls *Post Star* broke the news with this lead: "A world-renowned rock star will move to the area in the coming days, and he'll be staying at least three months."

The consequences of failing to complete the program were severe and unequivocal: If he failed, he would receive a one-to three-year prison sentence. On the other hand, if he succeeded, the sentence would be dropped to five years of probation. However, if at any time in the next ten years he was convicted of another felony, a prison sentence would be mandatory.

Anastasio made the most of his opportunity. He'd always exhibited tremendous self-discipline when it came to the creative process— witness twenty years of prodigious song output, rigorous practice, and a legacy of nearly 1,500 Phish performances and hundreds more with his various solo bands and side projects. But regimentation imposed from outside, which he'd never really accepted or dealt with in his life, was the only realistic way to get the monkey of multiple addictions off his back. In the program, he did everything that was asked of him, including embracing the "higher power" concept that's a fundamental tenet of twelve-step programs.

He made one misstep, showing up late for a required counseling session. It wasn't because he'd relapsed; apparently, he'd gotten tied up in traffic. Still the judge was unyielding in insisting on absolute compliance, and Anastasio spent two nights in the lockup for this infraction. The stay, where he circulated among the general prison population, was described as "uneventful."

During his fourteen-month program in Washington County drug court, he cleaned up the county fairground, getting a taste of the world of humbling physical labor that existed on the other side of the stage lights. He internalized the lesson in a positive way.

He also seemed to be lightening his load. He changed the mission of the Barn—the mountainside studio that had served as his and Phish's recording studio, rehearsal space, and tree fort—in 2006, launching the Seven Below Arts Initiative (after the song "Seven Below," from *Round Room*). Now the Barn serves as a place where artists-in-residence live and work for terms of several months. Seven Below also provides arts education to underserved populations in Burlington.

Shortly after his prison weekend, Anastasio told *Rolling Stone*: "When Phish broke up I made some comment about how I'm not going to go around playing 'You Enjoy Myself' the rest of my life. . . . It's not so much I can't believe that I said that, but it's symbolic of how much I lost my mind or how much I lost my bearings or something. Because at this point in time I would give my left nut to play that song five times in a row every day until I die."

That was a far cry from "we're done," and it fanned hopes for Phish's return. The "left nut" quote lived on, inspiring the title of the bonus CD of unreleased live material from Walnut Creek Amphitheatre given away with preorders for the live DVD *Walnut Creek* on the band's Web site. Originally thinking they'd call it *Leftover Walnuts*, they shortened it to *Left Nuts*.

On the back cover of his solo album, *Bar 17*, released in fall 2006, Anastasio is pictured walking out of a tunnel. The photo was taken in Central Park, near the Upper East Side apartment where he and his family moved in 2005. A few footsteps ahead of him is the light. This hopeful image seemed obviously and perfectly symbolic of the corner he would soon turn in his life and the brighter days that awaited him—and Phish.

EIGHT

Reunion:
2008–2009

The four members of Phish reunited onstage on May 4, 2008, in New York City. They hadn't come to play but to accept a Lifetime Achievement Award at the Jammys (the Grammys of the jam-band world). Three days earlier, Trey Anastasio's mentor, Ernie Stires, had died of a heart attack at his home in Cornwall, Vermont. He was eighty-three years old. Anastasio referred to Stires in his speech at the Jammys.

"So much of that unique sound you heard with Phish was taught to me by him," said Anastasio of Stires.

He also touched on the Phish experience in broader terms:

"I want to express something that's been on my mind for the last five years," said Anastasio. "I've always wanted to somehow have a moment when I could convey to some degree what all of this meant to me and I know to the other guys, too.

"It always felt like we were part of something that was so much bigger than the four of us. I think in retrospect it feels like it was even bigger than our group of friends and our scene. It felt almost like a cultural kind of timing thing. As a musician, I feel like we're servants, and that musicians from the beginning of time have been there to express the mood and the musical feelings in the air for whatever's going on in that particular culture, whether it's like rock and roll or swing band music. You play at weddings, you play at funerals, and it's the greatest joy as a musician to be able to translate that, be part of something, and watch the scenery around you. That's what it felt like being in Phish all those years."

As it turned out, it wasn't only Anastasio who'd received tutoring from Stires. Mike Gordon visited Stires a few times in 2008, not long before he passed away.

"I was working on some composition stuff and getting really inspired by him, 'cause he's such a musical genius," Gordon recalled. On one such trip, he taped their conversation, which focused on his philosophy of composition and his general disdain for rock and roll.

"He wasn't really into rock and roll, because most rock bands use a simple melody and don't take the effort to do interesting stuff to accompany it," Gordon explained. "He thinks that music gains its essence in the harmony, in the harmonization more than the melody. Usually people would say the essence is in the melody, so that was pretty interesting to think about."

Stires's original approach to music merged aspects of jazz, as a performer's medium, and classical, as a composer's realm. Nowhere did his vision resonate into the world more than his influence on Anastasio and therefore Phish's repertoire. By extension, his philosophy got disseminated—though few may have realized it—among anyone who's ever enjoyed Phish's music.

The "braphecy" came true. The brotherhood of Phishheads who'd been prophesying a reunion apparently were reading the right tea leaves. The signs and symbols had been accumulating throughout summer 2008.

In June, Page McConnell posted a letter to Phish fans in response to reunion rumors. In it, he was both candid and encouraging: "I'm living a healthy lifestyle. I travel as little as possible and I sleep in my own bed. It took a couple of years after the breakup to begin talking to my old bandmates, but once the conversations began to flow, it wasn't long before the friendships were rekindled. And I can honestly say that I'm closer with all of them now than I've ever been in our 20-year relationship."

Over the 4th of July weekend, three band members were present for different reasons at the Rothbury Festival in Western Michigan. Anastasio and Gordon guested during each other's solo sets, and two new Anastasio–Marshall songs ("Backwards Down the Number Line," and "Alaska") were played that day. Jon Fishman joined in on drums for a set-closing cover of the Beatles' "She Said She Said," making it a three-quarters reunion. On September 6, the entire band performed three songs at the wedding of longtime road manager and friend Brad Sands. The tune selection—"Julius," "Suzy Greenberg," "Waste"—was less important than the gesture, which sent fans into a feeding frenzy. They were now fully there.

The reunion became official when this brief statement, followed by ticketing info, was posted on Phish.com on October 1: "Phish returns to the stage for three concerts at the Hampton Coliseum in Hampton, Virginia on March 6, 7 and 8, 2009." This trickle erupted into a torrent on January 7, 2009, when Phish announced plans for a two-part summer tour. Among those dates were two shows at Bonnaroo 2009. While it might seem like they—or Anastasio—had cried wolf by packaging their 2004 breakup with such seeming finality, the forgiving fans were glad to have them back, alive and healthy. In fact, demand for tickets briefly shut down both Ticketmaster's and Live Nation's online service.

Phish spent a few months working hard at a rehearsal space in New York City to ready themselves for their return.

On Friday, March 6, 2009, at around 8 P.M., Phish walked onto the stage of the Hampton Coliseum, in Hampton, Virginia. It was the foursome's first show since August 15, 2004—going on five years. The roar of welcome that greeted them was deafening. They had a strong opening gambit: "Fluffhead," including the six-part "Fluff's Travels," an extremely difficult piece of music whose precise delivery would demonstrate that they had their chops together. They performed the various sections nearly flawlessly. The roar of approval that greeted its conclusion sixteen minutes later was even louder. "Fluffhead" was just the start of two straight hours of music—an unheard-of length for a first set.

It made a resounding statement: After all the complications and time off, Phish was back. The general consensus was that Phish was once again playing with precision and focus. The chatter among Phishheads on the floor of Hampton was animated and approving: "Do you believe this?" "Can you believe how crisp they sound?" "They haven't sounded this good in [ten or twelve or fifteen] years."

Page McConnell was playing completely out of his mind.

Anastasio was obviously well in his right mind.

Fishman and Gordon were solid, Zen-like, and controlled as they anchored the band.

Everyone was exactly where they needed to be.

The group seemed to be back in that fugal frame of mind where four strong, independent voices meshed as one. Chris Kuroda was back on lights, locked in as well as ever, creating unprecedented visual panoramas to accompany the music.

The jams made room for all four members. Their complementary musicianship recalled all those collective-improv practice sessions where they'd honed their skill to a fine point in the first half of the nineties. Moreover, they'd figured out a way for McConnell to be an assertive instrumental voice without necessitating that Anastasio recede ambiently into the background. In fact, McConnell was probably the biggest surprise and the MVP of the three-night run, with his assertive yet integrated playing.

Over those three nights, they played long shows and lots of songs. The jams themselves weren't so very long—no fifty-minute "Tweezer" or jammed-together strings of songs. The sheer number of songs performed was impressive: twenty-eight on Friday, twenty-seven on Saturday, thirty (if you count "Happy Birthday," which they sang to Fishman's dad) on Sunday. Nearly ninety songs, and not a single repeat. And they sounded sharp and tight, executing the hairpin-turn shifts in the composed sections with aplomb.

Hampton is an old survivor of a coliseum—an oval-shaped small arena dating from 1970, which was roughly the dawn of the arena-rock era. It was entirely appropriate that Phish, a band of survivors themselves, chose to launch their reunion there.

Countless bands have played there, and Phish's epic stands would rate among its greatest moments. Counting the reunion stand, Phish has performed fifteen nights at Hampton Coliseum since 1995, including three of their first four post-hiatus reunion shows in 2003.

Hampton came even more alive in March 2009, when Phish proved beyond a shadow of a doubt that they were a band reborn. Demand for tickets was so great that people were paying as much as $1,000 per night. Hampton's big, swampy bowl of a main floor was packed sardine-tight with delirious Phishheads. Despite the lack of elbow room, people found a way to dance. And everyone was friendly. I'd forgotten that part of it: falling into conversations with strangers like you'd known them all your life. Sharing facts, trivia, road stories, and the excitement of having Phish back in the house.

The band didn't talk much to the audience. The music, and the effort and energy they put into it, said plenty. Before the encore on the final night, Anastasio did step to the mike to utter a few words: "This has been an incredible weekend," he said, and 14,000 tired but jubilant fans roared their agreement. "Obviously, it's felt a lot like a reunion … family members and friends, all of us together again … "

Sharing in the groove.

The good vibes and solid playing resumed in the summer with a tour kickoff at Boston's Fenway Park (their first supersized stadium show). In Asheville, I sat behind the stage, where I got a close view of the interactions among the band members and the faces of the crowd pressed against the rail. Onstage, Anastasio stood between Gordon (to his left) and McConnell (ensconced among banks of keyboards to his right). It was a return to their classic Nectar's set up. There was much conferring among the three of them between songs, with Anastasio walking back and forth to consult with each of them and Gordon relaying the group's next move to Fishman. One couldn't help but notice the shared smiles and relaxed demeanor. Anastasio's posture, and constantly tapping foot, conveyed his contentment and engagement.

Several nights after Asheville, Phish performed two shows at the Bonnaroo Music Festival, outside Manchester, Tennessee. Even though Bonnaroo was basically built from the blueprint of Phish's festival campouts, Phish had never before played there as a group. Their first show at Bonnaroo broke new musical ground and their second show at Bonnaroo 2009 made a bit of history, as Phish performed for three hours, including a three-song mini-set with Bruce Springsteen. They did spirited versions of Wilson Pickett's "Mustang Sally" and two old favorites by the Boss: "Bobby Jean" and "Glory Days." It was another memorable moment in a career full of them.

The projects started coming fast and furious as Phish gained momentum. In early September came the release of a new album, *Joy* (their first studio album in five years). On a personal front, Anastasio took his boldest step yet into the world of classical-rock fusion by performing with the New York Philharmonic at Carnegie Hall in September. Phish announced a three-day festival in California at the end of October. Festival 8, as it was dubbed, combined an outdoor campout concert marathon with a chance to cover another artist's album on Halloween. Who would disagree that a world with a healthy Phish in it is a better place?

As Mike Gordon put it, "We've come up with a body of music that is unique, and we've developed a way of going on musical adventures on a regular basis and brought a lot of people along with us.

"It's a very rare and lucky occupation and combination of people. Just a uniquely fortunate situation."

EPILOGUE

An Interview with Trey Anastasio

I spoke with Trey Anastasio in July 2009, after I'd finished—or thought I'd finished—this book. We had last talked prior to the release of his solo album *Shine*, and then came the bust and a period of years during which he worked hard on getting himself together. It was good to talk with him again under such positive circumstances.

We began with the new beginning, discussing Phish's three-night run of shows in Hampton, Virginia, which kicked off their reunion in March 2009. As the conversation unfolded, Anastasio spoke openly and emotionally about the changes that life has brought in recent years. The word *gratitude* came up quite a bit. So did the word *happy*.

ME: I saw the reunion shows at Hampton Coliseum. I did not want to miss that moment when you all came onstage and hit the first note on the first night. Describe that moment from your perspective.

ANASTASIO: It felt great. The most exciting thing for me was that all seven kids were onstage. They might have been a little hidden, but they were in the back corner. The reason I bring that up is because when we left the stage at Coventry, there were 3,500 people on the guest list. No exaggeration. Our scene had devolved to where it was eating itself. At Hampton, there were approximately ten people backstage, and seven of them were our kids. And it was such a relief. It was quiet backstage. I had my wife and my kids with me. It was all family, and everything just seemed to be back to normal.

Not that we don't love all of our friends, and there were many of our friends at the Hampton shows. But the most important thing to me was that we managed to get back on track. We had a practice room backstage. We were working on music. We weren't socializing. And it showed, I think. That's the way the whole tour's been going, and it's made me very happy. When we went onstage, I saw a lot of people I knew in the audience. It all just felt . . . I was moved and filled with gratitude to be back with my friends playing music again.

Over the four years we were apart, everybody took time to get their personal lives back on track. The fact is, we'd started at the age of eighteen and had been going at a ferocious pace without a real break. I mean, we took that hiatus, but I just went right back on the road during the hiatus without a real break. It's a much more healthy atmosphere, and it's made me so happy. I really can't describe how filled with gratitude and happy I was at those three shows. And actually I've felt that way the entire the tour, every night.

ME: You talked about the backstage scene. I've known you guys long enough that when I first came in, it was more similar to what you're describing now than what it became from 1997 on. It was family and close friends backstage, and it wasn't a wild, overrun scene.

ANASTASIO: Not at all! I'm so glad you remember that. You know, I don't drink anymore, which is great for me. I'm thrilled about that and have been for years now, actually. Sometimes people will say, "Is it strange with the band?" And I say, "No, it's not strange at all. As a matter of fact, it's a lot stranger that that ever really happened. If you had been around, the amount of time that that *wasn't* going on was so much bigger than the amount of time that it was."

It all seems like it's back to normal. I think we just were not equipped—as so many people are not equipped—to contend with the tricky landscape of becoming big or famous. I don't like the word *big*, but whatever it was, we had it. We even had a bit of a naïve attitude toward employing people. Everyone was our friend and we loved to have our friends around, so we just said, "Hey, yeah, you can come back, too." I remember in '96 when we started playing arenas, there was nobody backstage, not one person. To the point where it was kind of boring, actually. [*laughs*] And then in '97 and '98, we opened the door, and there it went.

Anyway, when you take the distractions away, there's so much energy to focus on practicing and the show. So now, before the shows start, we find ourselves back in the practice room. One of my favorite parts of Phish is that when it's just the four of us practicing, there's such a deep sense of humor. I mean, everybody's laughing and cracking these jokes that you have to know all the previous references to get. It's like seven jokes deep. Mike will say three words, and it's referring to a joke that happened last year. It makes me really happy that we have the ability to have that time together.

ME: One of the things that you noted and mourned after the breakup was the fact that Phish had stopped practicing. You've actually said that you liked practicing as much as performing.

ANASTASIO: I do. Do you know that twentieth-anniversary film Mike made? Well, there's all these shots in there from band practice. Like when we're doing "All Things Reconsidered" and Fish falls down in front of the camera. That was our practice room in Winooski, and it just brought me right back. But now we are practicing. As a matter of fact, we're starting practice again in a couple of days.

It wasn't just that we weren't practicing as much. It was that practice had gone from being just the four of us to having a lot of crew members around. If you're a club band, you don't really have a big crew, so whatever. Then you become an arena band and there's a keyboard tech, bass tech, drum tech, guitar tech, soundman, monitor mixer, and so on. So it's kind of accepted that when you do band practice, all those guys come in, and they're all wonderful people, but it's just not the same. You'd think it would be simple for us to say, "You know, we'd prefer to practice alone in a little room, thank you." But we never really did that, and now we *are* doing that. When we practiced before Hampton, we got a little room with a Fender amp and said, "Have the guy from the studio unlock the door, and we'll lock it when we leave."

It's funny because I notice it in . . . I have a pretty strong personality versus Page, who's a little quieter. And when there are a lot of people around, he might not—he's different when it's just the four of us, and he's very, very smart and has a great point of view that is crucial to the decision-making dynamic. Page comes at things from a more rational point of view, and that's really important. When there's a bunch of people around, he might just retreat, and all of a sudden the whole balance is off. And that's when it falls apart.

That's at the base of what actually happened before. I remember a lot of frustration from Page, and there were times when I was thinking, "What is the problem here?" And now I get it. God's honest truth is that as long as the four of us are together and have a protected, quiet and comfortable atmosphere around us, then we can make decisions with the dynamic that has always existed.

ME: I have a philosophical question for you about risk-taking. You're a risk-taking musician, and personally, you know what it's like to take risks as well. How do you separate the two? Is it possible to separate creative risk-taking from personal risk-taking?

ANASTASIO: I think that today my view would be that a solid personal life and a solid spiritual life is a necessity for creative risk-taking. I feel very grounded today on a personal level, and yesterday we announced that I'm going to play with the New York Philharmonic at Carnegie Hall. I can tell you, that's a musical risk, and it's a pretty significant piece of music we're going to be playing.

That's why I keep mentioning how happy I was that my family was with me onstage. I feel so lucky to have this wonderful family, and I always wanted to find a way to combine family life with life on the road. That's tricky terrain, and it wasn't working out so well seven years ago and today it is. And lo and behold, here comes this big orchestral piece, "Time Turns Elastic," and Phish is playing long sets, and it's like a springboard.

ME: For Phish's second show at Bonnaroo this year, you played for three hours and were joined at one point by Bruce Springsteen.

ANASTASIO: A little singer-songwriter from New Jersey! That was a blast. He's a very nice guy.

ME: How did it work out that Springsteen appeared with you?

ANASTASIO: He was there and somebody said, "Do you want to go on Bruce's bus and meet him?" And I said, "Yeah, of course." My wife Sue grew up in Freehold, New Jersey. Jersey girl! Sue's dad—and this is a completely true story—sat next to Bruce's dad all through grammar school up until Freehold High, so they had a lot of mutual friends. So we got on the bus and Sue and Bruce started talking and names were flying. I kind of felt like a fly on the wall while they were talking. But we all got talking on the bus, and it was a thrill.

ME: When we spoke in 2004, it struck me that you had about as much on your plate as any one person could handle, just in terms of musical projects: working with an orchestra, your solo band, Dave Matthews, and, of course, Phish. I thought to myself,

"How does he do it?" and "Is this healthy?" Are you pacing your-self differently nowadays?

ANASTASIO: Well, I've spent the last three years working on my per-sonal health and my family. The last tour, we all went together for the whole tour. If you look at the calendar, tour started the day after school got out and ended when the kids' Shakespeare camp was about to begin. Then we're going back out, and it ends again before the school year starts. I'm not saying that's always going to be the case, but that was such a. . . . [*trails off*]

Crazy stuff happened in those last three years. Obviously, I publicly went through an arrest, and I had to stop and re-evaluate. I was racing around too fast, and I was putting my health last. And today I go to bed early and keep myself in shape. Most im-portantly, it's more about spiritual health than anything and try-ing to keep priorities in line. As long as I do that, everything else seems to not be a problem.

I just feel a lot of gratitude today. It's a subject that's constantly coming up among the band, that we're very lucky to still be to-gether with all four original members twenty-six years into our career. Fish has said to me a number of times that when Phish stopped, he didn't even know where he lived. He had a house, but he hadn't even really moved in because we were on the road all the time. We stopped, and he was able to move up to the place where he lives now. He lives on a beautiful farm with animals, and they've got three children. They're very settled in. Same with Mike. We stopped, he got married during the break, had his first child, built a studio in his home, and got his own band together so he could play outside of Phish. I think we all really had to do that, and when we come back together now, there's such a feeling of gratitude that we made it over a big hurdle.

ME: Do you see any reason Phish can't have longevity now?

ANASTASIO: I don't see any reason today not to believe that. But I think that today I'm really trying to—okay, one of the things with this last tour, I said, "Before I set foot on this tour, I'm going to set a rule for myself that whatever show we're playing is the only show. There is no tour." Because with all those projects you mentioned, I was getting really tired of spreading myself too thin, racing around and thinking of too many things at once. What I try to do now is look at one show, and it all seems to take care of itself.

I remember we were in St. Louis and somebody was asking, "Are you excited about Alpine Valley?" And my response was, "I'm in St. Louis. This is the most important show. This is it. Tomorrow may never come." So I think if you have that attitude, there's no reason that Phish couldn't go on for quite some time.

ME: As long as you take it one day at a time, right?

ANASTASIO: It's pretty much one day at a time. Am I talking like a sober guy now? [*laughs*] I could tell you right now that getting arrested in that car was the best thing that ever happened to me. I wrote a thank-you letter to that guy. Just to slow down and reassess and put everything back in its proper perspective.

ME: One of the best new songs, and it bears on the whole issue of survival and moving forward, is "Backwards Down the Number Line." Tom Marshall told me about sending it to you as a birthday poem, and that became the point where you two resumed your collaboration.

ANASTASIO: Yeah. And it's the first song on the new record. It *had* to be the first song on the record. I love that song. When I was in upstate New York, I wasn't actually allowed to leave my apartment for fourteen months. The first year, I basically didn't talk to anyone except my wife. Literally, no one. I just turned off the phone. I didn't visit with anyone. I couldn't, really, except for people I met in my tiny little world there. And it was such a necessary thing and a relief. It just had been such a whirlwind for twenty-three years.

I hadn't talked to Tom or anybody, really. I'd not really seen the guys in the band—I mean, I called Page every once in a while just to say hi. And then on my birthday Tom sent me this e-mail, which was "Backwards Down the Number Line," the lyrics. I had a multitrack, an eight-track machine, in my apartment, and I recorded the demo in about ten minutes.

The guys from Phish eventually came up a couple of months later, and we had dinner together for the first time since Coventry. We had seen each other before. Mike and I had gone on tour. But we hadn't been all together alone, and we went out to dinner, and it was such a great night.

I'm just thinking that song really summed up the way I feel about the guys in the band and stretching out to the people in our community and the Phish fans. I mean, it's all in there, with those lines about, "You decide what it contains / How long it goes / But this remains / The only rule is it begins / Happy happy, oh my friend." And, you know, "We pushed through hardships, tasted tears." It's really strange how it just emerged, *boom*! I couldn't wait to play it and invite everybody else back into the party.

ME: It's a real rebirth sort of song, and I have to say I almost got choked up when Phish played it for the first time.

ANASTASIO: I *was* choked up the first time we played it to the point I might have even missed a line or two. I still get choked up when I hear it.

ME: You've taken on new management, and the band appears to be deliberately traveling a lot lighter these days. Is that a fair statement?

ANASTASIO: Much lighter. It was a huge, enormously important change for us. That being said, can I say for the record that my dear friend John Paluska [who ran Dionysian Productions, Phish's original management company] is not only the most wonderful person and brilliant manager ever, but I miss my daily five-hour talks with him. He's just loaded with integrity and vision. This is a guy who used to walk around arenas and cover up ads. He was such an enormous part of what people loved about

Phish. The attention to detail and the focus on integrity—a lot of that was embodied in him, and I hope that we continue to carry forward that tradition.

He was the perfect manager for us right up until the end, and it was a great run. But we just couldn't go on with a management company that we had to shoulder the financial burden for. It was way too much pressure by the end. I know on a personal level it was keeping me up at night. And Page was clearly not psyched about the situation, either.

But again, that is not a personal statement about any of the wonderful people who worked in that office. As you know, it was very much a family affair. They put on all those wonderful festivals. But it was—again, I use the word *naïve*—we were a little bit naïve putting together what was our vision as eighteen- or twenty-year-olds: "Oh, we'll just hire all our friends and everything will go perfectly forever and we'll make tons and tons of money every month and cover all the overhead, never take a break and never slow down."

And that's not the way it went.

ME: Have you noticed any changes in the jamming? Has it taken on any different characteristics or new directions since the reunion?

ANASTASIO: The first thing I noticed at Hampton, and especially as the tour went on, was a little bit more of an emotional weight based on life coming into the picture. Anybody our age, once you've had divorces and deaths and arrests. . . . It's funny, because it makes me appreciate young bands even more. I can't stop listening to this record *Oracular Spectacular* by the band MGMT, because it's so full of this attitude of, "I'm twenty-one and the world's my oyster." It's part of rock and roll. But I like music by people who have lived a little. Hopefully you don't have to live *too* much! [*laughs*] In any case, I hear an element of humility, an extra added element of humility, in our music now.

APPENDIX 1

Phish's Live Performances, By Year and By Locale

Year	US	Canada	Europe	Japan	Total
1983	2				2
1984	3				3
1985	28				28
1986	19				19
1987	42				42
1988	97				97
1989	127	1			128
1990	148				148
1991	135				135
1992	111	2	8		121
1993	106	5			111
1994	119	6			125
1995	80	1			81
1996	52	1	18		71
1997	45		34		79
1998	57		9		66
1999	61	2		4	67
2000	41	1		7	49
2001	0				0
2002	1				1
2003	44				44
2004	17				17
	1,336	19	69	11	1,435

Note: 60 percent of Phish's shows were played from 1988 through 1994. This period of time represents just 31.8 percent of the twenty-two years from formation to breakup.

Phish's 2009 reunion stand and summer tour added 31 more shows, making for a total of 1,466 Phish concerts through August 2009.

Here's a breakdown of European shows, by country:

Austria (1)–1997 (1)
Belgium (3)–1992 (1), 1996 (1), 1997 (1)
Czech Republic (3)–1997 (1), 1998 (2)
Denmark (7)–1992 (1), 1997 (2), 1998 (4)
England (5)–1992 (1), 1996 (1), 1997 (3)
France (11)–1992 (1), 1996 (5), 1997 (5)
Germany (18)–1992 (4), 1996 (5), 1997 (9)
Ireland (2)–1997 (2)
Italy (11)–1996 (5), 1997 (6)
Netherlands (4)–1996 (1), 1997 (3)
Spain (4)–1997 (1), 1998 (3)

APPENDIX 2

The Missing Set Lists

The following set lists can be regarded as an addendum to *The Phish Companion*, whose set lists were complete through the April 2004 run in Las Vegas. Just as they were going to press with the second edition, Phish made its breakup announcement. These fifteen set lists did not make it into the *Companion*, so here they are, for the sake of completeness.

Summer Tour 2004

06/17/04 KeySpan Park, Brooklyn, NY
Set I Song I Heard the Ocean Sing, Dinner and a Movie, The Curtain (With), Sample in a Jar, The Moma Dance>Free, Nothing, Maze, Frankenstein
Set II 46 Days>Possum, The Oh Kee Pa Ceremony>Suzy Greenberg, Axilla, Also Sprach Zarathustra, Birds of a Feather, Kung, Mike's Song>I Am Hydrogen>Weekapaug Groove
Encore The Divided Sky

06/18/04 KeySpan Park, Brooklyn, NY
Set I AC/DC Bag, Camel Walk, Crowd Control, Stash, Cars Trucks Buses, Carini, My Sweet One, Character Zero, Tweezer
Set II Wilson, Down With Disease, 99 Problems, Big Pimpin', Chalk Dust Torture, Harry Hood>Taste
Encore Bug, Tweezer Reprise

06/19/04 *Saratoga Performing Arts Center, Saratoga Springs, NY*
Set I Reba, Runaway Jim, NICU>Scents and Subtle Sounds, Wolfman's
  Brother, Walls of the Cave>David Bowie
Set II Song I Heard The Ocean Sing, Piper>Gotta Jibboo>Limb By Limb,
  Cavern
Encore Wading in the Velvet Sea

06/20/04 *Saratoga Performing Arts Center, Saratoga Springs, NY*
Set I Rift, Julius, Won't You Come Home Bill Bailey, Waves, Gumbo,
  Water in the Sky, Horn, Poor Heart, Drowned
Set II Seven Below>Ghost>Twist, You Enjoy Myself
Encore Good Times Bad Times

**06/21/04 *Ed Sullivan Theatre,* New York, Late Show With David
Letterman** (Note: the group performed atop the *Late Show* marquee
overlooking Broadway. Soundcheck included a rough version of what
is believed to be Phish's first take on "Quantegy," sans lyrics.)
Set I Scents and Subtle Sounds, Also Sprach Zarathustra, Wilson,
  Chalk Dust Torture, Tweezer, Tweezer Reprise

06/23/04 *Verizon Wireless Music Center, Noblesville, IN*
Set I Llama, Bouncing Around the Room, Bathtub Gin, Ya Mar, Pebbles and
  Marbles, Army of One, Split Open and Melt
Set II Halley's Comet>Crosseyed and Painless, Slave to the Traffic Light,
  Nothing>46 Days>Scents and Subtle Sounds>Brian and Robert,
  Limb By Limb, Cavern
Encore Waste

06/24/04 *Verizon Wireless Music Center, Noblesville, IN*
Set I Loving Cup, Cities, Back on the Train, Vultures, My Mind's Got a
  Mind of Its Own, Down With Disease>Rock and Roll
Set II Tube, Run Like an Antelope, The Wedge, Timber (Jerry),
  Prince Caspian>Simple, Walls of the Cave
Encore The Squirming Coil

06/25/04 *Alpine Valley Music Theatre, East Troy, WI*
Set I Julius, Roses Are Free 1>AC/DC Bag, Glide, Anything But Me,
David Bowie, Wolfman's Brother, Golgi Apparatus
Set II Seven Below>Buffalo Bill>Lawn Boy>Mike's Song>I Am Hydrogen>
Weekapaug Groove, You Enjoy Myself>Also Sprach Zarathustra>
You Enjoy Myself
Encore Sample in a Jar

06/26/04 *Alpine Valley Music Theatre, East Troy, WI*
Set I Access Me, Scents and Subtle Sounds, Stash, The Moma Dance,
The Divided Sky, Wilson, Funky Bitch, Character Zero
Set II Boogie On Reggae Woman>Ghost>Free, Friday>Piper >Harry Hood
Encore Possum

08/09/04 *Hampton Coliseum, Hampton, VA*
Set I Chalk Dust Torture, Bathtub Gin>Runaway Jim, Walls of the Cave,
Loving Cup
Set II All of These Dreams, Limb By Limb, Lifeboy, Crowd Control,
Seven Below>Stash>NICU, Bug, Contact, Character Zero
Encore David Bowie

08/10/04 *Tweeter Center Boston, Mansfield, MA*
Set I AC/DC Bag, Heavy Things, Punch You in the Eye, Wolfman's
Brother, Theme from the Bottom, Birds of a Feather
Set II Mike's Song>I Am Hydrogen>Weekapaug Groove, Song I Heard
The Ocean Sing>Piper, Makisupa Policeman, Dog Faced Boy, Friday,
Harry Hood
Encore Possum

08/11/04 *Tweeter Center Boston, Mansfield, MA*
Set I The Divided Sky, Suzy Greenberg>Down With Disease>Prince
Caspian>Scent of a Mule>Tears of a Clown>Scent of a Mule,
Mexican Cousin
Set II Run Like An Antelope>Also Sprach Zarathustra, Golgi Apparatus,
Waves, Tweezer>Hold Your Head Up>Terrapin, Hold Your Head Up,
Timber (Jerry), Sample in a Jar
Encore Bouncing Around the Room, Tweezer Reprise

08/12/04 Tweeter Center at the Waterfront, Camden, NJ

Set I Wilson, You Enjoy Myself>Ghost>Maze>Catapult>Maze, The Moma
   Dance, Horn, Pebbles and Marbles

Set II Piper, Sneaking Sally Through the Alley, Cavern, Limb By Limb,
   Julius, Rock and Roll, Scents and Subtle Sounds

Encore Lawn Boy, Frankenstein

08/14/04 Newport State Airport, Coventry, VT

Set I Walls of the Cave>Runaway Jim>Gotta Jibboo, You Enjoy Myself,
   Sample in a Jar, Axilla, Poor Heart, Run Like An Antelope, Fire

Set II AC/DC Bag>46 Days, Halley's Comet>Ya Mar, David Bowie, Character
   Zero Set III Twist>The Wedge, Stash>Free, Guyute, Drowned>Jam, Friday

Encore Harry Hood

08/15/04 Newport State Airport, Coventry, VT Coventry

Set I Mike's Song>I Am Hydrogen>Weekapaug Groove, Anything But Me, Reba,
   Carini, Chalk Dust Torture>Possum, Wolfman's Brother>Jam, Taste

Set II Down With Disease, Wading in the Velvet Sea, Glide, Split Open and
   Melt>Ghost Set III Fast Enough For You, Seven Below, Simple,
   Piper>Bruno>Dickie Scotland, Wilson, Slave to the Traffic Light

Encore The Curtain (With)

Reunion Shows, Spring 2009

03/06/09 Hampton Coliseum, Hampton, VA

Set I Fluffhead, The Divided Sky, Chalk Dust Torture, Sample in a Jar, Stash,
   I Didn't Know, Oh Kee Pah Ceremony>Suzy Greenberg, Farmhouse, NICU,
   Horn, Rift, Train Song, Water in the Sky, Squirming Coil, David Bowie

Set II Backwards Down the Number Line, Tweezer>Taste, Possum, Theme
   from the Bottom, First Tube, Harry Hood, Waste, You Enjoy Myself

Encore Grind, Bouncing Around the Room, Loving Cup

03/07/09 Hampton Coliseum, Hampton, VA

Set I Back On the Train, Runaway Jim, Brian & Robert, Split Open and Melt,
   Heavy Things, Punch You in the Eye, Gumbo, Reba, Mexican Cousin, It's

Ice, Halley's Comet, Beauty of a Broken Heart, Guelah Papyrus, Lawn Boy, Run Like an Antelope

Set II Rock & Roll>Limb by Limb, Ghost>Piper>Birds of a Feather, Wolfman's Brother, Prince Caspian, Mike's Song>I Am Hydrogen>Weekapaug Groove, Character Zero

Encore A Day in the Life

03/08/09 Hampton Coliseum, Hampton, VA

Set I Sanity, Wilson, Foam, Bathtub Gin, Undermind, AC/DC Bag, My Friend, My Friend, Scent of a Mule, All of These Dreams, Maze, She Thinks I Still Care, Army of One, Tube, Cars Trucks Buses, Free, Frankenstein

Set II Down With Disease>Seven Below, The Horse>Silent in the Morning, Twist>2001, The Moma Dance, While My Guitar Gently Weeps, Wading in the Velvet Sea, Slave to the Traffic Light

Encore Happy Birthday, Contact, Bug, Tweezer Reprise

Summer Tour 2009

05/31/09 Fenway Park, Boston, MA

Set I Star Spangled Banner, Sample in a Jar, The Moma Dance, Chalk Dust Torture, Ocelot, Stash, Bouncing Around the Room, Poor Heart, Limb by Limb, Wading in the Velvet Sea, Down with Disease, Destiny Unbound, Character Zero

Set II Tweezer>Light, Bathtub Gin, David Bowie, Time Turns Elastic, Free, (The Ballad of) Curtis Loew, You Enjoy Myself

Encore Cavern, Good Times Bad Times, Tweezer Reprise

06/02/09 Nikon at Jones Beach Theater, Wantagh, NY

Set I Runaway Jim, Foam, Stealing Time from the Faulty Plan, Timber (Jerry), Cities, Driver, Reba, Possum, Farmhouse, If I Could

Set II Mike's Song>Simple>Wolfman's Brother>Weekapaug Groove, When the Circus Comes, Kill Devil Falls, Harry Hood, Loving Cup

Encore Suzy Greenberg

06/04/09 Nikon at Jones Beach Theater, Wantagh, NY
Set I Grind, The Divided Sky, Ocelot, The Squirming Coil, Punch You in the Eye,
    Dirt, NICU, Ghost, Run Like an Antelope
Set II Water in the Sky, Birds of a Feather, Drowned, Meatstick,
    Time Turns Elastic, Waste, You Enjoy Myself
Encore Rock and Roll

06/05/09 Nikon at Jones Beach Theater, Wantagh, NY
Set I Wilson, Buried Alive, Kill Devil Falls, AC/DC Bag>I Didn't Know,
    My Friend My Friend, Ya Mar, Theme from the Bottom, Boogie On
    Reggae Woman, Split Open and Melt
Set II Down With Disease>Twist>Piper>Backwards Down the Number Line,
    Free, Twenty Years Later>2001>Slave to the Traffic Light
Encore A Day in the Life

06/06/09 Comcast Center (formerly Great Woods), Mansfield, MA
Set I Stealing Time from the Faulty Plan, Nothing, Back on the Train,
    Golgi Apparatus, Sparkle, Gotta Jibboo, Lawn Boy, Let Me Lie, Taste,
    Makisupa Policeman, Prince Caspian
Set II Seven Below, Fluffhead, Scent of a Mule, Heavy Things, Harry Hood,
    Possum, Bug
Encore Contact, Julius

06/07/09 Susquehanna Bank Center, Camden, NJ
Set I Chalk Dust Torture, Fee, Wolfman's Brother, Guyute, My Sweet One,
    46 Days>The Lizards, The Wedge, Strange Design, Tube, First Tube
Set II Sand, Suzy Greenberg, Limb by Limb, The Horse>Silent in the Morning,
    Sugar Shack, Character Zero>Tweezer
Encore Joy, Bouncing Around the Room, Run Like an Antelope,
    Tweezer Reprise

06/09/09 Asheville Civic Center, Asheville, NC
Set I Kill Devil Falls, The Moma Dance, Sample in a Jar, Stash,
    Dog Faced Boy, Gumbo, Tube, Lengthwise, The Divided Sky,
    When the Cactus Is in Bloom, Bold as Love

Set II Backwards Down the Number Line>Ghost>Fast Enough for You, Halley's Comet>Maze, Alaska, Theme from the Bottom, Golgi Apparatus, Possum
Encore Loving Cup

06/10/09 Thompson-Boling Arena, Knoxville, TN
Set I Runaway Jim, Punch You in the Eye, Ocelot, Foam, Train Song, Undermind, Mike's Song>I Am Hydrogen>Weekapaug Groove, The Squirming Coil, Character Zero
Set II Back on the Train, Waves>A Song I Heard the Ocean Sing>David Bowie, Army of One, Reba, Hello My Baby, Julius>Cavern>Harry Hood
Encore Frankenstein

06/12/09 Bonnaroo Music & Arts Festival, Manchester, TN
Set I Chalk Dust Torture, Stealing Time from the Faulty Plan, The Divided Sky, Possum, Down with Disease, Alaska, Stash, Golgi Apparatus, Wolfman's Brother, Poor Heart, Kill Devil Falls>Free, Wading in the Velvet Sea, Harry Hood>Highway to Hell>2001>You Enjoy Myself>Wilson>You Enjoy Myself
Encore A Day in the Life

06/14/09 Bonnaroo Music & Arts Festival, Manchester, TN
Set I AC/DC Bag>NICU, Gotta Jibboo, Punch You in the Eye>Sparkle>Bathtub Gin, Character Zero>Tweezer>The Horse>Silent in the Morning, Run Like an Antelope, Mustang Sally*, Bobby Jean* Glory Days*
Set II Rock & Roll>Light>46 Days, Limb by Limb, Farmhouse, Backwards Down the Number Line>Prince Caspian, First Tube
Encore Suzy Greenberg>Tweezer Reprise
*with Bruce Springsteen

06/16/09 The Fabulous Fox Theatre, St. Louis, MO
Set I Kill Devil Falls, Ocelot, Brian and Robert, Sample in a Jar, Rift, Ya Mar, Reba, Train Song, Horn, Possum Slave to the Traffic Light
Set II Halley's Comet>Runaway Jim, Frankie Says, Time Turns Elastic, Sleep, Mike's Song>I Am Hydrogen>Weekapaug Groove, Boogie On Reggae Woman, Character Zero
Encore The Star-Spangled Banner, McGrupp and the Watchful Hosemasters, While My Guitar Gently Weeps

06/18/09 Post Gazette Pavilion, Burgettstown, PA

Set I Golgi Apparatus, Chalk Dust Torture, Bouncing Around the Room, Wolfman's Brother, The Divided Sky, Heavy Things, Walk Away, Wilson, Tube, Alaska, David Bowie

Set II Down With Disease>Free, Guyute, Piper, When the Circus Comes, Harry Hood>The Squirming Coil, You Enjoy Myself

Encore Grind, Hello My Baby, Hold Your Head Up>Bike>Hold Your Head Up, Loving Cup

06/19/09 Verizon Wireless Music Center (formerly Deer Creek), Noblesville, IN

Set I Backwards Down the Number Line, AC/DC Bag, Limb By Limb, The Moma Dance, Water in the Sky, Split Open and Melt, Lawn Boy, The Wedge, Stealing Time from the Faulty Plan, The Connection, Ocelot, Fluffhead

Set II A Song I Heard the Ocean Sing>Drowned>Twist, Let Me Lie, Tweezer>2001>Suzy Greenberg>Possum

Encore Sleeping Monkey>Tweezer Reprise

06/20/09 Alpine Valley Music Theatre, East Troy, WI

Set I Punch You in the Eye, Runaway Jim, Stash, Ya Mar, Bathtub Gin, Kill Devil Falls, Train Song, Farmhouse, Sparkle, Run Like an Antelope

Set II Waves>Sample in a Jar, Maze, Makisupa Policeman>Ghost>The Lizards, You Enjoy Myself>NICU>Prince Caspian>Waste>Fire

Encore Character Zero

06/21/09 Alpine Valley Music Theatre, East Troy, WI

Set I Brother, Wolfman's Brother, Funky Bitch>The Divided Sky, Joy, Back On the Train, Taste, Poor Heart, The Horse>Silent in the Morning, The Man Who Stepped Into Yesterday>Avenu Malkenu>The Man Who Stepped Into Yesterday, Time Turns Elastic

Set II Crosseyed and Painless>Down With Disease>Bug>Piper> Wading in the Velvet Sea, Boogie On Reggae Woman, Slave to the Traffic Light

Encore Grind, Frankenstein

07/30/09 Red Rocks Amphitheatre, Morrison, CO

Set I The Divided Sky, Ocelot, the Wedge, Poor Heart, The Moma Dance, Horn, Stash, The Horse>Silent in the Morning, Possum

Set II Mike's Song>I Am Hydrogen>Weekapaug Groove, Ghost>Wolfman's Brother, Limb By Limb, Billy Breathes, The Squirming Coil>David Bowie

Encore Loving Cup

07/31/09 Red Rocks Amphitheatre, Morrison, CO

Set I Runaway Jim, Chalk Dust Torture, Bathtub Gin, Time Turns Elastic, Lawn Boy, Water in the Sky, Stealing Time from the Faulty Plan, Split Open and Melt

Set II Drowned>Crosseyed and Painless>Joy, Tweezer>Backwards Down the Number Line>Fluffhead Piper>A Day in the Life

Encore Suzy Greenberg>Tweezer Reprise

08/01/09 Red Rocks Amphitheatre, Morrison, CO

Set I AC/DC Bag, The Curtain (With), Mound, Gotta Jibboo, Guyute, Punch You in the Eye, Tube, Alaska, Run Like an Antelope

Set II Rock and Roll>Down with Disease>Free, Esther, Dirt, Harry Hood

Encore Sleeping Monkey, First Tube

08/02/09 Red Rocks Amphitheatre, Morrison, CO

Set I Roses Are Free, Wilson, NICU, Prince Caspian, Back On the Train, Reba, Grind, Beauty of a Broken Heart, Sample in a Jar, Sugar Shack, Waste, Kill Devil Falls

Set II Boogie On Reggae Woman, You Enjoy Myself>Undermind>Drums>Seven Below>2001>Waves, Character Zero

Encore Bittersweet Motel, Bouncing Around the Room, Slave to the Traffic Light

08/05/09 Shoreline Amphitheatre, Mountain View, CA

Set I Golgi Apparatus, Halley's Comet, Chalk Dust Torture, The Divided Sky, When the Circus Comes, Time Turns Elastic, Ya Mar, Stealing Time from the Faulty Plan, Suzy Greenberg, David Bowie

Set II Backwards Down the Number Line, Down With Disease>Limb By Limb, Oh Sweet Nothin', Cities>Maze, Mike's Song>Simple, Weekapaug Groove

Encore Let Me Lie, Bold As Love

08/07/09 The Gorge Amphitheatre, Gorge, WA
Set I Down With Disease, Ocelot, Pebbles and Marbles, Possum, Sleep,
    Destiny Unbound, Stash, Sneakin' Sally Through the Alley>Cavern
Set II The Moma Dance>Light>Taste, Fluffhead, Joy, Bathtub Gin>Harry Hood
Encore Slave to the Traffic Light

08/08/09 The Gorge Amphitheatre, Gorge, WA
Set I The Mango Song, Chalk Dust Torture, Middle of the Road, Tweezer,
    Driver, Twenty Years Later, Ya Mar, It's Ice, Wolfman's Brother,
    Character Zero>Run Like an Antelope
Set II Rock & Roll>Makisupa Policeman, Alaska, The Wedge, You Enjoy
    Myself, Backwards Down the Number Line>Piper, Grind
Encore Good Times Bad Times, Tweezer Reprise

08/11/09 Toyota Park, Bridgeview, IL
Set I Kill Devil Falls, Sample in a Jar, Ocelot, Paul and Silas, Windy City,
    The Curtain (With), Train Song, Gumbo, Heavy Things, Time Turns Elastic
Set II Backwards Down the Number Line>Carini>Gotta Jibboo,
    Theme from the Bottom, Wilson>2001>Chalk Dust Torture, Harry Hood,
    the Squirming Coil
Encore Loving Cup

08/13/09 Darien Lake Performing Arts Center, Darien Center, NY
Set I Sample in a Jar, Dinner and a Movie, Wolfman's Brother, My Friend,
    My Friend, Possum, Farmhouse, Sugar Shack, Brian and Robert,
    David Bowie, Bathtub Gin, How High the Moon, Golgi Apparatus
Set II Drowned>Prince Caspian>Rift, The Horse>Silent in the Morning,
    Sparkle, Run Like an Antelope, Suzy Greenberg, Fluffhead
Encore Joy, First Tube

08/14/09 Comcast Theatre, Hartford, CT
Set I Punch You in the Eye, AC/DC Bag, NICU, Colonel Forbin's Ascent
    Fly>Famous Mockingbird, Birds of a Feather, Lawn Boy, Stash, I Didn't
    Know, Middle of the Road, Character Zero
Set II Down With Disease>Wilson>Slave to the Traffic Light, Piper>
    Water in the Sky, Ghost>Psycho Killer>Catapult>Icculus>You Enjoy Myself
Encore While My Guitar Gently Weeps

08/15/09 Merriweather Post Pavilion, Columbia, MD

Set I Crowd Control, Kill Devil Falls, The Sloth, Beauty of a Broken Heart, Axilla I, Foam, Esther, Ha Ha Ha, Party Time, Tube, Stealing Time from the Faulty Plan, Strange Design, Time Turns Elastic

Set II Tweezer>Taste, Alaska, Let Me Lie, 46 Days, Oh! Sweet Nuthin', Harry Hood

Encore Good Times Bad Times, Tweezer Reprise

08/16/09 Saratoga Performing Arts Center, Saratoga Springs, NY

Set I Llama, The Moma Dance, Guyute, Anything But Me, Cars Trucks Buses, Chalk Dust Torture, Golgi Apparatus, David Bowie, Cavern, Possum, Ocelot, Run Like an Antelope

Set II Backwards Down the Number Line>Twenty Years Later, Halley's Comet>Rock & Roll, Harpua>I Kissed a Girl>Hold Your Head Up>Harpua, You Enjoy Myself

Encore Grind, I Been Around, Highway to Hell

APPENDIX 3

Phish On Record:
From Studio to Stage

The conventional wisdom is that Phish are best experienced live and that the studio albums are frozen relics lacking the interaction and spontaneity that allow the group to soar in concert. That is the fans' take, and this mindset is peculiar to the jam-band world. Improv-oriented bands face a perpetual dilemma: How do you bottle the lightning of live performance in the studio? You can play live in the studio, which is kind of pointless without an audience to generate energy and feedback. Or you can take advantage of studio technology and craft a piece of music that lives and breathes on its own terms.

Phish took the latter tack, making records in different locations and with different producers (including several self-productions) in an effort to galvanize the typically static recording process. *Billy Breathes* is the acknowledged classic and must-own Phish studio album. But there are other non-live highlights in their catalog: *Rift*, their most ambitious and conceptually cohesive album; *Hoist*, a lively, extroverted endeavor featuring interesting guest musicians; and *Farmhouse*, the song-rich first Phish album recorded at the Barn, the studio that Trey Anastasio built outside Burlington.

For the full, uncut Phish experience, the double-disc *A Live One* is an essential acquisition. If you are now fully hooked on Phish, then backtrack and listen to where it all began (*Junta, Lawn Boy, A Picture of Nectar*). Finish up by fast-forwarding to see how it all ended (*Round Room, Undermind*)— that is, before it resumed again in 2009.

Incidentally, there's lots more available in the way of live Phish: official (LivePhish CDs and downloads), unofficial (online downloads, fan-swapped tapes and CDs), and unacceptable (bootlegs).

Was Phish a disappointing chart act, as is widely assumed? Hardly. Phish has racked up nine gold albums (500,000 copies sold), two of which have been certified platinum (1 million copies sold). Only three of their ten major studio releases have failed (as of yet) to attain gold status. Somewhat amazingly, the first sixteen volumes in the LivePhish series all made Billboard's Top 200 album chart—for exactly one week—from *Live Phish 02* (No. 93) to *Live Phish 08* (No. 154).

Charts don't always tell an accurate tale. A slow but steady seller that "bubbles under" the Hot 200, in *Billboard* lingo, might surprise years later with a gold or platinum certification. This held true in Phish's case, affirming their slow, steady, long-haul approach. *Junta, Lawn Boy,* and *A Picture of Nectar* were all certified gold long after their release (and in 2004, *Junta* went platinum), yet none of them ever appeared—even for a week—on *Billboard*'s Top 200 album chart.

A few Phish albums did make impressive showings on the charts, due to strong initial sales in the SoundScan era, when album sales began to be tracked more accurately. *Billy Breathes* and *The Story of the Ghost* both went Top Ten. (Ironically, *Ghost* never reached the gold plateau—go figure.) Among Phish releases, *Hoist, A Live One,* and *Billy Breathes* hold the records for chart longevity, at thirteen, fourteen, and fifteen weeks, respectively.

Just as it's clear that the industry underestimated the popularity of Phish's studio recordings, it's also true that two later studio releases began to tell a different tale. Numbers don't lie, and the relatively poor showings of Phish's final studio albums—*Round Room* and *Undermind*—suggest that interest had begun waning by the time of their 2004 breakup.

Five years later, the regrouped Phish has released another studio album, *Joy*, not on Elektra but on their own JEMP label. *Joy* debuted at No. 13 on *Billboard*'s Top 200—ironically, the exact position that *Undermind* debuted at in 2004—and at No. 5 on *Billboard*'s Rock Chart.

Phish's Studio Recordings

Title	Release Date	Chart Peak	RIAA
Junta	April 1989 (Absolute a Go Go); October 26, 1992 (Elektra)		platinum
Lawn Boy	September 21, 1990 (Absolute a Go Go); June 30, 1992 (Elektra)		gold
A Picture of Nectar	February 18, 1992		gold
Rift	February 22, 1993	51	gold
Hoist	March 29, 1994	34	gold
Billy Breathes	October 15, 1996	7	gold
The White Tape*	August 1, 1998		
Story of the Ghost	October 27, 1998	8	
The Siket Disc	July 15, 1999 (Phish Dry Goods); November 7, 2000 (Elektra)		
Farmhouse	May 16, 2000	12	gold
Round Room	December 10, 2002	46	
Undermind	June 15, 2004	13	
Joy	September 8, 2009	13	

Note: All releases are on Elektra Records unless otherwise noted. RIAA certification: gold = 500,000 units, platinum = 1 million units.

*Phish's first recordings, from 1984–1986

Phish's Live Releases

Title	Venue/Locale	Concert Date	Release Date	Chart Peak	RIAA
A Live One	various	Summer and Fall 1994 tours	June 27, 1995	18	platinum
Slip Stitch and Pass	Markthelle, Hamburg, Germany	March 1, 1997	October 28, 1997	17	
Hampton Comes Alive	Hampton Coliseum, Hampton, VA	November 20–21, 1998	November 23, 1999	120	gold
Live Phish 01: 12.14.95	Broome County Arena, Binghamton, NY	December 14, 1995	September 18, 2001	97	
Live Phish 02: 7.16.94	Sugarbush Summerstage, North Fayston, VT	July 16, 1994	September 18, 2001	93	
Live Phish 03: 9.14.00	Darien Lake Performing Arts Center, Darien, NY	September 14, 2000	September 18, 2001	118	
Live Phish 04: 6.14.00	Drum Logos, Fukuoka, Japan	June 14, 2000	September 18, 2001	127	
Live Phish 05: 7.8.00	Alpine Valley Music Theater, East Troy, WI	July 8, 2000	September 18, 2001	115	
Live Phish 06: 11.27.98	The Centrum, Worcester, MA	November 27, 1998	September 18, 2001	105	
Live Phish 07: 8.14.93	World Music Theatre, Tinley Park, IL	August 14, 1993	April 16, 2002	128	
Live Phish 08: 7.10.99	E Centre, Camden, NJ	July 10, 1999	April 16, 2002	154	
Live Phish 09: 8.26.89	Townshend Family Park, Townshend, VT	August 26, 1989	April 16, 2002	141	
Live Phish 10: 6.22.94	Veterans Memorial Auditorium, Columbus, OH	June 22, 1994	April 16, 2002	147	
Live Phish 11: 11.17.97	McNichols Sports Arena, Denver, CO	November 17, 1997	April 16, 2002	145	
Live Phish 12: 8.13.96	Deer Creek Music Center, Noblesville, IN	August 13, 1996	April 16, 2002	138	
Live Phish 13: 10.31.94	Glens Falls Civic Center, Glens Falls, NY	October 31, 1994	October 29, 2002	112	
Live Phish 14: 10.31.95	Rosemont Horizon, Rosemont, IL	October 31, 1995	October 29, 2002	146	
Live Phish 15: 10.31.96	The Omni, Atlanta, GA	October 31, 1996	October 29, 2002	144	
Live Phish 16: 10.31.98	Thomas & Mack Center, Las Vegas, NV	October 31, 1998	October 29, 2002	139	
Live Phish 17: 7.15.98	Portland Meadows, Portland, OR	July 15, 1998	May 20, 2003		
Live Phish 18: 5.7.94	The Bomb Factory, Dallas, TX	May 7, 1994	May 20, 2003		
Live Phish 19: 7.12.91	The Colonial Theatre, Keene, NH	July 12, 1991	May 20, 2003		
Live Phish 20: 12.29.94	Providence Civic Center, Providence, RI	December 29, 1994	May 20, 2003		

Title	Venue/Locale	Concert Date	Release Date	Chart Peak	RIAA
Live Phish: 02.28.03	Nassau Coliseum, Uniondale, NY	February 28, 2003	December 16, 2003		
Live Phish: 07.15.03	USANA Amphitheatre, West Valley City, UT	July 15, 2003	December 16, 2003		
Live Phish: 07.29.03	Post-Gazette Pavilion at Star Lake, Burgettstown, PA	July 29, 2003	December 16, 2003		
Live Phish: 04.02.98	Nassau Coliseum, Uniondale, NY	April 2, 1998	July 19, 2005		
Live Phish: 04.03.98	Nassau Coliseum, Uniondale, NY	April 3, 1998	July 19, 2005		
Live Phish: 04.04.98	Providence Civic Center, Providence, RI	April 4, 1998	July 19, 2005		
Live Phish: 04.05.98	Providence Civic Center, Providence, RI	April 5, 1998	July 19, 2005		
New Year's Eve 1995: Live at Madison Square Garden	Madison Square Garden, New York, NY	December 31, 1995	December 20, 2005		
Live in Brooklyn	KeySpan Park, Coney Island, Brooklyn, NY	June 17, 2004	July 11, 2006	62	
Colorado '88	Roma Bar and Fly Me to the Moon Saloon, Telluride, CO	July 29–August 5, 1988	November 20, 2007		
Vegas '96	Aladdin Theatre, Las Vegas, NC*	December 6, 1996	November 20, 2007	23**	
Live Phish: 08.13.93	Murat Theatre, Indianapolis, IN	August 13, 1993	November 20, 2007		
Live Phish: 10.21.95	Pershing Auditorium, Lincoln, NB	October 21, 1995	November 20, 2007		
Live Phish: 11.14.95	University of Central Florida Arena, Orlando, FL	November 14, 1995	November 20, 2007		
Live Phish: 12.01.95	Hersheypark Arena, Hershey, PA	December 1, 1995	November 20, 2007		
Live Phish: 12.29.97	Madison Square Garden, New York, NY	December 29, 1997	November 20, 2008		
Live Phish: 05.08.93	Field House, University of New Hampshire, Durham, NH	May 8, 1993	August 5, 2008		
Live Phish: 12.07.97	Ervin J. Nutter Center, Dayton, OH	December 12, 1997	August 5, 2008		
Live Phish: 07.06.98	Lucerna Theatre, Prague, Czech Republic	July 6, 1998	August 5, 2008		
At the Roxy	Roxy Theatre, Atlanta, GA	February 19–21, 1993	November 18, 2008		

*also available as a deluxe edition with bonus DVD
**on *Billboard*'s Top Independent Albums chart

Phish's Live DVDs

Title	Venue/Locale	Concert Date	Release Date	RIAA*
Bittersweet Motel**	The Great Went, Loring Air Force Base, Limestone, ME and various European venues	August 16-17, 1997 (Great Went) and Summer 1998 (Europe)	March 6, 2001	
Live in Vegas	Thomas & Mack Center, Las Vegas, NV	September 30, 2000	November 12, 2002	gold
It	Loring Air Force Base, Limestone, ME	August 2-3, 2003	October 12, 2004	platinum
Live in Brooklyn	KeySpan Park, Coney Island, Brooklyn, NY	June 17, 2004	July 11, 2006	
Walnut Creek	Walnut Creek Amphitheatre, Raleigh, NC	July 22, 1997	August 5, 2008	
The Clifford Ball	Plattsburgh Air Force Base, Plattsburgh, NY	August 16-17, 1996	March 3, 2009	

*Earned certification in the video-longform format
**Not a concert documentary but a band documentary with concert footage

APPENDIX 4

Deadheads and Phishheads: An Academic's Perspective

Rebecca Adams has a unique overview of the relationship between the Grateful Dead and Phish, particularly as regards their respective followings and parking-lot scenes. She holds a PhD in sociology and is a professor of sociology at the University of North Carolina at Greensboro. A Deadhead from the beginning, she saw her first Dead show at New York's Fillmore East in 1970. She continued seeing the Dead with some regularity through 1978, at which point negative aspects of the increasingly younger crowd's behavior turned her off the scene.

She reconnected in 1986, when she attended a Dead concert in Hampton, Virginia. At that show she ran into Matt Russ, a student of hers (and a bona fide Deadhead) who suggested that she consider studying the Deadhead phenomenon from a sociological perspective. And so she did, offering a course for credit during which her students followed the band on tour, interviewing Deadheads at gigs and in the parking lots. What resulted was the first published academic study of the Deadhead phenomenon and community. She has written and edited a few books, including *Deadhead Social Science*, as well as numerous journal articles and a well-circulated video about the Deadheads. She's become something of a celebrity in her own right within the Dead community. Garcia himself approached her backstage at a 1989 gig, saying, "Hey, you're famous!"

Adams saw Phish for the first time in 1994 and began taking note of the Phishheads. A good number of them, she realized, were younger Deadheads who'd jumped to Phish, bringing with them elements of the Deadhead scene. Because most of these Phish newbies had been Dead newbies as well, they were never particularly well socialized into either camp, causing problems for both bands—but especially for Phish, in Adams's opinion.

"For the Dead, after *In the Dark* and 'Touch of Grey,' there was this huge influx of new Deadheads, and the older Deadheads developed derogatory terms like 'Touchhead' and 'In the Darker' for these new people. So there was this problem with bunches of young people coming into the Dead scene and not enough old people to convince them they had to behave and take care of themselves. Not that there was ever any suggestion they should stop doing what they were doing, but they needed to contain it, not impose on other people and not create problems for the scene as a whole.

"From my perspective as an infrequent visitor to the Phish scene, I saw some of the fringe elements of the Dead community who hadn't been totally integrated into the phenomenon moving over and establishing themselves in the Phish parking lots. I saw two problems in the Phish scene: (1) It was a very young crowd without much older wisdom to guide it from the beginning. (2) The fans tried to bring over what they remembered from the Dead parking lot and re-create it in a way that didn't work if you didn't have an age-mix crowd."

As for hard-drug use—the infiltration of cocaine, heroin, and various other substances into Phish's parking-lot scene in the mid nineties—Adams is less inclined to blame Deadheads who wandered over.

"I know that Phish had a lot of trouble with hard-core drug users," she said. "It may very well have been Deadheads who brought those drugs into the parking lots, but at that time if you look at white-powder drug use among young people in general, that's when it went up nationally. Rather than it being necessarily attributable to a huge influx of Deadheads, I think that might have happened in the Phish scene anyhow."

APPENDIX 5

A Talk With Brad Sands

Brad Sands was more than Phish's road manager. He was their closest friend, confidante, and counselor. He kept them on schedule (as best he could). He oversaw access to them, instinctively learning who they did and didn't need around them at any given moment. He came to understand their moods and idiosyncrasies, acting to adjust and defuse situations so they could focus on music. He was, as Mike Gordon told writer Randy Ray, "the innermost person of all of the people in our organization." From the time he hopped aboard in 1991 as an unpaid roadie, Sands witnessed the unfolding of Phish history like no one else.

In the reunion era, Sands no longer works for Phish, as the group resumed with a clean slate. Subsequent to Phish's breakup and Anastasio's bust, Sands has worked for Gov't Mule, Les Claypool, and the Police. In a sense, things have come full circle with Sands' role as a consultant on Phish's Festival 8—the Halloween festival that revived the group's tradition of concert campouts in 2009. In this far-ranging interview, Sands looked back with humor and pride at his many years as chief aide-de-camp for Phish and for Trey Anastasio as a solo artist.

ME: I'd like to go back to the beginning and ask how you came onboard.

BRAD: I first heard of Phish in the summer of 1991. My friend Greg came home with the *Lawn Boy* album, and we were immediately drawn to it. We saw that they were playing at the Arrowhead Ranch in upstate New York and drove up there. They were passing out flyers for Amy's Farm, which was eight days later. We were like, "Who's gonna drive all the way to Maine to see these guys? Ha ha ha!" Arrowhead Ranch was great and we saw them the next night, too. Then we all decided, "Hey, let's go to Maine! What the hell!"

Since I was collecting unemployment, we decided to drive across the country to see the Dead in Oakland on Halloween, which is my birthday. Along the way, we planned to see Phish in New Mexico and Arizona. At the Club West in Santa Fe, a friend of mine and I showed up early, hanging out with nothing to do. They didn't have anybody to help load in their gear, so we asked Andrew Fischbeck, who was the tour manager at the time, "Hey, you guys want some help?" "Yeah, sure." So we helped load in their stuff and I helped Chris Kuroda set up the lights. Chris and I got along immediately, because we were both huge New York Giants fans and loved the Grateful Dead.

They asked if I would sell T-shirts for them that night. Later that evening, they were like, "Do you think you'd be interested in doing something like this, 'cause we're hiring somebody," I said, "Yeah, yeah," and went to the next 15 shows. I always bought my ticket, never asked them for anything, and just basically kept my mouth shut and helped. I weaseled my way in there and wasn't going to let this opportunity slip away. That's how I got the job. I started helping Chris set up the lights, selling merch and driving the truck. I was 21 years old and making $250 per week. And I was as happy as shit. Those were the happiest days of my life.

ME: Moreover, you were now getting into the shows for free.

BRAD: Yeah, and as a bonus Paul Languedoc let me start taping the shows with my little tape recorder. I'd patch into the soundboard. If you notice, there are a lot of soundboards from '93 and '94 out there. Those are my tapes, the "Bradboards."

ME: What were you hearing that would make you want to tape every show?

BRAD: I was immediately drawn to Trey's playing, and he had this shit-eating grin on his face that was totally contagious. I just couldn't believe what a good time it looked like they were having. They seemed totally weird but cute and funny. The drummer's wearing a dress. A lot of it was the energy of the crowd as well. People were really psyched back then. I knew they were going to be big. Maybe not as big as they ended up getting, but I could tell there was a movement that was going to happen with these guys.

ME: I know there weren't titles per se in the Phish organization, but when did you become "road manager"?

BRAD: In 1993 and 1994, we were getting bigger and starting to play some amphitheaters. They hired their first real production manager and tour manager/accountant. They made me production assistant because I wasn't a very good guitar tech. Drums, I was okay. Guitars, no. What they found happening was that the tour manager job was the hot seat. They could never find a guy the band liked. As I was production assistant for two years, it got to the point where I was the one who was always around the band. I knew exactly what they needed, how they wanted it to be finessed, and the right time to say something and the right time to shutup. So eventually, in 1996, I became road manager.

ME: How would you define the job of road manager?

BRAD: The job of the road manager is basically to make sure the band feels like they're looked after 24/7. I did a lot of travel planning and day-to-day logistics. And I'd take care of their guests. Make sure their people were having a good time. Make sure the band members were all in a good mood. Basically, my job was to make sure that all Phish had to think about was playing music. That was a big part of it. The thing about Phish is they're four totally different people.

ME: I don't think people realize how different they are, because they project so much unity and oneness of vision.

BRAD: People just know them as "the band." But they're all completely unique individuals and they all have their own patterns. For example, I might say, "Bus call is at four o'clock." Everybody has to be on the bus at four, right? Well, here's how it would break down. Page would come down early. He'd be down about 3:45. Trey would show up anywhere between 3:55 and 4:05. So Page and Trey are both there, and they're asking, "Where's Mike? Where's Fish?" "They're not here yet." "Okay, we're gonna go get coffee." So they're gone. Mike might roll down around 4:15, 4:20. Fishman's still nowhere to be found. Then Mike's gone because no one is there. Trey and Page come back. Then Fishman finally comes down. He sees that Trey and Page are there but Mike went back up to his room. Imagine trying to keep your sanity when you're dealing with those guys on that kind of stuff [laughs].

ME: It's like herding cats.

BRAD: Yeah, it is! You always had to build in a half-hour buffer. But to be honest, it was almost impossible to be mad at any of them. Fishman would be late all the time and I could never get mad at the guy. He just has that personality. He comes out, "Hey, man," and he smiles, and you'd forget everything. "Hey, Fish, how's it going?" All is forgiven all the time.

So it was really keeping those four people and their four different worlds aligned. Also I did the guest list and was in charge of backstage and not-really-but-kind-of personal security. They never traveled with a bodyguard. They had John Langenstein handling security in the parking lots and different guys over the years doing interior security, but they never had anybody traveling with them.

So basically the road manager's job is to put out fires all day. And no matter what's happening, you have to remain calm. Because if you're freaking out, everybody will start to freak out. I prided myself on retaining at least some semblance of calmness amidst chaos.

ME: It sounds like there's a significant psychological component to the job.

BRAD: Very much so. And for better or worse, you're often the only person on tour they talk to. It's very much a mind game all the time— what to say when, listening. You're like their counselor for everything, for right or wrong. There's always a lot of moral dilemmas involved with the job. If you see somebody doing something they shouldn't be doing, then do you talk to them about it or do you say something to someone else? It's all that kind of stuff.

ME: Very complicated interpersonal dynamics, I'm sure.

BRAD: Exactly. You can almost get too close to it. For me, the hardest part was that Phish was so big that it became your identity. It became who you are. I used to find it was very hard to adjust to being off-tour, because when you're out on the road, you're part of this energy that's churning. You're at the center of it, and everything is just building around your world. Then you get home and you're just another guy. It's that high and low, the peaks and valleys, that kind of messed with your head. Being on the road is like summer camp. It's so great, you're with your friends, everything is provided for you. It's like you're in the World Series every day. Then you get home and it's like, "What do I do now?"

ME: That may partly explain why they toured so heavily, because that life became their reality.

BRAD: I think that was part of it. In the beginning, there was a sense of purpose among all of us that we were trying to prove something. Even in the crew. Our crew—like the crews of Blues Traveler, the Spin Doctors, the Dave Matthews Band—always tried one-upping each other to be the best crew out there. The bands were like that, too. There was a sense of community, but the dedication the Phish guys put into stuff was crazy.

ME: I've never seen anything like their work ethic.

BRAD: When I first started, it was pretty intense. When I came up to work for them in Vermont, I stayed at Paul's and Trey's house. I slept on the couch. Those guys practiced for five hours every day in the livingroom. I was like, "Wow, those guys really do practice."

ME: What were your favorite years for Phish?

BRAD: The year 1994 was a real turning point. I really thought they were hitting their stride that summer. There were just some great shows. The playing was a little different. That was the year *Hoist* came out, and that batch of songs was great in concert. I also thought 1997 and 1998 were great years.

ME: What about those two years did you like?

BRAD: This is sort of good and bad, but by '97 there started to be somewhat of a dark side seeping into the whole thing. That isn't what you want in the lifestyles. But at the beginning, I thought it translated into some amazing music. To me, what made the Grateful Dead so great was Jerry Garcia and the fact he was this down-and-out character with a positive attitude, and he had soul. And I thought in those years, the soul came into Phish.

It was like this. People would ask why I thought Phish was a better jam band than, say, moe. or String Cheese Incident. My reply was that the other bands were like seeing *Star Wars* without Darth Vader. You've got the hero, you've Han Solo, and it's all great, but without Darth Vader you're not going to see *Star Wars* over and over. Because it's the dark side, and it needs to be in there as well. It's inevitable with anything that the dark side gets in too much and then ruins it. But in '97 and '98 you can hear a bit more attitude in the playing, maybe some more confidence, and those were the years we actually—"we" meaning the band—thought that we were the best band in the world. It was al-most like a swagger, you know, from the fall of 1997 up until Big Cy-press. That was the feeling.

ME: What did you do during the hiatus?

BRAD: I worked for Trey. One of the biggest problems was that a lot of the pressure of being Phish just got transferred to Trey. We all just started working for Trey. So I don't think he ever really got a break from the whole thing until after the second breakup. Trey was doing good business, but the merchandise company and all that were still there. That wasn't really addressed during the hiatus.

ME: Was it a matter of Trey not being able to put his foot down?

BRAD: I think he was always looking for [manager] John Paluska to do it, and John didn't want to do it, for whatever reason. Because Trey never wanted to be the bad guy. That's not in his nature. He wants to take care of people. He would've been happy for people to come in and say—and there were people saying this—"You need to get rid of a lot of this." Maybe not all of it, but some of it, for sure. We didn't need our own merchandise company. Because what happens is, these guys are humans and they're great people. They go down to the office and see all these people working, and they don't want them to lose their jobs. But at what point does it become an expense of your own? Not just monetarily but emotionally. It was hard because it was a big family, but where there's big families, there's problems.

It can go both ways. One of the reasons I was on payroll was that Trey wanted somebody 24/7 that he could talk to or do something with, hash out ideas or whatever. I was happy to be working for Trey. I loved working for Trey. It was great. I didn't want to lose my job, either.

ME: Regarding the 2004 breakup, I'm drawn to the metaphor of the Art Tower they burned down at the Great Went. Phish had built up this incredible organization with all these super-talented people—some of the best in the business—and torched it. Do you have any theories as to why they—and, particularly, Trey—felt the need to end it so dras-tically and absolutely?

BRAD: It's hard to say. There were plenty of times where I thought to my-self—and I know everybody else thought to themselves—"Why do we have to break up? Why not just go away for awhile?" And Trey would say, "I can't do that." I'd say, "Why?" And it was always that he couldn't see it that way. He saw it in the way of "I've got to tear it apart" or "It can't just be sitting there, too big." I don't know if I agreed with that, but it wasn't my thing. It was his thing. I think when they got back together [after the hiatus], it was for all the wrong reasons. It just wasn't good.

ME: I have to say, though, I thought they played well on the summer 2003 tour.

BRAD: Yeah, there were some good shows and good moments in '03. The summer tour had some good stuff. The It festival certainly had some great playing. The Tower Jam was incredible. The Miami New Year's run was good, too. But I think 2004 took a turn for the worse. Las Vegas was a disaster on all fronts, pretty much. There were some good shows at the beginning of the summer, but the last week was terrible. It was just like a wake. It was really depressing, to be honest. That was a point where the drugs really were a lot worse for everybody.

ME: I was there on the second night of the post-hiatus stand at Hampton in January 2003 when they had to start "You Enjoy Myself" over again. Didn't you have to come out with a cup of coffee or something for Trey?

BRAD: Uh, I remember it [laughs]. I know that he was pretty hurtin' that day. That was not a good run. There were a few moments with all of them that we kind of had to rescue them from themselves. And there's probably a few times it looked like I needed rescuing as well. I think with Trey, though, it was more because he wears it on his sleeve so much.

Trey's personality is like this. Say we find a pack of fireworks—you, me, Page, whoever. We say, "Let's set these off. This will be great, right?" We set them off. Trey says, "There's got to be more fireworks around here. Let's go find more. Let's find the factory. *And let's blow them all up!*"

That's Trey, and this is why he writes such great, amazing songs. It's that kind of insane drive he has that will also get you into trouble. There's so many greats that are like that. He's the one who practices in his room for eight hours. He obsesses about stuff. So when it came to partying, the guy set the world on fire. And you know what? We were all happy to follow him as much as we could a lot of the time. Because Trey was our leader, you know?

The great thing about Phish was when they were all in their roles and flourishing. Obviously, it's the band dynamic that makes them so great. The first thing I was drawn to with them was the relationship between Trey and Fishman back in the early nineties. To me, it was like Pete Townshend and Keith Moon of the Who. If you watch old interviews with Townshend and Moon, and you watch Trey and Fishman interact, it's the same thing. It's like two goofballs who are brothers bouncing off each other.

ME: And pushing each other to musical heights, as well.

BRAD: Exactly. It's like when you listen to the Who, a lot of the time the guitar and drums are more connected than the bass and the drums. Now Fishman doesn't really play like Moon, but it's a similar vibe. It's no surprise they named the band after him. He really embodies the spirit of the whole thing. And then Page is like a backbone up there. He's solid strength, like a tree with deep roots. Mike is just genuinely strange. He gives the band their weirdness. When you put all four of them together, it's like Trey used to say: "A wop, a mick and a couple of hebes." [*laughs*]

ME: Amy Skelton said to me, "We almost lost Trey." Did you ever have that fear?

BRAD: Yeah. I mean, it was a strange time, because I was around him a lot in that period and one of the things he always used say to me was, "I don't ever want you to have an intervention for me or anything like that." Which to me meant he knew he was in trouble. But knowing Trey well enough, he was going to have to find that out on his own. He tried a few times from other people prodding him to do this or that. It just didn't stick. It was gonna have to come from him. It did because he was sort of forced into it by a court case. But I think a lot of it was just a cry for help. 'Cause Trey's a really smart guy. He's not stupid, you know, and a lot of what was going on was just stupid on everybody's part.

ME: In your interview with Randy Ray, you said, "We liked the partying. We liked the rock and roll atmosphere. But it all just became too much."

BRAD: Well, that was the thing, you know? From 1997 to 2000, we had all of our friends around all the time. There was a big party. The whole thing was a big, fun, happy experience. Amy Skelton is the one who came up with the Betty Ford Clinic. Don't let anybody tell you that was my fault. That was her idea! [*laughs*] She was like, "I've got a ton of friends. Why don't we get a room backstage and stock it with booze?" Trey was like, "Great idea!" But after the third night, when there was all this hard liquor, people were back there getting shit-faced, just wasted. So then we went to all beer, and that's when we started calling it the Betty Ford Clinic, because it looked like every single person in there needed help.

To us it was funny. It seemed like good times. Arguably, for four years you could say we were throwing the best party in rock and roll. Which is pretty cool! When we first met Stewart Copeland from the Police, he came to see us in Vegas. It was him and his brother Ian. They flew in, and when Stewart saw the setup he was like, "Man, you've got this shit down! This is hospitality." Ian was like, "This is amazing. . . . I haven't had such a good time in 20 years." And we're thinking to ourselves, "Wow, these are real legendary guys here."

We enjoyed that reputation. But then it took over, and it just got too crazy. The whole thing took on its own momentum, 'cause that's what they wanted at that time. I couldn't drag those guys out of there at set break half the time. They loved their friends, and they wanted them to be having a good time

ME: You've called Big Cypress "the best weekend of our lives," and it was a career pinnacle.

BRAD: It was like climbing Mount Everest. It was the biggest festival, the longest set. Everything was just *big*, you know? When I got on the property, which was on December 27th, 1999, there wasn't anybody there yet. But there was already this magnetic energy that was just undeniable. Like, *this is gonna be special*. You could feel it in the air. And because it was on an Indian reservation, it really did feel like anything goes, like anything can happen out here.

Phish totally rose to the occasion on all fronts with the playing. I don't remember much about the 30th at all, to be totally honest, because it was all about the 31st. It's funny because they closed the 31st with "After Midnight," and from that moment on, it was a crazy buildup of energy—I get goosebumps just talking about it—until we finally drove the band through the crowd to the stage on the airboat hot-dog thing.

The playing was pure adrenalin and joy. I remember moments in the set where it started to lull, and then they played something that pulled it right back into the energy. You know, if you stay up all night with a friend, it's a cool night. Could you imagine doing that with 85,000 people? It's pretty intense! To be able to pull that off, all of us as a group, I never felt so much satisfaction in my life, professionally.

INDEX